Sex for Sale in Scotland

Prostitution in Edinburgh and Glasgow, 1900–1939

Louise Settle

EDINBURGH
University Press

For Linda and Vince Settle

Edinburgh University Press is one of the leading university presses in the UK. We publish academic books and journals in our selected subject areas across the humanities and social sciences, combining cutting-edge scholarship with high editorial and production values to produce academic works of lasting importance. For more information visit our website: www.edinburghuniversitypress.com

Edinburgh University Press Ltd
The Tun – Holyrood Road
12 (2f) Jackson's Entry
Edinburgh EH8 8PJ

First published in hardback by Edinburgh University Press 2016

Typeset in Ehrhardt by
Servis Filmsetting Ltd, Stockport, Cheshire,
and printed and bound in Great Britain by
CPI Group UK (Ltd), Croydon CR0 4YY

A CIP record for this book is available from the British Library

ISBN 978 1 4744 0000 8 (hardback)
ISBN 978 1 4744 2931 3 (paperback)
ISBN 978 1 4744 0001 5 (webready PDF)
ISBN 978 1 4744 1428 9 (epub)

Contents

Acknowledgements iv
List of Figures and Tables v

1 Introduction 1
2 Controlling the 'Social Evil': Policing Prostitution 17
3 The Social Geography of Prostitution 52
4 Reforming the 'Fallen': Voluntary Organisations, Probation and the Informal Regulation of Prostitution 81
5 Women's Experiences of Prostitution 113
6 Dance Clubs and Ice-cream Tubs: Clandestine Prostitution and the Kosmo Club 156
7 Conclusion 185

Bibliography 197
Index 213

Acknowledgements

First and foremost I would like to thank my doctoral supervisors Professor Louise Jackson and Dr Gayle Davis for their invaluable expertise, support and guidance. I would also like to thank Dr Andrew Davies and Professor Viviene Cree for their expert advice and Dr Chris Grocott for providing me with the initial encouragement to pursue this research.

I gratefully acknowledge the support of the Arts and Humanities Research Council for providing the financial support that was essential for this project. I am also grateful to the Institute for Advanced Studies in the Humanities (IASH) for providing me with further financial support and a wonderful academic environment in which to work. Thank you also to the very helpful archivists and members of staff at the Edinburgh City Archives, the Glasgow City Archives, the National Records of Scotland, the National Library of Scotland and the Glasgow Police Heritage Society. I would also like to thank Professor Richard Rodger and Karen Howie for all their help with databases and digital mapping, Varpu Lauchlan for her contribution to the book's cover design and the anonymous reviewers of Edinburgh University Press, whose suggestions helped to make this a better book.

I would like to express my deepest gratitude to the many friends, colleagues and family members who have helped with the editing process and provided me with advice, friendship and laughter. In particular, I would like to thank all my friends at IASH and the University of Edinburgh – those regular lunchtime chats and Friday night drinks kept me going! Finally, thank you to Pertti Ahonen for all your patience and support.

Figures and Tables

Figures

2.1 Comparison of National Solicitation Offences Statistics with Edinburgh and Glasgow 19
2.2 Chief Constable James Verdier Stevenson 25
2.3 Chief Constable Andrew Donnan Smith 25
2.4 Chief Constable Percy Joseph Sillitoe 27
2.5 Chief Constable Roderick Ross 27
2.6 Sentence Given for Importuning Offences in Edinburgh,1911 35
2.7 Sentence Given for Importuning Offences in Edinburgh, 1921 36
2.8 Sentence Given for Importuning Offences in Edinburgh, 1931 36
2.9 Sentence Given for Importuning Offences in Edinburgh, 1903 37
2.10 Sentence Given for Importuning Offences in Edinburgh 1911 37
2.11 Sentence Given for Importuning Offences in Edinburgh, 1921 38
2.12 Sentence Given for Importuning Offences in Edinburgh, 1931 38
2.13 Brothel Convictions in Edinburgh, 1897–1936 43
2.14 Brothel-keeping and Immoral Traffic Act Prosecutions and Convictions in Glasgow, 1892–1933 44
3.1 Importuning Convictions, Edinburgh Districts, 1903 53
3.2 Location of Importuning Convictions on Edinburgh Map, 1903 54
3.3 Importuning Convictions, Edinburgh Streets, 1911 55
3.4 Importuning Convictions, Edinburgh Districts, 1911 55
3.5 Location of Importuning Convictions on Edinburgh Map, 1911 56
3.6 Importuning Convictions, Edinburgh Streets, 1921 56
3.7 Importuning Convictions, Edinburgh Districts, 1921 57
3.8 Location of Importuning Convictions on Edinburgh Map, 1921 57
3.9 Importuning Convictions, Edinburgh Streets, 1931 58
3.10 Importuning Convictions, Edinburgh Districts, 1931 58
3.11 Location of Importuning Convictions on Edinburgh Map, 1931 59
3.12 Home Addresses of Women Convicted for Importuning in Edinburgh, 1903 63

3.13 Home Addresses of Women Convicted for Importuning in Edinburgh, 1911 63
3.14 Home Addresses of Women Convicted for Importuning in Edinburgh, 1921 64
3.15 Home Addresses of Women Convicted for Importuning in Edinburgh, 1931 64
3.16 Map of Police Districts in Glasgow in 1933 75
5.1 Occupations of Women Arrested for Importuning 119
5.2 Birthplace of Women Convicted for Importuning 120
5.3 Nationality of the Women, 1903 122
5.4 Nationality of the Women, 1911 122
5.5 Nationality of the Women, 1921 122
5.6 Nationality of the Women, 1931 123
5.7 Age of the Women, 1903 124
5.8 Age of the Women, 1911 124
5.9 Age of the Women, 1921 125
5.10 Age of the Women, 1931 125
5.11 Home Addresses of Women Convicted for Importuning, Edinburgh, 1903–31 143

Tables

2.1 Prosecutions and Convictions for Importuning Offences in Scotland, 1906–55 18
2.2 Immoral Traffic Act Convictions in Glasgow 45
3.1 Percentage of Visits to Brothels in each Police District of Glasgow 74

CHAPTER 1

Introduction

I think that if our prostitutes were driven off the streets there would be a danger to respectable women.
Edinburgh Chief Constable Roderick Ross, 1927[1]

Chief Constable Roderick Ross' 1927 statement highlights the ambiguities surrounding both the policing of prostitution and attitudes towards the role of prostitution in Scotland during the early twentieth century. On the one hand, Ross' proposal that 'our prostitutes' should not be 'driven off the streets' suggests that he was against criminalising street prostitution because it performed a necessary role in society. On the other hand, he clearly saw the women who were involved in prostitution as being unrespectable and less important than other women. Nonetheless, his use of the possessive pronoun 'our' suggests that he did not necessarily see them as outcasts from society entirely.[2]

It was not only police officers who held apparently contradictory attitudes towards prostitution. Then, as today, the British public were equally divided in their opinions regarding prostitution and what should be done about it. Whilst some wanted to abolish prostitution because of its harmful influence on women and society, others saw prostitution as a necessary evil required to placate men's natural sexual desires. Likewise, many practically minded observers were also concerned about controlling the disease and public disorder that might result from unregulated prostitution. The figure of 'the prostitute', therefore, was used as a symbol for wider concerns within society and appropriated for different causes. On the one hand, she was held up as a figure of pity by the reformers who wanted to 'save her' and the feminists who used her plight to rally against the double sexual standard and problematise women's unequal position in society. On the other hand, she was portrayed as a dangerous source of contagion and social disorder by the army, police and medical profession who wanted to inspect, sanitise and control her. These varying opinions and attitudes had a tangible impact on the regulation of prostitution during this period and, consequently, on the lives of the women who sold sex. The ways in which laws and policing policies were implemented had the potential to influence how and where these women could work, and the actions of religious voluntary organisations shaped the ways in which 'fallen women' were given access to welfare and alternative employment opportunities. However, these were not the only, or necessarily the most influential, factors that shaped everyday life for the women involved in prostitution. Technological developments and changes in entertainment patterns were also highly important, as were the wider socio-economic changes that shaped the experiences of all those who lived during this period, and this is to say nothing of the role that individual choice played in this equation.

Since the legitimisation of sex and sexuality as a serious subject for historical research in the 1970s, the historiography of prostitution has increased dramatically, resulting in the formation of a considerable field – one which covers a wide variety of periods and geographic locations.[3] These works range from individual studies of specific cities, countries and time periods to more popular studies which attempt to give a general overview of international trends across several centuries.[4] The focus of these studies is equally wide-ranging, covering topics such as law, policy and policing; venereal disease and medical intervention; the role of religious and other voluntary organisations; and the policing of sexuality, women's bodies and public spaces.[5] This diverse research has greatly increased our knowledge of prostitution across the world and provides useful analytical frameworks for analysing the wider social implications of prostitution in different contexts. Moreover, these studies on prostitution have provided a helpful vantage point for understanding much wider changes in society, especially those relating to gender, power and sexual relations. This book will explore these themes further by examining how the police, magistrates, voluntary organisations and probation officers in Edinburgh and Glasgow worked together during the early twentieth century to control female prostitution and influence the lives of the women involved.

In 1843 the writer and social reformer William Tait estimated that there were 200 brothels in Edinburgh with over 800 women working within them.[6] He calculated that the ratio of men to prostitutes was therefore 80:1 and that over £200,000 was spent on buying sex each year. He described the many different types of establishments in which prostitution took place, such as brothels, taverns, eating houses and private lodgings, and judged the 'class' of prostitute who lived there. He also listed the many reasons why he thought women entered prostitution, a list that included: licentious inclination; pride and love of dress; seduction; poverty; intemperance and a bad home life. Clearly these calculations and observations were highly subjective, and their accuracy is questionable. Nonetheless, these questions regarding why women entered prostitution, where they worked and what kind of life they led remain central for understanding the history of prostitution. Whereas historians have begun to answer many of these questions relating to the nineteenth century[7], this is less true for the twentieth century, especially in relation to Scotland. Whilst there has been research which focuses on England during the first half of the twentieth century, and on London in particular, there has previously been no research on prostitution in early-twentieth-century Scotland.[8] This is surprising, considering that Scotland has distinctive traditions of law, religion, medical practice and practical policing.[9]

This book will explore how these Scottish traditions influenced the organisation of prostitution in Edinburgh and Glasgow between 1900 and 1939 and shaped the methods that were used to police it, both formally and informally. In particular, the book will examine the extent to which the informal system of lock hospitals and asylums that was used to regulate prostitution in Scotland during the nineteenth century continued to hold sway, and explore the ways in which this system adapted to meet the wider socio-economic trends of the period. The experiences of the women who were involved in prostitution are central to this book. Although the nature of the available source materials make it difficult to ascertain unmediated accounts of women's experiences, by using a collective biography approach it is possible to determine some of the reasons as to why women became involved in prostitution and explore the impact it had on their lives. Whilst abuse, exploitation and poverty affected many of the women involved in prostitution, this book will also explore the ways in which women negotiated the challenges posed by the individuals and institutions that attempted to control or exploit them.

Prostitution and the Law

Prostitution has never technically been illegal in Britain; however, several acts and by-laws have been used to make various prostitution-related offences illegal, such as soliciting, brothel-keeping and living off the immoral earnings of prostitution. During the early nineteenth century prostitution was mainly regulated using vagrancy laws. These laws were not designed specifically to police prostitution, but they were used to prosecute women who caused public annoyance and disorder or committed indecent and riotous behaviour through their involvement in prostitution. In Scotland the common law offence 'breach of the peace' was used for this purpose prior to the late nineteenth century.

In the 1860s the British government introduced new legislation to tackle the spread of venereal diseases in the armed forces. Whilst most other European countries adopted the French system of licensing and state-regulated brothels, Britain opted for regulation based on disease control, and the 1864, 1866 and 1869 Contagious Diseases Acts made compulsory the genital examination of any women suspected of being a 'common prostitute' in particular port and garrison towns. This legislation was only enacted in specific towns, none of which were in Scotland. However, the widespread opposition to the acts did influence Scottish debates concerning the policing of prostitution. Opposition to the Contagious Diseases Acts came from a wide range of social, moral and political campaigners. These included working-class men and women who recognised the class bias inherent in the selection of suspect women, evangelicals who condemned the state regulation of vice, and early feminist campaigners who objected to the licensing of a double standard of sexual morality which resulted in the oppression and ill-treatment of women. When the Acts were successfully repealed in 1886, many of these reformers, collectively known as the 'social purity movement', turned their attention towards campaigning against 'white slavery'.[10] The moral panic surrounding white slavery, which was ignited by the tales of young British girls being abducted and forced into sexual slavery abroad and fuelled by sensationalist newspaper articles such as W.T. Stead's 'The Maiden Tribute of Modern Babylon', resulted in the enactment of the 1885 Criminal Amendment Act. Among several sections which aimed at policing morality, the Act raised the age of consent from thirteen to sixteen and made brothel-keeping illegal. In addition to the Act, the National Vigilance Association (NVA) was founded in order to help uphold and enforce these new morality laws throughout Britain, and this was soon followed by the establishment of the Scottish National Vigilance Association (SNVA).[11]

However, whilst these organisations and national legislation were important, when considering the day-to-day policing of prostitution in Scotland, the separate Scottish legislation was more influential. The most far-reaching legislation in Scotland was the 1892 Burgh Police (Scotland) Act. This Act stipulated that to 'loiter about or importune for the purposes of prostitution' by a 'common prostitute or streetwalker' was an offence punishable by a fine of up to forty shillings for each offence.[12] In addition to the 1892 Burgh Police Act, individual cities within Scotland also had their own separate acts. In Edinburgh, the 1879 Edinburgh Municipal and Police Act stated that the 'common prostitute' or 'night walker' who:

> loiters or importunes passengers for the purposes of prostitution in or near any street or court, or any common stair or passage, or in

> any public park or garden, Holyrood park, or any other open space frequented by the public, shall be liable to a penalty not exceeding five pounds, or in the discretion of the judge or police, may, without a penalty being inflicted, be committed to prison for a period not exceeding that of 60 days.[13]

Although it was very similar to the 1892 Act, the Edinburgh Act of 1879 gave the courts considerably more power to impose harsher fines and sentences. However, in Glasgow the Glasgow Police (Further Powers) Act of 1892 meant that women could only be fined up to forty shillings and be sentenced to prison for a period no longer than 60 days in default of payment.[14] Local licensing acts were also used for regulating prostitution. For example, the 1903 Licensing (Scotland) Act prohibited a publican or a hotel keeper from 'permitting men or women of notoriously bad fame from assembling and meeting within his premises.'[15] Other important Scottish legislation included the 1902 Immoral Traffic (Scotland) Act that was introduced to target men who trafficked women into prostitution and lived off their immoral earnings, and men who 'in any public place persistently solicit or importune for immoral purposes.'[16] The Act allowed for imprisonment for up to six months, and the 1912 Criminal Law Amendment Act introduced the use of the cat tail whip as further punishment for these offences.[17]

Although these acts were in many ways similar to their English and Welsh counterparts, there were some significant differences. In England and Wales the police had to prove that a woman had been soliciting to the 'annoyance of the inhabitants or passengers.'[18] This was often difficult to prove and slowed down the prosecution process, sometimes resulting in the fabrication of evidence by the police, which led to accusations of corruption and feelings of mistrust. In Scotland, however, it was not necessary to prove annoyance, which lessened the need to fabricate evidence. Unlike in England and Wales, under Scottish law the uncorroborated evidence of one witness was not sufficient to prove a charge, and the Procurator Fiscal, not the police, was responsible for initiating prosecutions. These factors reduced the need to manufacture false charges, which was perceived to have become a problem in England, and reduced the likelihood of accusations of corruption and malpractice.[19] Furthermore, in Scotland the police also employed a system of cautioning which meant that a woman had to be seen importuning on three separate occasions before she could be arrested. Only if the woman was cautioned and reported several times was she formally charged and categorised as a 'common prostitute'.[20] This helped to stop cases of mistaken identity and meant that women who were only occasionally turning to prostitution had less chance of being arrested and officially labelled as a 'common prostitute'.

Finally, the 1902 and 1912 Immoral Traffic (Scotland) Acts placed more focus on prosecuting men for their involvement in prostitution than did the equivalent legislation south of the border.

Chapter Outline

The book focuses on Edinburgh and Glasgow because a large majority of all prostitution-related offences in Scotland occurred in these two large urban centres. However, whilst comparisons will be made between the two cities, the nature of the different sources available in Edinburgh and Glasgow means that a 'like-for-like' comparison is not possible. Instead, Edinburgh and Glasgow are used as case studies to further our understanding of urban prostitution in Scotland's two largest cities between 1900 and 1939.

The book opens with a chapter on the policing of prostitution in Edinburgh and Glasgow which explores how contemporary attitudes towards prostitution influenced the methods that were used to police it during the early twentieth century. The first half of the chapter focuses on street solicitation and questions the extent to which it was criminalised during this period. The second half of the chapter focuses on the policing of brothels, 'pimps' and 'brothel-keepers'. Julia Laite's recent research has shown how prostitution in London was increasingly criminalised between 1885 and 1950.[21] This criminalisation forced women to rely more heavily on third parties for protection against detection and facilitated a move to more clandestine forms of indoor prostitution. This trend towards the use of more clandestine methods of prostitution can also be seen in Edinburgh and Glasgow. However, the extent to which a targeted campaign of increased criminalisation was the main factor in this development is less certain. London is a unique city: its size and diversity mean that to generalise the findings from London to Scotland would be misleading. In Edinburgh and Glasgow arrest and conviction rates for soliciting offences declined sharply during the early twentieth century, and chapter two will explore the many complex reasons for this decline.

By analysing police and court records over a forty-year period, including witness reports, general order books, annual reports and returns of crime for Edinburgh and Glasgow, chapter two will examine how the law was translated into practical everyday policing. How, in other words, did the attitudes and experiences of the police and magistrates influence methods of surveillance, arrest and prosecution? Crucially, the witness reports given by police officers for the Burgh Court hearings provide detailed descriptions of their surveillance methods and provide examples of the everyday interactions between the police and the women involved in prostitution, allowing us to gain insights into individual and collective police attitudes towards prostitution. Memoirs of more senior police officers also give an interesting insight into the attitudes of the men in charge of determining day-to-day policing strategies. Whilst the police memoir genre follows its own stylistic traditions, casting some doubt on these works' factual accuracy, the memoirs do help us understand the motivations of the men who designed and implemented prostitution-related policies.

The importance of understanding the ways in which the unique Scottish context affected the organisation and regulation of prostitution during the early twentieth century is particularly pertinent in light of recent research which has highlighted the importance of space and place for understanding the history of prostitution. Philip Howell's study of two English cities (Liverpool and Cambridge) and several British colonies (including Malta, Gibraltar and Corfu) during the nineteenth century shows that the 'particularities of place' were fundamental for shaping the regulation of prostitution.[22] Howell argues that in Liverpool and Cambridge prostitution was policed by separating it into specific locations away from respectable society.[23] Chapter three will use police and court records to examine the extent to which this occurred in Edinburgh and Glasgow during the early twentieth century and to question whether space was used as a form of social control, separating the undesirable women from respectable society. Were those in a position of authority able to organise space so that it corresponded with the dominant social system and reinforced distinctions between moral and immoral spaces?[24] Although middle-class discourses about prostitution portrayed prostitutes as outcasts, and many 'respectable' members of society may have wanted this separation to be reflected in the physical and social landscape, was this desire ever fully realised? Were the police willing and able to control the movement and activities of women who engaged in prostitution, or did these women find ways of crossing and subverting these invisible boundaries? What role did other factors, such as property prices or proximity to entertainment districts, play in shaping where prostitution was located? By exploring these themes the chapter will ultimately determine whether prostitution was physically and psychologically confined to the margins of society, and the extent to which women themselves understood, internalised or resisted this association with the immoral landscape.

Scotland has a long-established tradition of voluntary, philanthropic and Kirk-led organisations enjoying a strong influence within communities. Barbara Littlewood, Linda Mahood and Roger Davidson have demonstrated the various ways in which Scotland had a 'preference for local and voluntary initiatives' that was based on strong religious and community-based philanthropic networks.[25] What is more, Davidson points out that the Scottish state has traditionally had little interest or involvement in matters of morality prior to the twentieth century.[26] However, while Mahood has studied the role of Magdalene Asylums in Scotland during the nineteenth century, and Davidson and Davis have examined prostitution policy in Scotland after 1950, there has been little research undertaken on prostitution and reform institutions in Scotland during the early twentieth century. One important exception is the work of Viviene Cree, who has tracked shifts in the remit of the National Vigilance Association in Scotland across the twentieth century as it reconfigured (and renamed) itself to become primarily an adoption society.[27] However, there has yet to be any detailed analysis of how different voluntary reform organisations worked together with the police to influence the day-to-day regulation of prostitution and the experiences of the women involved.

Whilst voluntary organisations were also involved in the reformation of 'fallen women' in England, the nature and extent of their role in the twentieth century differed considerably in Scotland. Most importantly, the nineteenth-century 'Glasgow system' described by Linda Mahood, which relied on the cooperation between the police, voluntary and medical institutions, continued to play a vital role in Scotland well into the twentieth century. Central to the survival of this system were the ways in which voluntary organisations adapted to wider socio-economic developments and changes in the criminal justice system, especially after the introduction of probation in 1907. The willingness of voluntary organisations to allow their volunteers to work as probation officers and to accept probationers into their reform homes meant that women who were arrested for soliciting were increasingly placed on probation rather than given prison sentences. The close connection between religious voluntary organisations and the probation service that resulted from this cooperation meant that the official approach towards policing prostitution was partly shaped by the ideology of these religious voluntary organisations.[28]

Chapter four will use probation reports and the records of the Magdalene Asylums and other voluntary organisations in Edinburgh and Glasgow, such as the National Vigilance Association of Scotland (Eastern Division) and the Women Patrols, to explore the ways in which this collaboration encouraged a more penal-welfare approach towards policing prostitution.[29] By looking in depth at the day-to-day running of these institutions and the expectations placed on probations, the chapter will explore the different responses women had to this system and assess both the positive and negative aspects of this penal-welfare approach. To what extent did the efforts to care for and to reform 'fallen women' in the domestic sphere mean that women were forced to adopt middle-class standards of respectable femininity, or did they reject this ideology?[30] Whilst the restriction of their freedom and intrusion into their private lives for long periods may have been a high price to pay in order to avoid prison, did some women benefit from this opportunity to avoid incarceration and gain help with finding alternative employment?

William Tait's 1840 study (referred to earlier) not only consisted of lists of the causes of prostitution but also included some more personal and sympathetic musings about the harsh realities of life for women working as prostitutes in Edinburgh during the nineteenth century. For example, he stated that:

> Many are the insults which these wretched creatures receive from passengers and police; but how few feel or know the difficulties they have to contend with, and that theirs is no calling of pleasure or choice.[31]

This book is also interested in the everyday realities of the lives of women who sold sex and the 'difficulties they had to contend with'. Much of the historiography on prostitution in the nineteenth century certainly supports Tait's assessment that their life was 'no calling of pleasure'.[32] Frances Finnegan's study of prostitution in York during the nineteenth century highlights the extreme poverty and lack of economic opportunities which drove women to work as prostitutes, concluding that 'poverty was the result as well as the cause of their taking to prostitution.'[33] Similarly, Linda Mahood and Judith Walkowitz describe the many dangers and difficulties faced by women involved in prostitution in Scotland and England, respectively. However, Mahood and Walkowitz, alongside others working on the twentieth century, such as Julia Laite and Victoria Harris, have pointed out that, whilst women had to contend with the harsh realities of abuse and poverty, portraying these women solely as victims risks denying their historical agency. Whilst it is important to communicate the experiences of the 'unsuccessful', the types of sources available for historians, such as the records of the court, police, prison and the poor law, mean that there is a tendency to focus on this aspect of women's experiences. Whilst being careful not to unfairly glamorise their lives, where possible this study aims to include sources which enable us to learn more about the ways in which women resisted those who tried to control or exploit them.

These issues surrounding victimhood and agency are particularly important in light of long-standing debates within feminism regarding the position of prostitution in society.[34] On the one hand there are those who want prostitution legalised and decriminalised. They believe that individuals should have the right to choose what they do with their own bodies and that it is the 'whore stigma' associated with sex work that is the main problem – something which decriminalisation would potentially begin to undermine.[35] One of the most vocal groups who support this stance and typically want legalisation are the sex workers themselves.[36] Some feminists agree with these arguments, vying for a more pragmatic approach which listens to the women who know the most about prostitution. They argue that if women choose to work in the sex industry, then they deserve the opportunity to work in a safe environment with the same employment rights and regulations as other jobs.[37] Moreover, the illegality of prostitution does little to reduce supply and demand or protect women; instead it furthers the dangers associated with sex work because women must rush safety procedures and feel they cannot turn to the police for protection. However, others argue that prostitution is inherently harmful to women and it is a cause, symptom and symbol of the gender inequalities still prevalent within society; hence it must be abolished. They are sceptical about the claim that women freely choose prostitution, pointing out that underlying socio-economic factors, such as poverty, inequality, harmful childhood experiences, drugs and alcohol dependency, limit the scope of their 'choices' and make some women more likely to resort to prostitution. Therefore, criminalisation (albeit of those who buy sex as opposed to those who sell it) is necessary to protect women and to promote gender equality.[38]

These issues are at the centre of a considerable split within feminism, one in which the issues of sexuality, power, human rights, equality and freedom of choice are fundamental. These different approaches are reflected in the historiography. There is a noticeable contrast between historians who have focused on the evidence which gives accounts of the oppression suffered by women under patriarchy and those who have been more concerned with showing women's historical agency. For example, Sheila Jeffreys argues that abolitionism is the only solution for ridding society of this harmful and exploitative activity which no woman truly chooses.[39] Her monograph *The Spinster and her Enemies, 1880–1930* consequently places a strong emphasis on the role of the early feminists who campaigned for the abolition of prostitution but ignores the other feminist organisations active during this period, such as the Association for Moral and Social Hygiene (AMSH), which was more concerned about campaigning against the oppressive solicitation laws in favour of women's rights and liberties.[40] However, historians such as Victoria Harris, Julia Laite and Linda Mahood have been critical of this approach and instead chosen to focus more on balancing the realities of women's agency with those of economic hardship.[41]

Chapter five will also attempt to find this balance whilst keeping women's experiences at the heart of the narrative. The chapter will examine the ways in which women negotiated the pressures placed on them by those who attempted to exploit, reform, regulate and control them. Where possible, I intend to build a clearer picture of who these women were and explore the complex relationships that developed between different individuals within the sex industry, especially those between 'prostitutes', 'pimps' and 'brothel-keepers'. Whilst it is acknowledged that only fragments of these women's experiences can be obtained, the chapter will use a wide range of sources, including census and demographic data, poor law, prison, court and police records, to piece together as many different fragments of their experiences as possible. One of the most valuable sources that will allow me to do this is the Glasgow poor law records that include detailed information about the women over the extended period that they sought support from the Glasgow parishes. They provide details of the claimants' place of birth, their family backgrounds (including information about their parents and children), their 'character', religion, education, state of health, economic circumstances and many other factors that may have facilitated their move into and out of prostitution. The poor law records for Edinburgh were destroyed and, therefore, it is not possible to use the same approach for Edinburgh. However, the Edinburgh Criminal Conviction Registers offer a similar insight, albeit one which is more heavily focused on the women's criminal histories. By bringing together such a range of sources it is possible to build a clearer picture of individuals' lives and to develop a better understanding of the wider patterns and themes that influenced how people became involved in prostitution. Whilst these sources relate primarily to women who were caught up in the legal system or needed financial assistance, meaning they often provide accounts of hardship, abuse and exploitation, they also demonstrate the many ways in which the women negotiated these difficulties and found different ways of coping.

Chapter six expands on the themes established in chapter five by widening the scope of the focus to include women who were involved in more lucrative forms of clandestine prostitution and did not require poor law assistance or have their activities scrutinised by the authorities. The chapter revolves around the 1933 trial of Asher Barnard, the owner of the Kosmo dance club in Edinburgh, who was accused of running a clandestine prostitution operation in the club that involved women dance partners being hired for the evening and taken to off-site locations for sex. The trial provides in-depth details about this method of clandestine prostitution and how new technologies, such as the telephone and the motor car, were used to make this system possible. Furthermore, the trial provides new insights into the experiences of those women who worked as dance partners and provides examples of the types of dangers and exploitation they faced, while also highlighting the benefits they gained from working in a higher-paid and safer environment than the street. However, as with all court testimony, the witness statements were 'staged performances' and the context of the court setting must be taken into consideration.[42] Newspaper reports are also used, both to provide more details about the trial, and to analyse the reaction of the public towards this new form of clandestine prostitution. The reports are used tentatively, with the understanding that the accounts were often influenced by editors' tendencies to emphasise the more sensationalist material and to follow long-standing narratives that shaped the way in which prostitution stories were reported.[43] The chapter ends by examining the role that men played in prostitution, as pimps and managers, but also as customers. The final chapter will bring all of the different themes together and explore how the conclusions made from this research could contribute to contemporary debates about prostitution.

Notes

1. *The Scotsman*, 28 January 1927, p. 11.
2. The word prostitute will sometimes be used within the book but with the understanding that this was a label used by contemporaries to describe and categorise women who engaged in acts of prostitution.
3. For examples of studies on various countries and time periods see, for example: Jacques Rossiaud, *Medieval Prostitution* (Oxford: Basil Blackwell, 1988); Judith Walkowitz, *Prostitution and Victorian Society: Women, Class and the State* (Cambridge: Cambridge University Press, 1980); Sumanta Banerjee, *Under the Raj: Prostitution in Colonial Bengal* (New York: Monthly Review Press, 1998); Maria Luddy, *Prostitution and Irish Society 1800–1940* (Cambridge: Cambridge University Press, 2007); Mary Gibson, *Prostitution and the State in Italy, 1860–1915* (Athens, OH: Ohio State University Press, 1986); Victoria Harris, *Selling Sex in the Reich* (Oxford: Oxford University Press, 2010); Alain Corbin, *Women for Hire: Prostitution and Sexuality in France after 1850* (London: Harvard University Press, 1990); Laurie Bernstein, *Sonia's Daughters: Prostitutes and their Regulation in Imperial Russia* (Berkeley: University of California Press, 1995); Christian Henriot, *Prostitution and Sexuality in Shanghai: A Social History, 1849–1949* (Cambridge: Cambridge University Press, 2001); Gail Hershatter, *Dangerous Pleasures: Prostitution and Modernity in Twentieth Century Shanghai* (Berkeley: University of California Press, 1997); Kay Daniels, *So Much Hard Work: Women and Prostitution in Australian History* (Sydney: Fontana, 1984); Donna J. Guy, *Sex & Danger in Buenos Aires: Prostitution, Family, and Nation in Argentina* (Lincoln: University of Nebraska Press, 1991); Ruth Rosen, *The Lost Sisterhood: Prostitution in America, 1900–1919* (London: Johns Hopkins University Press, 1982); Timothy J. Gilfoyle, *City of Eros: New York City, Prostitution, and the Commercialization of Sex, 1790–1920* (London: W.W. Norton, 1992); Marilynn Wood Hill, *Their Sisters' Keepers: Prostitution in New York City, 1830–1870* (London: University of California Press,

1993); Mark Connelly, *The Response to Prostitution in the Progressive Era* (Chapel Hill: University of North Carolina Press, 1980); Daniel Francis, *Red Light Neon: a History of Vancouver's Sex Trade* (Vancouver: Subway, 2006); Anne Butler, *Daughters of Joy, Sisters of Misery: Prostitutes in the American West, 1865–1890* (Urbana: University of Illinois Press, 1985); Sue Gronewold, 'Beautiful Merchandise: Prostitution in China, 1860–1936', *Women and History*, 1 (1982) pp. 1–114.

4. For general overviews and popular histories see, for example, Nils Johan Ringdal, *Love For Sale: A World History of Prostitution* (New York: Grove Press, 2004); Neil Philip, *Working Girls: An Illustrated History of the Oldest Profession* (London: Bloomsbury, 1991).

5. For studies on policing, law and policy see, for example: Julia Laite, *Common Prostitutes and Ordinary Citizens: Commercial Sex in London, 1885–1960* (Basingstoke: Palgrave Macmillan, 2012); Helen Self, *Prostitution, Women and Misuse of the Law: the Fallen Daughters of Eve* (London: Frank Cass, 2003); Stefan Slater, 'Pimps, Police and Filles de Joie: Foreign Prostitution in Interwar London', *The London Journal*, 32, 1 (2007) pp. 53–74; Roger Davidson and Gayle Davis, *The Sexual State: Sexuality and Scottish Governance, 1950–1980* (Edinburgh: Edinburgh University Press, 2012); For studies on venereal disease and medicine see, for example, Philippa Levine, *Prostitution, Race and Politics: Policing Venereal Disease in the British Empire* (London: Routledge, 2003); Roger Davidson and Lesley Hall (eds), *Sex Sin and Suffering: Venereal Disease and European Society since 1870* (London: Routledge, 2001); Roger Davidson, *Dangerous Liaisons: a Social History of Venereal Disease in Twentieth-Century Scotland* (Amsterdam: Rodopi, 2000); Mary Spongberg, *Feminizing Venereal Disease: The Body of the Prostitute in Nineteenth-Century Medical Discourse* (London: Macmillan, 1997); For studies on the role of religion, voluntary organisations and the social purity movement see, for example: Mariana Valverde, *The Age of Light, Soap, and Water: Moral Reform in English Canada, 1885–1925* (Toronto: Toronto University Press, 2008); Linda Mahood, *The Magdalenes: Prostitution in the Nineteenth Century* (London: Routledge, 1990); Paula Bartley, *Prostitution, Prevention and Reform in England, 1860–1914* (London: Routledge, 2000); For studies on the policing of women's bodies and public space see, for example, Philip Howell, *Geographies of Regulation: Policing Prostitution in Nineteenth Century Britain and the Empire* (Cambridge: Cambridge University Press, 2009); Timothy Gilfoyle, 'The Urban Geography of Commercial Sex: Prostitution in New York City, 1790–1860', *Journal of Urban History* 13, 4 (1987) pp. 371–93; Judith Walkowitz, *City of Dreadful Delight:*

Narratives of Sexual Danger in Late-Victorian London (London: Virago, 1992).

6. William Tait, *Magdalenism: An Inquiry into the Extent, Causes and Consequences of Prostitution in Edinburgh* (Edinburgh, 1840).
7. See, for example, Mahood, *The Magdalenes*: Walkowitz, *Prostitution and Victorian Society*; Francis Finnegan, *Poverty and Prostitution: A Study of Victorian Prostitutes in York* (Cambridge: Cambridge University Press, 1979); Bartley, *Prostitution, Prevention and Reform*; Tony Henderson, *Disorderly Women in Eighteenth-Century London: Prostitution and Control in the Metropolis, 1730–1830* (London: Longman, 1999).
8. See, Laite, *Common Prostitutes and Ordinary Citizens*; Self, *Prostitution, Women and Misuse of the Law*; Slater, 'Pimps, Police and Filles de Joie'. For research on prostitution in Scotland after the Second World War see, Roger Davidson and Gayle Davis, '"A Festering Sore on the Body of Society": The Wolfenden Committee and Female Prostitution in Mid-Twentieth-Century Scotland', *Journal of Scottish Historical Studies*, 24 (2005) pp. 80–98.
9. See, for example, David Barrie, *Police in the Age of Improvement: Police Development and the Civic Tradition in Scotland, 1775–1865* (Cullompton: Willan, 2008); Douglas Grant, *The Thin Blue Line: The Story of the City of Glasgow Police* (London: Long, 1973); Lindsay Farmer, '"The Genius of our Law": Criminal Law and the Scottish Legal Tradition', in *Law in History: Histories of Law and Society* Vol. II, (ed.) David Sugarman (Aldershot: Ashgate, 1996) pp. 97–115; Richard Cowley, *A History of the British Police: From its Earliest Beginnings to the Present Day* (Stroud: History Press, 2011); David Hamilton, *The Healers: A History of Medicine in Scotland* (Edinburgh: Mercat Press, 1981).
10. Edward Bristow, *Prostitution and Prejudice, the Jewish Fight against White Slavery, 1870–1939* (Oxford: Clarendon, 1982).
11. Walkowitz, *Prostitution and Victorian Society*.
12. The Burgh Police (Scotland) Act 1892 (55 & 56 Vict. c. 55).
13. The Edinburgh Municipal and Police Act 1879 (42&43 Vict. c. cxxxii).
14. The Glasgow Police (Further Powers) Act 1892 (55&56 Vict. c. 165).
15. The Licensing (Scotland) Act 1903 (3 Edw 7, c. 25).
16. The Immoral Traffic (Scotland) Act 1902 (1&2 Geo 5, c. 20).
17. The Criminal Law Amendment Act 1912 (3&4 Geo 5, c. 38).
18. Report of the Street Offences Committee, pp. 1928–9 (cmd.3231), IX, 13, 16, 24–5, as cited in Davidson and Davis, 'A Festering Sore on the Body of Society'.
19. Lindsay Farmer, *Criminal Law, Tradition and Legal Order: Crime and the Genius of Scots Law 1747 to the Present* (Cambridge: Cambridge University

Press, 1997), p. 82; Clive Emsley, 'Sergeant Goddard: The Story of the Rotten Apple, or a Diseased Orchard?' in Amy Gilman Srebnick and Rene Levy (eds), *Crime and Culture: A Historical Perspective* (Aldershot: Ashgate, 2005) pp. 85–104.

20. Davidson and Davis, 'A Festering Sore on the Body of Society', p. 83.
21. Julia Laite, 'Prostitution in London 1885–1930' PhD thesis (Cambridge University, 2008); Laite, *Common Prostitutes and Ordinary Citizens.*
22. Philip Howell, *Geographies of Regulation.*
23. Ibid, p. 11.
24. For further discussion on the social and cultural production and use of space see: Henri Lefebvre, *The Production of Space* (Oxford: Basil Blackwell, 1991); Michel de Certeau, *The Practice of Everyday Life* (London: California University Press, 1984).
25. Linda Mahood and Barbara Littlewood, 'Prostitutes, Magdalenes and Wayward Girls: Dangerous Sexualities of Working Class Women in Victorian Scotland', *Gender and History*, 3, 2 (1991) pp. 160–175, p. 161.
26. Davidson and Davis, *The Sexual State.*
27. Viviene Cree, *From Public Streets to Private Lives: The Changing Task of Social Work (Aldershot: Avebury, 1995).*
28. See, for example, Maurice Vanstone, *Supervising Offenders in the Community: A History of Probation Theory and Practice* (Aldershot: Ashgate, 2004).
29. See, David Garland, *Punishment and Welfare: A History of Penal Strategies* (Aldershot: Gower, 1985).
30. See, for example, Amanda Anderson, *Tainted Souls and Painted Faces: The Rhetoric of Fallenness in Victorian Culture* (London: Cornell University Press, 1993); Amanda Vickery, 'Golden Age to Separate Spheres? A Review of the Categories and Chronology of English Women's History', *The Historical Journal*, 36, 2 (1993) pp. 383–414; Leonore Davidoff and Catherine Hall, *Family Fortunes: Men and Women of the English Middle Class, 1780–1850* (London: Hutchinson, 1987).
31. William Tait, *Magdalenism*, p. 18.
32. Ibid, p. 18.
33. Finnegan, *Poverty and Prostitution*, p. 17 and 32.
34. Katie Beran, 'Revisiting the Prostitution Debate: Uniting Liberal and Radical Feminism in Pursuit of Policy Reform', *Law and Inequality: A Journal of Theory and Practice*, 19 (2012) pp. 19–56; Ann Heilmann, 'Gender and Essentialism: Feminist Debates in the Twenty-First Century', *Critical Quarterly* 53, 4 (2011) pp. 78–89.
35. See, for example, Belinda Brooks-Gordon, 'Bellwether Citizens: The Regulation of Male Clients of Sex Workers', *Journal of Law and*

Society 37, 1 (2010) pp. 145–70; Teela Sanders, 'Blinded by Morality? Prostitution Policy in the UK', *Capital & Class* 29, 2 (2005) pp. 9–15.

36. See for example, Melisa Gira Grant, *Playing the Whore: The Work of Sex Work* (Verso, 2014); http://prostitutescollective.net (last accessed 30 May 2015); http://www.nswp.org (last accessed 30 May 2015); http://www.scot-pep.org.uk/(last accessed 30 May 2015).
37. See, for example, Jill Nagle, *Whores and Other Feminists* (London: Routledge, 1997); Sarah Bromberg, *Feminist Issues in Prostitution* (1997); from feministissues.com: http://feministissues.com/ (last accessed 30 May 2015); Lisa McLaughlin, 'Discourses of Prostitution/Discourses of Sexuality', *Critical Studies in Mass Communication* 8, 3 (1991) pp. 249–72.
38. See, for example, Sheila Jeffreys, *The Industrial Vagina: The Political Economy of the Global Sex Trade* (Oxford: Routledge, 2009); Kathleen Barry, *The Prostitution of Sexuality* (New York: New York University Press, 1995); Melissa Farley '"Bad for the body, bad for the heart"': Prostitution Harms Women Even If Legalized or Decriminalized', *Violence Against Women*, 10 (2004) pp. 1087–125; Christine Overall, 'What's Wrong with Prostitution? Evaluating Sex Work', *Signs* 17, 4 (1992) pp. 705–24.
39. Sheila Jeffreys, *The Idea of Prostitution* (Melbourne: Spinifex Press, 1997).
40. For more on the Association of Moral and Social Hygiene see, for example, Julia Laite, 'The Association for Moral and Social Hygiene, Abolitionism, and Prostitution Law in Britain, 1915–1959', *Women's History Review*, 17, 2 (2008) pp. 207–23; Sheila Jeffreys, *The Spinster and her Enemies, Feminism* and *Sexuality 1880–1930* (London: Pandora, 1985).
41. Mahood, *The Magdalenes*; Harris, *Selling Sex in the Reich*; Laite, *Common Prostitutes*.
42. Shani D'Cruze, *Crimes of Outrage: Sex Violence and Victorian Women* (London: UCL Press, 1998).
43. Adrian Bingham, *Family Newspapers? Sex, Private Life and the British Popular Press, 1918–1978* (Oxford: Oxford University Press, 2009).

CHAPTER 2

Controlling the 'Social Evil': Policing Prostitution

By the late nineteenth and early-twentieth centuries a wide range of national legislation and local by-laws meant that the Scottish police had considerable powers to arrest those involved in prostitution. However, rather than prosecutions increasing due to this legislation, the number of arrests and convictions sharply declined after the First Word War. There are many possible reasons behind this decrease, but one of the most significant was down to how the police and magistrates in Edinburgh and Glasgow chose to implement the law on an everyday basis. This chapter will examine how police attitudes towards prostitution influenced the methods that were used to police different types of indoor and outdoor prostitution, and how this approach shaped the ways that individual men and women were treated under the law. The first half of the chapter will begin by examining the policing of street prostitution and the second half will explore the policing of brothels and 'pimps'.

Policing Street Prostitution

Three key acts were used to police prostitution in Scotland during the early twentieth century. The most commonly used piece of legislation was the 1892 Burgh Police (Scotland) Act.[1] Section 381, subsection 22, made it an offence for a 'common prostitute or street walker' to importune for the purposes of prostitution, and subsection 23 criminalised anyone who 'habitually and persistently importunes or solicits, or loiters about for the purpose of importuning or soliciting women or children for immoral purposes'.[2] In addition to this there were two main local by-laws. In Edinburgh this was the 1879 Municipal and Police Act which penalised the '"common prostitute" or "night walker" who loiters or importunes passengers for the purposes of prostitution in or near any street or court'. In Glasgow, the Glasgow Police (Further Powers) Act 1892 – section 18 stated that:

> Every street prostitute or street walker who on or near any street loiters about or importunes passengers for the purposes of prostitution shall be liable to a penalty not exceeding forty shillings for each offence.[3]

During the late nineteenth century and the first decade of the twentieth century these laws resulted in a large number of arrests. However, the number of prosecutions declined drastically after the First World War. Table 2.1 shows that, whereas in 1908 there had been 3,192 proceedings against women for soliciting offences in Scotland, by 1918 there were only 460. After the war

Table 2.1 Prosecutions and Convictions for Importuning Offences in Scotland, 1906–55.

Year	No. proceeded against	No. of charges proved	Year	No. proceeded against	No. of charges proved
1906	2,757	2,544	1931	452	420
1907	2,997	2,790	1932	325	309
1908	3,192	2,989	1933	349	319
1909	2,969	2,750	1934	281	265
1910	2,870	2,496	1935	286	267
1911	2,485	2,219	1936	336	322
1912	2,487	2,147	1937	312	293
1913	1,884	1,642	1938	238	229
1914	1,696	1,481	1939	141	132
1915	1,328	1,141	1940	41	36
1916	956	812	1941	43	41
1917	580	470	1942	138	129
1918	460	389	1943	268	255
1919	635	515	1944	328	302
1920	803	641	1945	254	240
1921	686	589	1946	141	135
1922	648	585	1947	105	95
1923	837	807	1948	103	94
1924	608	558	1949	91	86
1925	425	387	1950	82	76
1926	544	476	1951	72	71
1927	472	413	1952	95	91
1928	480	438	1953	136	126
1929	439	402	1954	168	160
1930	394	362	1955	202	201

Source: Wolfenden Committee Report, 1957.

ended there was a slight increase in prosecutions, but the numbers did not return to the high levels found before the First World War. During the 1920s and 1930s there were several fluctuations in the number of prosecutions but the long-term pattern was one of gradual decline, so that by 1939 the number had reached just 141 per year.

The crime returns for Edinburgh and Glasgow show that these two cities accounted for the vast majority of solicitation prosecutions across the whole of Scotland. The prosecutions in Glasgow made up the largest percentage throughout the whole period, in part due to its considerably larger population size. However, the significantly larger number of arrests in Glasgow prior to the First World War may also reflect a more active approach to the policing of street solicitation that occurred in the city during this period, possibly a legacy of the nineteenth-century system that was characterised by Linda Mahood as being especially repressive.[4] Nonetheless, whilst there were some variations and fluctuations, the overall prosecution pattern in both cities

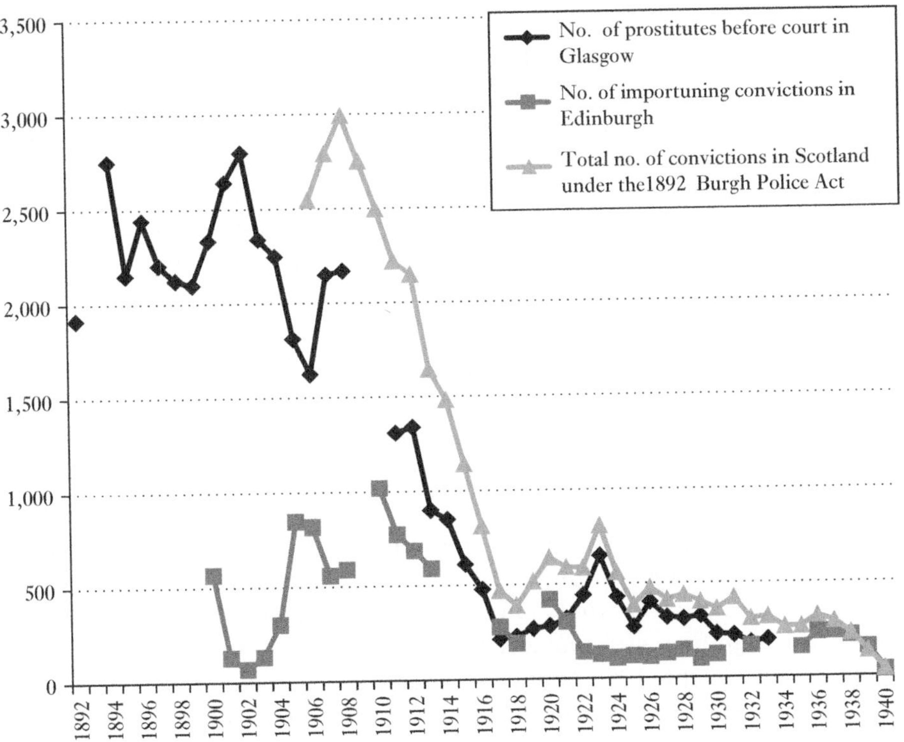

Figure 2.1 Comparison of National Solicitation Offences Statistics with Edinburgh and Glasgow.

Source: Wolfenden Committee Report, 1957; ECA, Edinburgh Police Annual Reports, 1900–1940; GCA, DTC 7/19/1, Glasgow Police Annual Reports, 1892–1933.

corresponded with the general pattern of decline that occurred in the national statistics after the First World War.

Although this sharp decline is quite striking, establishing exactly what it means is less simple. One possibility is that the statistics reflect a general reduction in the number of women engaging in prostitution. As average wages for women in Scotland increased during the early twentieth century and a wider variety of better paid jobs started to become available in new consumer industries and the service sector, it is likely that this reduced the number of women forced to resort to prostitution out of economic necessity. This certainly may have partly contributed to the decline, but to overemphasise the improvement in the majority of women's economic situations during this period would be misleading. Although there were some wage increases and real gains in the number of white collar and other higher-paid skilled jobs for women (particularly during the First World War), these opportunities primarily benefited middle-class women or included jobs which were given back to men once the war was over.[5] Moreover, viewing criminal statistics as an indication of the number of women involved in prostitution can be misleading. Whilst the police statistics do offer us some indication of the number of women involved, they only tell us about the number of offenders that were 'caught' and do not identify whether several offences were committed by the same woman. For example, whilst in Edinburgh in 1910 there were 1,020 arrests for importuning; the Edinburgh Police Chief Constable informed the inspector and Clerk of the Glasgow Parish Council that this actually only represented roughly 430 women.[6] Conversely, police statistics tell us little about the number of women who escaped arrest and worked unnoticed by the police in more clandestine settings.

Rather than a reduction in supply, another factor that could have contributed to a reduction in the number of prosecutions was a reduction in demand. During the First World War contemporaries were concerned that the war might lead to a 'loosening of sexual morals'.[7] In particular, concern was directed towards young women who engaged in promiscuous sex with soldiers due to 'khaki fever' which was apparently caused by their patriotic attraction towards men in uniform.[8] This was particularly alarming due to fears that these women would spread venereal disease to unsuspecting soldiers. Although they were not strictly engaging in acts of paid prostitution, because they accepted treats and gifts from their 'dates' rather than cold cash, these women were labelled as 'amateur prostitutes' due to the lack of an appropriate term for 'promiscuous' women. If promiscuity truly did increase dramatically during this period, then men would no longer have needed to turn to prostitution as their only option for pre-marital or extra-marital sex. However, while the Edwardian period did witness the beginning of what is seen as the 'sexualising of women', meaning women were seen as being capable of sexual response, this sexuality was expected to be passive and to occur only within marriage.[9] Moreover, attitudes towards sexuality were not as dramatically altered by the First World War as many assumed.[10] For those women who were not willing to engage in extra- or pre-marital sex before the war, it was unlikely that their attitudes towards sexuality drastically changed after the war.[11] It was not until the 1960s and 1970s, in the wake of the invention of the contraceptive pill and other cultural developments, that increased pre-marital sex was likely to have had a noticeable impact on the demand for prostitution.[12]

Nonetheless, The First World War may at least account for the dramatic reduction in the number of convictions between the years 1916 and 1918. Even though prostitution was thought to have increased during the war, it is fair to assume that during this period the police were occupied with duties more pressing to the war effort than solicitation offences.[13] The main concern the authorities had regarding prostitution was the potential threat it posed to soldiers who might contract venereal disease. It is possible, therefore, that arrests during this period were instead made under new wartime legislation such as the Defence of the Realm Act (DORA) regulation 13a and later 40D.[14] These Acts regulated where prostitutes could go and made it an offence for a woman who was infected with a venereal disease to have sex with a member of the armed forces. However, Julia Laite has shown that, in actuality, these laws did not result in a large number of arrests.[15] Moreover, these factors do not explain why the number of prosecutions remained low after the war.

Rather than the DORA Acts, Laite has shown that, in London, park regulations, 'breach of the peace' and licensing acts were increasingly used to police prostitution.[16] Therefore, whilst official solicitation statistics in London also declined, Laite suggests that the use of acts and regulations other than specific solicitation legislation masked the true number of women who were being arrested. However, although similar licensing acts and park regulations were also used in Edinburgh and Glasgow, there was less reason for the police to resort to them on a regular basis. Whereas in England the law required proof that a woman was soliciting to the annoyance of passers-by, something which routinely hindered the ability of the police to prosecute solicitation offences, in Scotland no such annoyance clause existed. This made it unnecessary for the police to use other acts when the relevant national and local solicitation legislation was adequate. This is supported by the lack of evidence in the Scottish police and court records of any significant increase in the use of these types of laws and regulations for the purposes of arresting prostitutes in Scotland during this period.

A more likely cause for the decline in the number of prosecutions was the movement of women from the street to indoor locations, making them less visible to the police. Chapters three and six will examine the development of clandestine prostitution in more depth, but it is fair to say that the movement of women indoors certainly did reduce the visibility of commercial sex. Nonetheless, street prostitution continued, and for those women who chose to move indoors, new commercial and technological developments arguably played at least an equally important role as policing in shaping their decision to move indoors. Rather than being forced to enter more clandestine venues due to increasing police persecution, as was the case in London, the criminalisation of street solicitation in Edinburgh and Glasgow did not increase in its intensity. On the contrary, the next section will show that the apathy and reluctance of the police and magistrates in Edinburgh and Glasgow to arrest and convict women for prostitution offences was one of the main reasons behind the decline in prosecutions after the First World War.

Police Attitudes

The impact and effectiveness of the solicitation legislation depended largely upon how the police chose to interpret and implement it on a day-to-day basis. It is therefore important to examine policing methods and attitudes towards prostitution. During the deliberations of the Street Offences Committee, which was set up in 1927 to investigate the effectiveness of solicitation laws, the Edinburgh Police Chief Constable Roderick Ross described to the committee the methods that were used to police prostitution: 'street offences were dealt with by plain clothes officers who were selected for their capability, experience and good conduct. There were about 30 officers out each night, 6 pairs in each division.'[17] The surveillance and arrest of prostitutes was primarily the responsibility of plain-clothes police; however, these plain-clothes officers were also engaged in different tasks, apart from 'merely seeking out prostitutes'.[18] Using plain-clothes policemen meant that they would go unnoticed by the women as they followed them on the streets, which allowed the officers to become 'acquainted with the habits of this class'.[19] Scots Law required there to be two witnesses before a conviction could be made; therefore the police officers worked in pairs so that they could verify each other's evidence.

The witness reports given by the Edinburgh Police describe in detail how the officers followed the women and recorded their movements.[20] The officers listed which streets the 'suspected prostitute' walked on, the different shops, pubs and parks she entered, who accompanied her and, most importantly, the details of each act of solicitation, including who, when and where. Once sufficient evidence had been gathered to establish that a particular woman was soliciting for the purposes of prostitution, the police approached her whilst she was talking with the man she was suspected to have solicited. The police then asked the man if he knew the woman and whether she had solicited him for the purposes of prostitution. After the man gave his reply, the police noted his answer and asked him to accompany them to the police station to act as a witness. In most cases the man declined to be a witness and was allowed to leave. The types of details the police recorded became very routine in nature, and the statements they wrote usually followed a set pattern. If one removed the specific details from each case (such as the names, dates and addresses), the extract below could represent any one of the numerous witness statements:

> At 10.50 pm on date of charge, I saw the two accused accost two sailors in Princes Street. They left them and then went down Leith Street where they loitered about and accosted a civilian. They left him and proceeded up Leith Street where they accosted 4 sailors. They were then arrested. The sailors were interviewed and they said that the two accused accosted them and declined to be witnesses. Both accused deny the charges.[21]

The hierarchical organisation of the police force meant that officers were expected to follow the strategies that were announced in the General Orders issued by the Chief Constable. These orders were, in turn, influenced by the policies that were decided by the council and magistrates committee, who were ultimately influenced by wider public and political concerns. Nonetheless, Joanne Klein has shown that in Liverpool, Manchester and Birmingham 'the personality of each force was in many ways dependent on the character of its Chief Constable.'[22] The attitude of the Edinburgh and Glasgow Chief Constables towards prostitution had a similarly important influence on the strategies that were adopted for policing prostitution in these cities and on the General Orders that the police were given to follow.

One of the most noticeable characteristics of this period in Scottish policing history is that many of the Chief Constables appreciated the difficult socio-economic circumstances that could lead some women to become involved in prostitution, making these women worthy of sympathy rather than moral condemnation. For example, the 1904 Glasgow Annual Police Report made by James Verdier Stevenson (the Glasgow Chief Constable from 1902 to 1922) described how prostitution was caused by 'the low rate of wages paid for female labour [which] tend[ed] to lead girls to the streets'.[23] In 1913 he explained that a woman entered prostitution because of an 'evil association' and that it was 'almost impossible for a young woman to break voluntarily with the associates whose interest it is to keep her in a state of degradation'.[24] After Stevenson's retirement in 1922, the new Glasgow Police Chief Constable, Andrew Donnan Smith, continued in a similar vein, making the following statement in April 1922:

> While it is true that many girls fall voluntarily, it is equally true that innocence, inexperience, poverty, and lack of employment are responsible for a great amount of prostitution, and great tact must be exercised in dealing with girls of this class if any headway in their reclamation is to be made.[25]

The Glasgow Police annual reports show that this understanding of prostitution translated into a more welfare-oriented approach towards policing prostitution that involved sending women to places where they could be reformed rather than punished. For example, in the annual report for 1922, Smith described how 'the imposition of a fine does not prove a deterrent, any person may pay the fine, and the woman may continue her mode of life'.[26] As an alternative to this, Smith suggested that prostitutes should be sent to a detention home. As will be further explained in chapter four, the idea of the reform home was not new, and institutions to reform 'fallen women' had been in existence in Scotland since the late eighteenth century. However, Smith's description of a reform environment of 'great human love' suggests that he was concerned about the welfare of these women and did not simply see them as a social nuisance in need of punishment. Smith wrote that the women should be sent to places with a 'homely description, and in charge of a person possessed of great human love and sympathy who would study each inmate in order to ascertain her individual tastes, and educate her on these lines'.[27] In 1928 the importance of reforming the women in a 'nice environment' was again stressed by Smith who stated that 'much money [was] spent on objects less worthy'.[28] Even if this show of compassion and charity was for publicity purposes, it is significant that the Glasgow Police Chief Constable thought a benevolent approach to be more appropriate than treating the women as criminals. His insistence that it was a worthy cause to spend money on reforming prostitutes suggests that he was committed to helping these women in practice and not just in theory.

In 1931 Percy Sillitoe replaced Smith as the Chief Constable of Glasgow. A. W. Cockerill, the author of Sillitoe's biography, describes how Sillitoe wanted 'prostitutes to look upon him as their father confessor'.[29] Cockerill generally portrays Sillitoe as a very dedicated, successful Chief Constable who was caring, understanding and sympathetic, yet also tough against crime, especially in dealing with Glasgow's gangs.[30] One of the main tactics

Figure 2.2 Chief Constable James Verdier Stevenson. The Glasgow Police Heritage Society.

Figure 2.3 Chief Constable Andrew Donnan Smith. The Glasgow Police Heritage Society.

he used to tackle the gangs was the use of informants, and these informers included 'barmen, ex-cons who Sillitoe helped over the years, prostitutes, a number of ex-boxers, and an ill assortment of gangsters'.[31] It appears that this cooperation with prostitutes continued in Glasgow at least until the mid-1940s. For example, the memoirs of Robert Colquhoun (a detective in Glasgow during the 1940s) describe how during the Second World War prostitutes would 'run amazing risks to tip us off'.[32] Another Glasgow policeman, David McNee, who was a plain-clothes officer during the 1940s, also described how the police frequently cooperated with 'the girls' and were keen to listen to any information they might provide. McNee describes how he spent time:

> Getting to know the 'girls' (indeed many of them were not much more than girls), listening to their gossip, exchanging pleasantries. They showed little or no antagonism towards the police and we in turn rarely judged them in moral terms. They knew the rules of the 'game' and there was a spirit of friendly competition between us.[33]

These statements suggest that not only were some members of the Glasgow police sympathetic and understanding towards the women who were involved in prostitution, but that they were also prepared to work together with them to solve crimes that they considered were more of a threat to society than prostitution.

It appears that this sentiment also held true in Edinburgh. The Chief Constable in Edinburgh between 1900 and 1935 was Roderick Ross, meaning his opinions and decisions had a large impact on the policy of the Edinburgh police during this period. Evidence given by Ross to the 1927 Street Offences Committee suggests that he was sympathetic towards some of the women involved in prostitution. When asked by committee chairman John McMillan whether he thought the street offences legislation should retain the words 'common prostitute', Ross stated that it was 'a harsh term to apply to young girls of sixteen or seventeen' and that he preferred the term 'habitually soliciting or importuning for prostitution' because it was 'a much kinder designation'.[34] This statement suggests that Ross made a distinction between the different women involved in prostitution. He was considerably more sympathetic towards the younger, less experienced women, but, when referring to the older women who had been involved in prostitution for a long time, he felt it was more acceptable to use harsh terms such as 'common prostitute' to describe them.

Although there are few surviving sources that provide an insight into the opinions and attitudes of the lower-ranking officers, there are some witness

Figure 2.4 Chief Constable Percy Joseph Sillitoe. The Glasgow Police Heritage Society.

Figure 2.5 Chief Constable Roderick Ross.

statements that suggest that in certain situations these officers were also sympathetic towards the women involved. For example, in 1912 Edinburgh Police Constable (PC) Alexander Robb described how Helen Garvie had 'been at different periods conducting herself as a prostitute . . . I have repeatedly cautioned the accused for such conduct . . . and on each occasion she promised to abandon that mode of living'.[35] Robb's continued attempts to deter Garvie from prostitution (without arresting her) suggest that he sympathised with her situation and was willing to give her several chances. He appears to have had faith that she might leave prostitution, and his description of how she 'has been at different periods conducting herself as a prostitute' suggests that he did not see her as 'a prostitute', but as someone who had to 'conduct herself' that way to earn a living.[36] Similarly, in November 1919, eighteen-year-old Freda Carson was cautioned and allowed away by the police on several occasions due to her 'youth' and because she 'promised to give up that mode of living'.[37] In another case during 1919, PC Robert Reid and PC William Webster tried to help nineteen-year-old Mary Kelly who was being abused by her husband, who was also acting as her pimp. Reid described how he had 'directed her to go to the central police station where she would get shelter as she said she was afraid to go home, and could stand [the] accused no longer.'[38] Webster corroborated this evidence by declaring that 'she impressed me that she was giving a truthful statement'.[39] The witness testimony given by the two officers illustrates that they were both sympathetic towards her situation and aware of the abuse that prostitutes were liable to face from the men who exploited them. Joanne Klein's research on police officers in Liverpool, Manchester and Birmingham during the interwar period shows that this sympathetic and understanding approach could be seen throughout police forces across Britain, and that 'most constables protected women from being victimised, regardless of their respectability, and even prostitutes sent for the police if they had problems with customers.'[40] However, the likelihood that abuse and corruption committed by the police may have gone unrecorded and therefore remained hidden from the historical record must also be acknowledged here.

William Merrilees, who was in charge of licensing in Edinburgh during the 1920s and 1930s (and therefore had some influence over how prostitution policy was implemented) also showed considerable empathy towards some of the women. In his autobiography he described how 'the problem of these unhappy girls nagged at me and my conscience'.[41] He explained how he believed that 'his duties lay not merely in bringing offenders to justice, but in helping, or seeking to help, at least some proportion of the girls towards a different and better life'.[42] Merrilees (like Glasgow Chief Constable Andrew Smith) also believed that this could be achieved by sending women to reform homes and finding them alternative respectable employment.[43] Similarly, he too selectively adopted the notion of 'the prostitute' as the victim of immoral men and in need of pity and compassion, depending on the circumstances of the individual women involved. For example, he explained that girls 'turned to prostitution . . . as a result of being wronged and abandoned by their lovers'.[44] However, his attitude was not always this understanding.

On several different occasions within his autobiography he referred to particular women as 'old pros', 'older known prostitutes' and 'old buns'.[45] He was clearly less concerned about the welfare of these 'common prostitutes' and later explained that the only women who were arrested were those who had ignored the opportunities they were given to be reformed. He therefore concluded that it was 'only fair' that these repeat offenders were sent to prison. Moreover, when referring to the problem of venereal disease he described how prostitution was a dangerous threat to society and it was therefore necessary that infected women should be forcibly sent to a lock hospital for treatment. Clearly Merrilees did not have the fate of *all* of these 'unhappy girls' on his conscience. Only those women who fitted the victim stereotype and were willing to reform were considered worthy of his compassion.

There were many more instances when the police made this type of distinction between young victims who had recently 'fallen' and 'old pros'. In 1920 Hilda Lind was arrested for importuning for the purposes of prostitution. The witness report described how she had never been before the court and had only been seen soliciting on the streets for the past few weeks, during which time she had been cautioned several times. The report ended by describing how she was 'at present in a very dirty state and seems a little soft' and it was therefore suggested that she needed to 'be found some place where she would be cared for'.[46] The officer evidently showed concern for her welfare and saw her as someone in need of care and protection rather than punishment. Hilda's age was not disclosed, although it appears that she might have been relatively young because she was living with her parents. Whether or not she was actually 'young' in terms of years, the fact that the officer believed that she was new to prostitution and did not describe her as a 'prostitute' appear to have been important reasons behind his more welfare-oriented approach.

This notion of a division between the 'victim' and the 'common prostitute' can be seen throughout the statements made by the police in both Edinburgh and Glasgow across the whole period. This distinction fits within a long-established way of viewing female sexuality that divided women into distinct groups depending on whether or not they were considered as either 'whores' or 'Madonnas'.[47] In particular, the 'sentimentalisation of the prostitute' encouraged by feminists and reform organisations meant that the image of her as the 'victim of circumstance' became more prominent during the early and mid-nineteenth century.[48] These reformers brought public attention to the socio-economic inequality women faced and to the double standard of sexual morality which led many women to turn to prostitution as a means of providing for themselves and their families – an attitude also clearly apparent in the writings and actions of the police officers. However, if the women were seen as 'old pros', then there was less sympathy towards them and they faced harsher punishments. The judgement of a woman's character was therefore a central aspect in determining how these women were treated under the law.

These attitudes and assumptions about women and prostitution were particularly influential thanks to the cautioning system which encouraged this process of categorising women according to whether they were seen as 'unfortunate girls' or 'hardened criminals'. The cautioning system relied on the profiling of women based on their appearance, behaviour and previous conviction history in order to decide whether or not they should be arrested, cautioned, or 'let away'. Those who caused little trouble and had no previous convictions for prostitution were given a caution and allowed to leave. Women were given three cautions before they were charged with an importuning offence and sent to the Burgh Court for a hearing and sentencing. This policy was closely followed by the police in both Edinburgh and Glasgow. For example, in 1911 the Glasgow Chief Constable wrote that:

> As a rule offenders are not brought before the court on the first apprehension – their names are taken and they are cautioned by the officer on duty and allowed away. If their parents or friends can be traced, they are asked to come and take them away.[49]

In Edinburgh, William Merrilees described the process of cautioning, starting from when a 'girl' was first caught soliciting:

> The girl herself was placed on record and given her first caution. If the same girl was caught again she was given a second caution, and possibly asked to call and see me. Some took advantage of this, others did not. If a girl was caught a third time, she was taken to the nearest police station where the officer in charge delivered a final caution.[50]

The Edinburgh Burgh Court records describe how this cautioning system was carried out on a daily basis. For example, in January 1928 the police caught Jessie Hope, Ann Paton and Catherine Delaney soliciting on the east side of Leith Street. Whereas Hope and Paton were described as 'being known to the police witness as being in the habit of frequenting the streets for the purposes of prostitution' and were consequently arrested and sentenced, 'the girl Delaney who had never been arrested for prostitution was cautioned and allowed away.'[51] The fact that this information had to be described in detail in order to justify the arrests of the women shows that the police took the cautioning procedure seriously. It also meant that the police could collect enough evidence to 'prove' in court that a particular woman was importuning for the purposes of prostitution. The whole system was therefore based on the assumption that this type of evidence could prove that the woman was a prostitute and that this knowledge of the woman's 'character' was the key to enabling a successful conviction.

In addition to providing the necessary evidence for a conviction, this evidence was also important because it could protect the police from accusations that they had falsely arrested an 'innocent' woman. Highly popularised cases of women being falsely arrested for soliciting and indecency, such as those of Elizabeth Cass in 1887 and Irene Savidge in 1928, made the police more concerned about the dangers of wrongly arresting women they suspected were prostitutes.[52] During the 1927 Street Offences Committee several questions were raised about the possibility of false arrest in Edinburgh and Glasgow, including how the forces ensured that it did not occur. The witnesses representing both police forces insisted that false arrest was extremely unlikely and uncommon because of their thorough cautioning system.[53] When questioned further, however, Mr Macpherson (public prosecutor for Edinburgh) recalled a case in 1926 in which a woman was falsely accused of importuning for the purposes of prostitution and awarded £500 damages by the court.[54] Lord Advocate Mr Craig also recalled a complaint of false arrest made by a woman in 1907 against the Glasgow Police which 'caused a good deal of trouble.'[55]

In Glasgow, the 1923 Glasgow Police Instruction Book laid out the procedures that officers were meant to follow when arresting women suspected of engaging in prostitution.

> A prostitute cannot be taken into custody simply because she is a prostitute; to justify her apprehension she must commit some distinct act which is an offence against the law. The police have no power to interfere with men and women merely speaking together in the streets so long as they behave themselves properly and do not cause an obstruction. When it is found necessary to interfere, it must be done civilly and firmly, without any offensive language.
>
> If a woman, suspected of being a prostitute, is observed in any street, she should be watched, and if she is seen to accost men or to endeavour to attract their attention she should be warned that if she persists in such conduct she may be apprehended, if after being warned, she is again found accosting men, and her actions leave no doubt that she is doing so for the purposes of prostitution, she may be apprehended. Before taking a woman into custody there must be sufficient evidence to satisfy the magistrate (1) that the woman is a prostitute, and (2) that she was loitering or accosting men for the purposes of prostitution.

> The fact that she is a prostitute may be proved either from previous convictions or her known character. Apprehensions should never be made in a doubtful case; a report should be made so that inquiry may be made into the woman's character. The police should be most careful to guard against the possibility of a mistake.[56]

Therefore, although there are some small differences in the exact nature of the cautioning system, the general principle in Glasgow of providing women with cautions before they were arrested was similar to that of Edinburgh. In both cities the police used this system of profiling to ensure that they had enough 'evidence' to prove that the woman was a 'prostitute' in order to safeguard themselves against accusations of wrongful arrest. In both cities this system led to the assumption that women with previous convictions or several cautions could be safely labelled as 'common prostitutes', arrested and assumed guilty. There were some exceptions to this pattern and several women were given more than three chances before they were arrested. For example, the police testimony relating to the case of May McArthur in 1919 described how she had 'never been before the court for prostitution, but she has been cautioned on six occasions'.[57] Nonetheless, once a woman had been convicted as a 'prostitute', it became much harder for her to escape arrest in the future. In this respect, it could be argued that this procedure enshrined in law a system of profiling that created a distinction between women that was based on their 'character', resulting in those women who were considered 'common prostitutes' being treated differently under the law than other 'non-prostitute' women.

Nevertheless, this did not mean that women with previous convictions were successfully prohibited from importuning on the streets. Prostitution was often not regarded as a 'real crime' because there was no obvious victim. Even if some officers agreed that prostitution was immoral, many believed that it was not their job to police morality. This, along with the tedious work involved in surveillance operations, meant that many police officers were less than enthusiastic about policing prostitution – a sentiment which was also held within many other police forces throughout Britain. For example, Mike Brogden describes how in Liverpool 'if [prostitutes] made a nuisance of themselves, they would be arrested. But as long as they were discreet, they were just left alone.'[58] Testimony given to the Street Offences Committee suggested that it was public knowledge (or at least a common suspicion) that the police sometimes turned a 'blind eye' towards instances of street prostitution. For example, the committee member Miss Kelly asked Edinburgh Police Chief Constable Roderick Ross about the likelihood that the officers could become so familiar with the women that they would 'wink at their offence'.[59] Ross denied that this was probable, but the fact that this question was raised suggests that these were commonly held concerns. Brogden's research on the Liverpool police force during the interwar period shows that this *laissez-faire* approach was common in Liverpool. Brogden explains how 'for the beat officer, prostitution was usually something to be tolerated. As long as the woman did not go out of her way to solicit customers, it was recognized that she, too, had a living to make.'[60]

The General Orders given to the police in both Edinburgh and Glasgow suggest that it was complaints from the public about the annoyance caused by prostitution which provided the main motivation for police action, rather than any strongly held belief in the criminality of prostitution. In Scotland it was not necessary to prove that importuning had caused annoyance (unlike in England and Wales during this period).[61] Nevertheless, it is evident that the police only became more concerned about importuning once they had received complaints from the public. For example, in Edinburgh, General Order 729 stated that 'many complaints have been raised about prostitution . . . therefore more needs to be done'[62], and General Order 707 stated that 'special attention should be paid to those characters likely to cause such annoyance' and that 'officers and men are directed to take such steps as will render these complaints impossible.'[63] Similarly, in Glasgow, the Chief Constable's reference to the fact that the issue of prostitution had been under 'observation by a proportion of the press' as a reason for why the police needed to stop 'the spread of immorality', suggests that he too was concerned about public opinion towards prostitution.[64] Furthermore, in 1930 the Glasgow Chief Constable explained that they must take action because 'many complaints have been made to the police [about] a detestable type of person . . . [who] drives a car and in a quiet thoroughfare importunes girls'.[65] Nonetheless, even though public complaints might have been one of the main reasons why the police decided to act, the overall number of these complaints was actually quite low.

In situations when the arrest was not prompted by public complaints or direct orders from senior officers, the choice of whether to arrest or caution women suspected of soliciting was ultimately left to the individual police officers – a situation which gave them considerable discretionary powers. It is likely, therefore, that the lack of enthusiasm for policing prostitution was not the only reason why some officers were reluctant to crack down on vice. In his autobiography, William Merrilees explained that there was corruption within the Edinburgh police vice squad during the interwar period. For example, he claimed that 'all was not well within the department itself. I was increasingly worried by things that were going on, that I knew to be contrary to the good name of the force'.[66] He later described how some criminals 'obviously depended upon a certain few police officers for a degree of protection'.[67] Merrilees then explained how he could not trust all of the police officers with information about when the raids on brothels would take place because he feared that they would inform the brothel owners, whom they 'were on friendly terms with'.[68]

Merrilees' claim that there was corruption surrounding the policing of prostitution is hard to verify. His autobiography tends to emphasise his role as the leader of a moral crusade against vice in Edinburgh, and his depiction of corruption in the force may have been exaggerated in an attempt to highlight his superior morality, in contrast to the other officers. Nevertheless, it is plausible that some corruption did occur in this particular area of policing. The substantial profits that were generated by prostitution would have made it tempting to 'turn a blind eye' towards particular prostitution offences if a large monetary incentive was involved. Considering that prostitution was often seen as a 'victimless crime', it is likely that certain officers may have been less concerned about the moral implications of turning a blind eye to this type of crime. A scarcity of evidence relating to police corruption makes it equally difficult to know the extent of corruption in Glasgow. However, evidence given by Glasgow Chief Constable Stevenson to the 1907 Metropolitan Police Committee suggests that some corruption did exist. For example, Stevenson stated that 'he had heard general statements made in regard to complaints of policemen receiving bribes from book-makers and prostitutes, but he did not think the practice was widespread.'[69]

This type of corruption is known to have occurred within the Metropolitan Police in London during the interwar period. On 29 January 1929 former Metropolitan Police Station Sergeant George Goddard was sentenced to eighteen months' hard labour for 'corruptly accepting and obtaining money' from brothel and restaurant owners.[70] Goddard worked in C Division, which included the main vice districts around Soho and thus allowed him to establish a system of bribery and protection:

> Each whore paid a regular sum to Goddard, which entitled her to be arrested in proper rotation with the other girls, never unexpectedly, and enabled her to give full attention to passing men without nervous wear and tear of keeping constant look-out for coppers. The arrangement was so convenient to the girls that on the appointed day, in places like Lisle Street, they formed small queues waiting to pay their dues to Goddard.[71]

Goddard was ultimately brought to justice, and some small changes were made to address the problem of police corruption. Nevertheless, Clive Emsley argues that Goddard was not merely 'one bad apple' who was corrupted but was part of a 'more significant and more deep-rooted' problem. Emsley suggests that in order to avoid the 'scandal of corruption that might go well beyond Goddard' the police did not seriously investigate the possibility that there was widespread corruption.[72] In 1906 the Royal Commission into Police Powers and Procedures reported that 'the enforcement of laws which are out of harmony with public opinion' (such as those relating to certain types of vice) were likely to result in some cases of police corruption.[73]Although the lack of reliable sources makes it difficult to prove the extent of corruption in Edinburgh and Glasgow, the same incentives and opportunities for corruption when policing vice would have been equally tempting in Scotland as they were in London. It is possible, therefore, that Glasgow's Chief Constable was equally unwilling to admit that corruption was a more widespread problem than the activities of a few 'black sheep'. If this was the case, then it would provide further evidence that the police were unofficially following a policy of toleration, albeit at a price. Rather than being increasingly criminalised, the women would have been free to work as long as they paid the bribes. If this type of corruption occurred, it is clear to see how this system would have led to abuses and exploitation by the police that would not have been recorded.

The sentencing decision of the magistrates was also an important factor in determining the policing of prostitution and the law's power to deter women from street solicitation. Importuning offences were heard at the Burgh and Police Court, and the magistrate was limited to the punishment they could give according to the Burgh Police Act (40 shillings' fine or a 60-day prison sentence in default of payment) or according to the local by-laws in each city.[74] In Edinburgh the Municipal and Police Act 1879 meant that the Burgh Court magistrates could award a fine of up to £10. If the fine was not paid, the woman could be sent to prison for a period of up to 60 days.[75] However, figures 2.6, 2.7 and 2.8 show that although the Edinburgh magistrates could

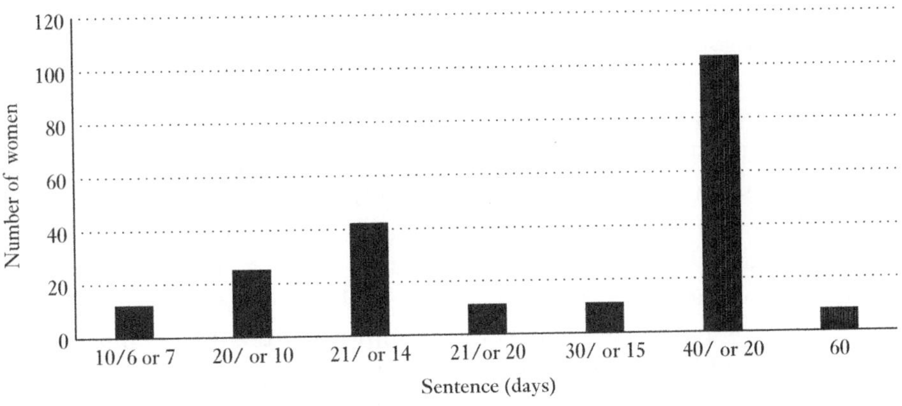

Figure 2.6 Sentences Given for Importuning Offences in Edinburgh, 1911.
Source: ECA, Edinburgh Burgh Court Records, 1911.

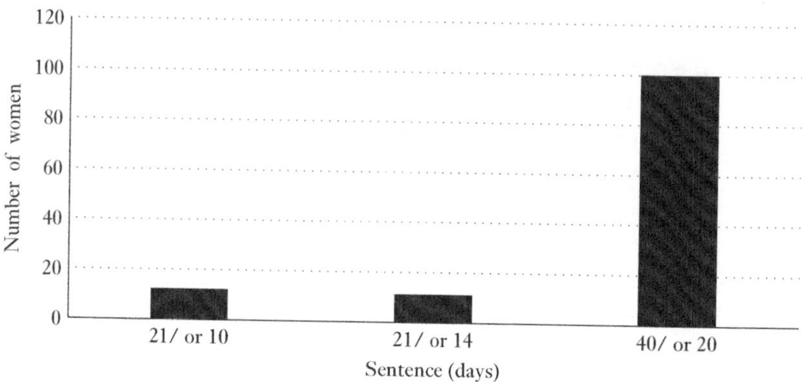

Figure 2.7 Sentences Given for Importuning Offences in Edinburgh, 1921.
Source: ECA, Edinburgh Burgh Court Records, 1921.

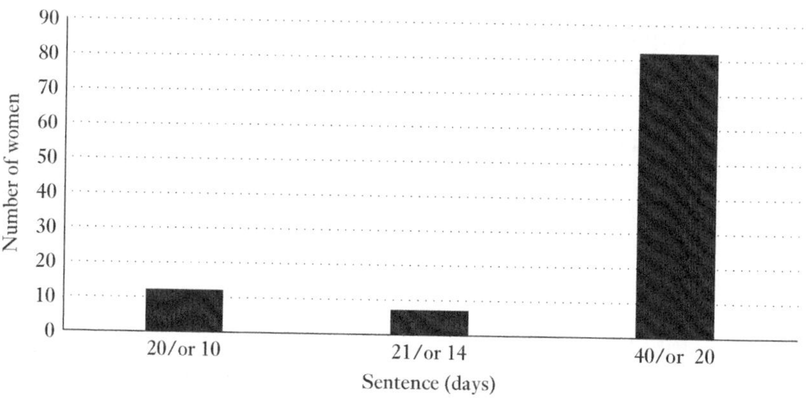

Figure 2.8 Sentences Given for Importuning Offences in Edinburgh, 1931.
Source: ECA, Edinburgh Burgh Court Records, 1931.

potentially charge up to £10 or give a prison sentence of up to sixty days, they did not usually choose this harsher punishment. Instead, the most common sentence was actually forty shillings or twenty days (suggesting that the Burgh Police Act was most commonly used in Edinburgh).

Furthermore, figures 2.9, 2.10, 2.11 and 2.12 show that although women were frequently sent to prison for short periods, many others were admonished, fined or put on probation. For example, in 1903 it was more likely that women would be admonished or fined than sent straight to prison, and although the chances of being sent to prison increased slightly in 1911, perhaps in response to the moral panics surrounding prostitution and white slavery that were particularly heightened in Scotland during that year, there were

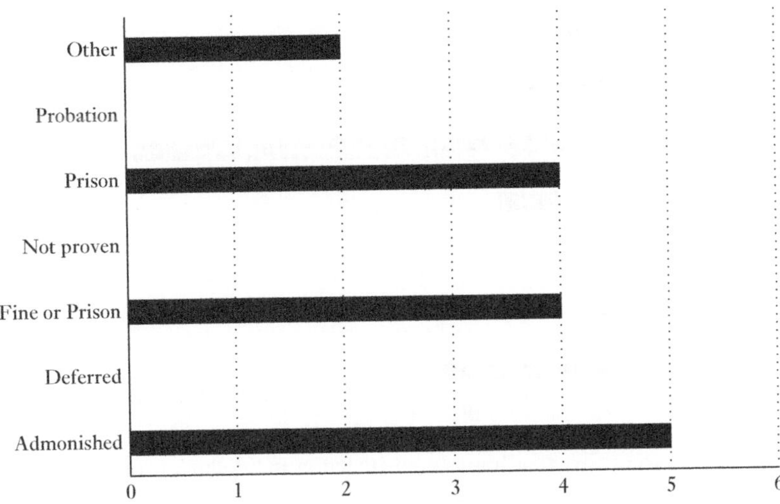

Figure 2.9 Sentences Given for Importuning Offences in Edinburgh, 1903.
Source: ECA, Edinburgh Burgh Court Records, 1903.

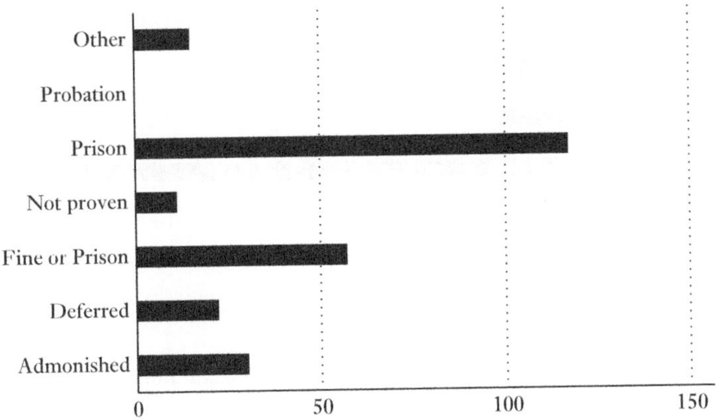

Figure 2.10 Sentences Given for Importuning Offences in Edinburgh 1911.
Source: ECA, Edinburgh Burgh Court Records, 1911.

still many women who were admonished, deferred, fined or given the verdict of 'not proven'. In 1921 the number of women being sent to gaol increased further, but so did the number of women being placed on probation, and it remained common for women to be fined or to have their cases deferred or found 'not proven'. By 1931 the percentage of women in Edinburgh who were sent to prison for importuning offences sharply declined, and the amount of women fined increased. This suggests that by 1931 it was only the poorest women who could not pay the fines who were sent to prison. Therefore, for

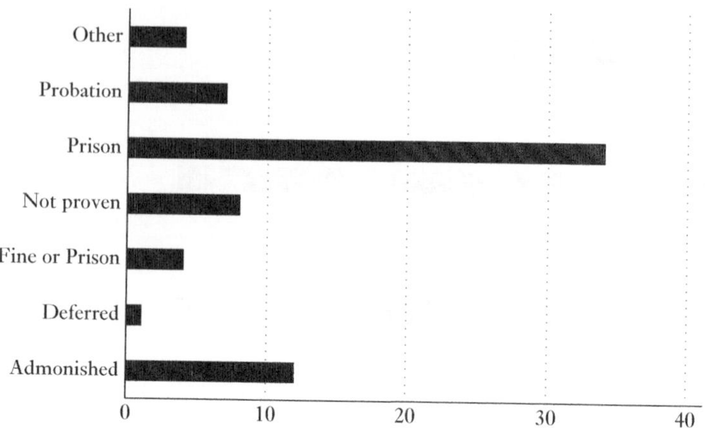

Figure 2.11 Sentences Given for Importuning Offences in Edinburgh, 1921.
Source: ECA, Edinburgh Burgh Court Records, 1921.

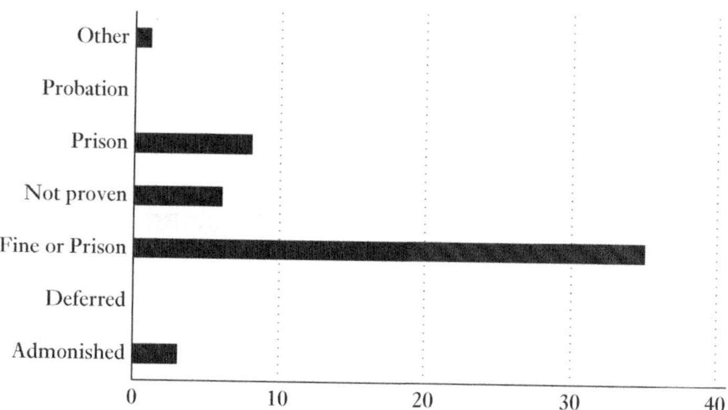

Figure 2.12 Sentences Given for Importuning Offences in Edinburgh, 1931.
Source: ECA, Edinburgh Burgh Court Records, 1931.

those women with enough money, the law's potential to deter was less potent. Indeed, the police officers in Glasgow and Edinburgh were well aware of this problem and on several occasions complained that 'the imposition of a fine is not a deterrent.'[76]

Overall, the sentencing patterns for this period show that the courts were not overly harsh towards the women and that the majority of women did not receive the full sentence possible. Instead, there appears to have been a sliding scale of punishment, meaning that the more frequently a woman was convicted, the higher her fine became, until eventually she would continue to receive the highest fine possible. The sentencing patterns therefore echoed the police cautioning system in that the magistrates were less lenient towards repeat offenders. This reiterated the idea that some women were 'hardened prostitutes' and therefore deserved more punishment, whereas the 'newly fallen' deserved kinder treatment and more 'second chances'. The impact that this policy had on the lives of those who were designated 'hardened prostitutes' will be examined further in chapter five. This pattern, however, was not absolute. There were many examples where the repeat offenders received lighter sentences and someone with no previous convictions received the maximum sentence. This undoubtedly reflected the individual magistrate's attitudes towards prostitution or simply their mood on the day. Just as the police were liable to individual discretion when arresting prostitutes, so too were the magistrates when convicting them.

The local town councils were also involved in making decisions about local solicitation legislation. For example, in 1922 Edinburgh Town Council set up a Provost's Committee to look into the issue. The councillors on the committee, in conjunction with the magistrates committee and organisations such as the Edinburgh Women's Citizen Association, made several suggestions concerning new by-laws that might be passed. It was suggested that penalties for various prostitution-related offences could be increased, that women who were known to persistently importune for the purposes of prostitution and were suspected of being infected with venereal disease should be subjected to forced medical examination and treatment, and that persons found in a brothel should be subject to penalties.[77] However, after considerable debate it was decided that all of these suggestions should be rejected and that no action should be taken. Therefore, although there were some calls for measures that would further criminalise prostitution, this more punitive approach was not sufficiently popular within the council for it to pursue any changes to the local by-laws.[78]

'Bullying Wretches' and 'Houses of Notorious Bad Fame': Policing Brothels and Pimps

Attitudes towards the policing of street prostitution and the women involved in it may have been varied and complex, but attitudes towards brothel-keepers, pimps and any other third parties who lived off the earnings of prostitution tended to be more clear-cut. The legislation shows that, rather than targeting the women who sold sex, it was those who exploited these women who were the real focus of police attention. For example, the 1902 Immoral Traffic (Scotland) Act made living off the earning of prostitution an offence, and in 1912 this Act was extended so that:

> every male person who loiters in any public place and persistently solicits or importunes for immoral purposes – shall be liable at the discretion of the court to be imprisoned for any term not exceeding 6 months with or without hard labour.[79]

This legislation built on the 1892 Burgh Police Act which also included a clause that sought to target men who solicited women and children. These acts combined went much further than the comparable English and Welsh legislation, and this strong commitment in Scotland to punishing the men involved in prostitution, rather than just the women, can be seen throughout the police records and General Orders. In response to the 1902 Immoral Traffic (Scotland) Act, Edinburgh's Chief Constable Stevenson issued General Order number 726 which emphasised that officers needed to find 'where prostitutes live, not just where they solicit' so that they can 'find the men living off the earnings . . . and the brothel-keepers.'[80] He then stated that 'every member of the police force should give this special attention' because it was 'a very important issue'.[81] The subsequent General Orders for the rest of the period detailed new ways in which the police should catch pimps and brothel-keepers. This approach was reflected in the attitudes of police officers such as William Merrilees who described those who lived off the earnings of prostitution as 'bullying wretches' and argued that 'brothel-keepers deserved the severest penalties'.[82] The Edinburgh police clearly seemed more concerned about arresting those living off the earnings of prostitution than the prostitutes themselves.

In Glasgow a similar picture emerged. The vast majority of General Orders that related to prostitution were more concerned with 'pimps' and 'brothel-keepers' than with the women who importuned on the streets. For example, the 1923 general instruction book informed the police that:

> The names and addresses of persons leaving pledges for or paying fines of prostitutes, or to whom messages are sent by prostitutes, detained on a charge of importuning, should be noted in the blotter opposite the case by the lieutenant on duty and communicated to the superintendent of the district in which such persons reside, to enable him to have them and their houses watched to ascertain whether they are keeping brothels or houses of accommodation, and, if male persons, whether they are living on the immoral earnings of the prostitutes concerned.[83]

The Glasgow Police were clearly keen to catch any third parties that were profiting from prostitution. Similarly, another General Order informed the

Glasgow Police that they should 'keep a strict watch on the drivers of those vehicles which are on the streets for hire principally after nightfall', as the Chief Constable was concerned that these drivers provided prostitutes and their clients with transportation to the different locations where prostitution took place and, in some instances, acted as a location for the act of prostitution itself.[84] The police were also involved in the observation of public houses and other licensed premises that might have 'harboured' prostitutes. The 1903 Licensing (Scotland) Act stipulated that licence holders must not 'knowingly permit or suffer men or women of notoriously bad fame' to assemble on their premises.[85] The police therefore used these licensing laws to discourage a wide variety of third parties from profiting from prostitution.

As with street solicitation legislation, it is important to examine how the police interpreted and implemented the legislation. The main approach used to police brothels was similar to that used for street prostitution, with surveillance by plain-clothes police officers again providing the main method. However, rather than walking the streets, the officers would find a location hidden from view and watch the activity that took place outside or within the brothel. Merrilees described how this could even include 'watching from roof tops and many strange places.'[86] A notebook was used to record the details of this activity, with particular attention paid to who entered the establishment, and at what time the men and women entered and exited. It was particularly important to note whether men 'stayed the night', a phrase that was frequently used throughout the witness reports. This surveillance would continue for several nights and could also involve watching through windows or holes in the walls. For example, in 1914 one officer described how by 'looking through the bedroom window I saw the man and the woman having carnal connection with each other', and in 1917 another officer described how he observed 'the soldier and the prostitute' through 'a small hole in the door of the house'.[87]

Once the officers had collected enough circumstantial evidence to justify their suspicions, they could apply to the magistrates for a warrant to enter the brothel. However, according to Merrilees, the police in Edinburgh 'seldom use[d] warrants when raiding brothels'; instead they relied on the cooperation of the occupant to let them enter.[88] On many occasions the occupier allowed the police into the building, but the occupier was not always so obliging. When refused entry, the witness reports show that the police frequently used their initiative to find other ways of entering the dwelling, often by following male customers into the flat, or entering once the door had accidentally been left open.[89] On entering, they looked for signs which might prove that prostitution had occurred there. The presence of unmarried men and women undressed and in bed together was seen as the most valuable evidence (especially if the woman could be identified as a 'known prostitute'). This type of evidence was frequently stated as 'proof' that prostitution had occurred in the premises.

Once inside, the officers would question the men concerning the reason for their visit. If they could obtain a statement from the men confirming that they had gone to this address for 'immoral purposes', that would provide useful evidence, and in the majority of cases the men did admit this. A case from 1914 provides a very good illustration of this: during the first raid on a brothel at 47 St Stephen Street in Edinburgh, the men who were found in the brothel stated that they met 'the women Robertson and Welsh in a public house in the Stockbridge district and accompanied them to the house for a night's entertainment'.[90] During another raid on the same brothel, when questioned by the police, William Thompson explained that the accused 'accosted him on Rose Street and he accompanied her to her house'.[91] During the final raid on the brothel, Robert Hannan stated that 'he was taken to the house by Sharp to get a woman'.[92] However, once the men had answered the questions, they were allowed to leave and were not forced to make an official witness statement at the police station. Consequently, the men rarely became official witnesses, instead choosing to leave before any insinuations could be made which might damage their reputation. In Glasgow, Chief Constable Smith wrote in the 1922 Annual Report that he felt that men should be charged when found in a brothel, 'but regrettably that was not so'.[93]

Whether or not the brothel-keeper was arrested often depended on his or her previous convictions. The witness reports show that in some cases the brothel-keepers were given a warning about their conduct before being arrested. For example, in March 1917, after several nights' surveillance, the police cautioned Mary Watt about conducting her house as a brothel. It was only following several more nights of observation that she was arrested for brothel-keeping.[94] This warning system, however, seemed less rigid than the cautioning system that was used for street solicitation, and in most cases the brothel-keepers did not receive a caution before they were arrested. For example, in 1914 the police observed Margaret Robertson's flat for seven nights, but she was only told that she would be reported for conducting a brothel during the last visit to the flat.[95] It appears that the police were more lenient towards women who worked on the streets than those who managed brothels. Nevertheless, just as the details of each brothel case varied, the decision made by the officers on whether they should arrest the brothel-keeper was open to discretion, and this opened up opportunities for corruption – a possibility that will be explored further in chapter six.

The police's targeting of the indoor locations where prostitution occurred inevitably would have had a negative impact upon the women working in these environments. In London, Laite has shown how this criminalisation of brothels and other indoor venues not only affected brothel-keepers, but also had a detrimental effect on the women who had previously used these premises. As brothels were increasingly targeted by the police, the women were consequently forced to engage in other, more risky, types of clandestine solicitation or to turn to pimps for protection. The legal definition of a brothel as a place where more than one woman resides for the purposes of prostitution meant that this could discourage women from working together indoors. Working alone exposed the women to more dangers, both from the men who bought sex and the men who lived off their earnings. As landlords became more reluctant to rent rooms to single women, 'bullies' exploited this situation by offering to act as their husbands. In Edinburgh and Glasgow these laws also led to a similar type of dangerous situation, particularly for the women who worked alone under the control of an aggressive pimp. Chapters five and six will explore these relationships further, but it is important to note that resorting to the protection of pimps was only one of the ways in which women responded to the closure of brothels and that not all of the women who worked alone in flats or other clandestine locations were controlled by pimps.

Finally, although the police may have wanted to close brothels and arrest 'pimps', in practice they were not always capable of achieving this. The conviction statistics for brothel-keeping in Edinburgh and Glasgow show that the police were not particularly successful. Figure 2.13 shows that in Edinburgh

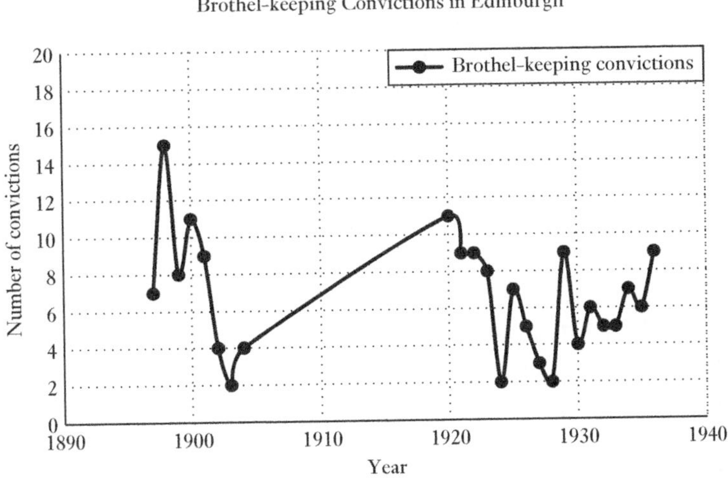

Figure 2.13 Brothel Convictions in Edinburgh, 1897–1936.

Source: ECA, Edinburgh Burgh Court Records, 1897–1936.

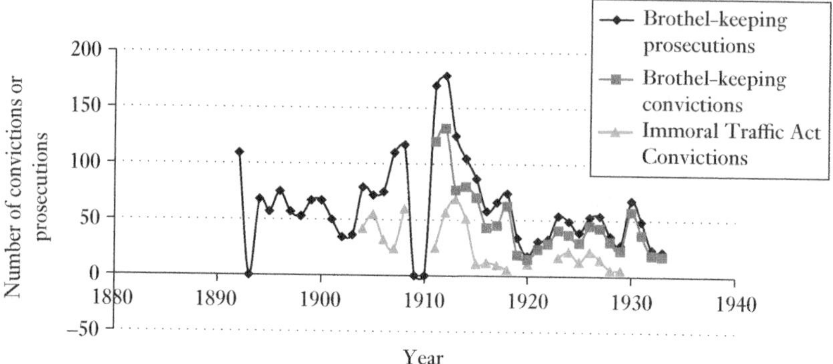

Figure 2.14 Brothel-Keeping and Immoral Traffic Act Prosecutions and Convictions in Glasgow.

Source: GCA, Glasgow Police Annual Reports, 1892–1933.

the number of brothel-keeping convictions per year rarely exceeded ten and peaked at eleven in 1900 and 1920. Figure 2.14 shows that there were more prosecutions in Glasgow, although Glasgow's considerably larger population may account for this discrepancy.

The number of brothel-keeping prosecutions in Glasgow increased considerably from 1907 to 1914. However, in 1911 prosecutions and convictions in Glasgow started to be recorded separately, which allows us to see that many prosecutions were not successful, often because the prosecutor had trouble getting the courts to produce a guilty verdict due to a lack of proof. Even when the police had collected a considerable amount of evidence from several nights' observation work, this did not guarantee a conviction. Moreover, many of the suspected brothel cases were not brought to court in the first place due to the Procurator Fiscal's decision that there was insufficient evidence.

This was equally true in relation to Immoral Traffic Act cases. However, attempts to arrest 'bullies' who lived off the immoral earnings of prostitution were slightly more successful. Table 2.2 shows that in Glasgow there were a considerable number of immoral traffic convictions between 1908 and 1914. This rise corresponded with a report that was published in 1911 by the Glasgow Parish Council, entitled 'Memorandum on the Social Evil in Glasgow'. The report gave lurid and sensationalist accounts of the prostitution that was occurring in Glasgow, in particular the dangers faced by young girls who worked in brothels or were seduced by 'foreigners' in ice-cream parlours.[96] Edinburgh, however, had far fewer immoral traffic convictions than Glasgow. In 1920 there were only six; in 1921 there were four, in 1922 two, 1923 also two; and in 1924 there was only one conviction.[97] It is likely

Table 2.2 Immoral Traffic Act Convictions in Glasgow.

Year	Immoral Traffic Act Convictions
1904	42
1905	55
1906	32
1907	24
1908	60
1909	–
1910	–
1911	25
1912	57
1913	69
1914	51
1915	11
1916	12
1917	10
1918	6
1919	–
1920	11
1921	–
1922	–
1923	17
1924	22
1925	13
1926	22
1927	15
1928	6
1929	6

Source: GCA, DTC 7/19/1 Glasgow Police Annual Reports, 1904–29.

that this was in part due to Edinburgh's considerably smaller population, although it may demonstrate a stronger enthusiasm for prosecuting 'pimps' in Glasgow, possibly due to the publication of the 1911 Memorandum on The Social Evil. Nonetheless, regardless of these slight differences, the overall number of convictions tended to decline in both cities after the First World War.

In 1920 Chief Constable Stevenson explained that the low prosecution rates were due to the difficulties the police faced. Stevenson complained how men who lived off the immoral earnings of their 'paramours' could 'move about with impunity, can change their venue from one part of the city to another, or from city to city as they get known to the police, and the police cannot interfere with them until they have committed a crime for which proof can be found'.[98] Similarly, in 1928 Chief Constable Smith made a statement describing how 'the police are often handicapped in their endeavours to bring these people to justice by the refusal of girls to give evidence.'[99] Therefore, whilst the police certainly wanted to target 'bullies' and sought more powers to do so, they were not always successful.

Conclusion

After examining the attitudes of the police towards prostitution and the methods that they used to police both outdoor and indoor forms of prostitution in Edinburgh and Glasgow, it is clear that the police followed a similar approach in both cities. Whilst many officers sympathised with the difficult economic and social factors that led some women to enter prostitution, they did not offer a compassionate approach towards all women. The police in both cities made a clear distinction between the young 'victims' who needed saving, and the 'common prostitutes' who were a public nuisance – an attitude that mirrored a wider public sentiment which made a distinction between 'amateurs' and the 'hardened prostitute'. The cautioning system that was developed in Edinburgh and Glasgow helped to realise this distinction even further due to the discretionary powers it gave the police to decide which women would be 'let away', cautioned, or arrested, based on this assessment of a woman's 'character'. Chapter four will examine this process further by exploring the ways in which increased cooperation between police and voluntary organisations shaped the police's decisions about which women would be 'helped' and which arrested.

The police in Edinburgh and Glasgow were not enthusiastic about policing street solicitation, and this was reflected in the decline in the number of importuning offences that were brought to court. Although street solicitation remained illegal and the police continued to arrest small numbers of women, there was no 'crackdown' on street prostitution equivalent to that in London. Instead, the women continued to solicit in the very centre of Edinburgh and Glasgow, relatively unencumbered by the threat of police persecution. Rather than increasing the persecution of the women involved in prostitution, the police often voiced a preference for sending women to reform homes. Chapter four will further explore the importance of this relationship between the police and voluntary organisations in shaping a more penal-welfare-oriented approach towards the policing of prostitution. The police did, however, attempt to increase the criminalisation of brothel-keepers and other third parties who lived off the earnings of prostitution. In both cities the police viewed the exploitative activities of brothel-keepers and pimps as a more serious crime than prostitution itself and focused their attentions accordingly. However, the difficulty in obtaining the necessary evidence for a successful prosecution considerably hindered their success, meaning that brothel and immoral traffic convictions remained low throughout the period. Consequently, it was unlikely that the new forms of clandestine prostitution which had begun to develop during this period were solely a direct result of increased criminalisation. The next chapter will therefore explore the role that other factors, such as technological development and changes in entertainment patterns, played in shaping the organisation of prostitution in Edinburgh and Glasgow during the first half of the twentieth century.

Notes

1. The Burgh Police (Scotland) Act 1892 (55 & 56 Vict. c. 55).
2. Ibid.
3. The Glasgow Police (Further Powers) Act 1892 (55&56 Vict. c. 165).
4. Mahood, *The Magdalenes: Prostitution in the Nineteenth Century* (London: Routledge, 1990), p. 15.
5. For further discussion about women's employment see, for example, Arnot *et al* (eds), *The Changing Experience of Women* (Oxford: Robertson, 1982); Ina Zweiniger-Bargielowska, *Women in Twentieth-Century Britain* (Harlow: Longman, 2001); Gail Braybon (ed.), *Evidence, History and the Great War: Historians and the Impact of 1914–18* (Oxford: Berghahn Books, 2003); Gail Braybon, *Out of the Cage: Women's Experiences in Two World Wars* (London: Pandora Press, 1987).
6. Glasgow City Archive (hereafter GCA), T. PAR 1.16, *Memorandum on the Social Evil in Glasgow*, p. 20.
7. Susan Grayzel, *Women and the First World War* (Harlow: Longman, 2002).
8. See, for example, Angela Woollacott '"Khaki Fever" and its Control: Gender, Class, Age and Sexual Morality on the British Home front in the First World War', *Journal of Contemporary History*, 29 (1994) pp. 325–47.
9. Lucy Bland, '"Guardians of the Race" or "Vampires on the Nation's Health"?' in Arnot *et al* (eds), *The Changing Experience of Women* (Oxford: Robertson, 1982).
10. Hera Cook, *The Long Sexual Revolution* (Oxford: Oxford University Press, 2004).
11. Ibid.
12. Ibid.
13. Lucy Bland, 'In the Name of Protection: The Policing of Women in the First World War', in Julia Brophy and Carol Smart (eds), *Women in*

Law: Explorations in Law, Family and Sexuality (London: Routledge and Kegan Paul, 1985) pp. 23–49.

14. Lesley Hall, 'War Always Brings it on': War, STDs, the Military, and the Civilian Population in Britain, 1850–1950', in Roger Cooter, Mark Harrison and Steve Sturdy (eds), *Medicine and Modern Warfare* (Amsterdam: Atlanta, 1999).
15. Julia Laite, 'Prostitution in London 1885–1930' PhD thesis (Cambridge University, 2008), p. 200.
16. Julia Laite, *Common Prostitutes and Ordinary Citizens: Commercial Sex in London, 1885–1960* (Basingstoke: Palgrave Macmillan, 2012).
17. *The Scotsman*, 28 January 1928, p. 11.
18. Ibid, p. 11.
19. Edinburgh City Archives (hereafter ECA), ED006/2/8 Edinburgh Police General Order 726, 2 May 1906.
20. ECA, Edinburgh Burgh Court Records (hereafter EBCR), witness reports 1903–1931.
21. ECA, EBCR, witness statement of P.C. George Irvine, 31 December 1920.
22. Joanne Klein, *Invisible Men, The Secret Lives of Police Constables in Liverpool, Manchester and Birmingham, 1900–1939* (Liverpool: Liverpool University Press, 2010), p. 6.
23. GCA, DTC 7/19/1 Glasgow Police Annual Report, 1904.
24. GCA, DTC 7/19/1 Glasgow Police Annual Report, 1913.
25. GCA, DTC 7/19/1 Glasgow Police Annual Report, 1922.
26. Ibid.
27. Ibid.
28. GCA, DTC 7/19/1 Glasgow Police Annual Report, 1928.
29. A.W. Cockerill, *The Memoirs of Percy Sillitoe* (London: W. H. Allen, 1975), p. 103.
30. For more on gangs and policing in Glasgow see, for example, Andrew Davies, 'Street Gangs, Crime and Policing in Glasgow in the 1930s: The Case of the Beehive Boys', *Social History*, 23, 3 (1998) pp. 251–68; Andrew Davies 'Glasgow's "Reign of Terror": Street Gangs, Racketeering and Intimidation in the 1920s and 1930s', *Contemporary British History*, 21, 4 (2007) pp. 405–27.
31. Cockerill, *The Memoirs of Percy Sillitoe*, p. 133.
32. Robert Colquhoun, *Life Begins at Midnight* (London: Long, 1962), p. 62.
33. David McNee, *McNee's Law* (London: Collins, 1983), p. 40.
34. *The Scotsman*, 28 January 1928, p. 11.
35. ECA, EBCR, case of Helen Garvie, 9 January 1915.
36. Ibid.

37. ECA, EBCR, case of Freda Carson, 21 November 1919.
38. ECA, EBCR, witness statement of Robert Reid, 23 July 1919.
39. ECA, EBCR, witness statement of William Webster, 23 July 1919.
40. Klein, *Invisible Men*, p. 224.
41. Merrilees, *The Short Arm of the Law, the Memoirs of William Merrilees, O.B.E., Chief Constable, the Lothians and Peebles Constabulary* (London: Long, 1966), p. 64.
42. Ibid, p. 65.
43. Ibid, p. 65.
44. Ibid, p. 67.
45. Ibid, p. 77.
46. ECA, EBCR, case of Hilda Lind, 1920.
47. See, for example, Lisa McLaughlin, 'Discourses of Prostitution/ Discourses of Sexuality', *Critical Studies in Mass Communication*, 8, 3 (1991) pp. 249–72; Eric Trudgill, *Madonnas and Magdalens: The Origins and Developments of Victorian Sexual Attitudes* (London: Heinemann, 1976).
48. Paula Bartley, *Prostitution: Prevention and Reform in England, 1860–1914* (London: Routledge, 2000).
49. GCA, DTC 7/19/1/98, Criminal Returns 1911.
50. Merrilees, *The Short Arm of the Law*, pp. 75–6.
51. ECA, EBCR, case of Jessie Hope, Ann Paton and Catherine Delaney, January 1928.
52. See, for example, Judith Walkowitz, 'Going Public: Shopping, Street Harassment, and Streetwalking in Late Victorian London', *Representation*, 62 (1998) pp. 1–30; Laite, 'Prostitution in London, 1885–1930', p. 170; Slater, 'Containment: Managing Street Prostitution in London', 1918–1959', *Journal of British Studies*, 49, 2 (2010) p. 343.
53. *The Scotsman*, 28 January 1928, p. 11.
54. Ibid.
55. *The Scotsman*, 2 December 1927, p. 13.
56. GCA, SR22/60/13 City of Glasgow Police Instruction Book 1923, pp. 356–7.
57. ECA, EBCR, case of May McArthur, 16 May 1919.
58. Mike Brogden, *On the Mersey Beat* (Oxford: Oxford University Press, 1991), p. 124.
59. *The Scotsman*, 28 January 1928, p. 11.
60. Brogden, *On the Mersey Beat*.
61. Laite, 'Prostitution in London', p. 168.
62. ECA, ED006/2/5 General Order 729, 13 July 1906.
63. ECA, ED006/2/5 General Order 707, 22 September 1903.

64. GCA, Glasgow Police Instruction Books: SR22/60/13, 25 November 1904.
65. GCA, DTC 7/19/1 Glasgow Police Annual Report, 1930.
66. Merrilees, *The Short Arm of the Law*, p. 69.
67. Ibid, p. 72.
68. Ibid, p. 88.
69. *The Scotsman*, 11 April 1907, p. 11.
70. Clive Emsley 'Sergeant Goddard: The Story of the Rotten Apple, or a Diseased Orchard?' in Amy Gilman Srebnick and Rene Levy (eds), *Crime and Culture: An Historical Perspective* (Aldershot: Ashgate, 2005), p. 85.
71. Ibid, p. 95.
72. Ibid, p. 93.
73. Ibid, p. 97.
74. Burgh Police (Scotland) Act 1892 (55&56 Vict. c. 55).
75. Edinburgh Municipal and Police Act 1879 (42&43 Vict. c. cxxxii).
76. GCA, DTC 7/19/1 Glasgow Police Annual Report, 1920.
77. TWL, 3AMS/B/04/02 Solicitation laws in Scotland 1892–1955, SL/1 Minutes of the Edinburgh Town Council, 2 February 1922, pp. 1–2.
78. Ibid.
79. The Immoral Traffic (Scotland) Act 1902 (1&2 Geo 5, c. 20) as amended by the Criminal Law Amendment Act 1912 (3&4 Geo 5, c. 38).
80. ECA, ED006/2/5 General Order 726, 2 May 1906.
81. Ibid.
82. Merrilees, *The Short Arm of the Law*, pp. 65–8.
83. GCA, SR22/60/13 City of Glasgow Instruction Book 1923, p. 357.
84. ECA, ED006/2/5 General Order 237.
85. GCA, SR22/60/13 City of Glasgow Instruction Book 1923, p. 186.
86. Merrilees, *The Short Arm of the Law*, p. 68.
87. ECA, EBCR, case of Margaret Robertson, 30 December 1914; ECA, EBCR, case of Mary Watt, 8 March 1917.
88. Merrilees, *The Short Arm of the Law*, p. 284.
89. ECA, EBCR, case of Margaret Robertson, 30 December 1914; ECA, EBCR, case of Mary Watt, 8 March 1917.
90. ECA, EBCR, case of Margaret Robertson, 30 December 1914.
91. Ibid.
92. Ibid.
93. GCA, DTC 7/19/1 Glasgow Police Annual Report 1922.
94. ECA, EBCR, case of Mary Watt, 8 March 1917.
95. ECA, EBCR, case of Margaret Robertson, 30 December 1914.
96. GCA, T. PAR 1.16, *Memorandum on the Social Evil in Glasgow, 1911*.

97. ECA, ED6/1/8 1920–1929, Edinburgh Police Return of Crimes.
98. GCA, DTC 7/19/1 Glasgow Police Annual Report, 1920.
99. GCA, DTC 7/19/1 Glasgow Police Annual Report, 1928.

CHAPTER 3

The Social Geography of Prostitution[1]

> The prostitutes . . . live as members of the proletariat, in the poorer districts, but their main beat is Princes Street, and it has in their eyes the prestige and familiarity of a business address.[2]

Edwin Muir's 1935 description of prostitutes in Edinburgh moving freely between the working-class areas of the city and those reserved for the middle and upper classes highlights their rare ability to transgress gender and class boundaries. Muir's statement suggests that prostitution in Edinburgh was not forced into the outskirts of society but remained in the very heart of the city centre. His recollections, whilst compelling, do not provide the full picture. This chapter will use court and police records alongside other contemporaries' writings on prostitution to gain a fuller understanding of how prostitution was organised and to explore the wider social implications attached to this use of space. By chronologically mapping the changing location of prostitution in Edinburgh and Glasgow, it is possible to track how emerging technologies and the development of new entertainment venues influenced the location of prostitution and shaped women's opportunities for successful solicitation. The first half of the chapter will focus on the geography of prostitution in Edinburgh, beginning with street solicitation and moving on to look at the location of brothels. The second half will then examine the location of prostitution in Glasgow, following a similar pattern. Whilst the previous chapter stressed the role that the state played in shaping the organisation of prostitution, this chapter will show that the women's utilisation of new commercial and technological developments was at least equally important in that process.

Selling Sex on Edinburgh's Streets

The development of the New Town at the end of the eighteenth and beginning of the nineteenth century meant that Edinburgh's wealthy elite moved from the overcrowded tenements of the Old Town to the wide streets and attractive town houses of the New Town.[3] Initially this meant that poorer inhabitants remained in the Old Town and so too did prostitution. For example, in 1840 Dr William Tait described how most prostitution occurred in the Old Town on streets such as Black Friar's Wynd, the Grassmarket and the High Street.[4] However, by the 1840s particular areas of the New Town had already started to become less elite, as lower-middle-class and then working-class families started to move into areas in the East End, such as St. James Square and Greenside Place.[5] It is no coincidence, then, that Tait also observed prostitution occurring in parts of the New Town's East End, such as St James Square, albeit to a lesser extent. The 1841 census also indicates that there were brothels on Greenside Place in the East End, again suggesting that prostitution was beginning to occur in the 'less respectable' East End areas of the New Town.[6]

By the early twentieth century this trend northwards started to become more firmly established. Figures 3.1 and 3.2 show that solicitation offences were spread across the city, including areas within both the Old and New Town.[7] However, the High Street in the centre of the Old Town still had one of the highest concentrations of importuning offences, and whilst there was some movement north, it is clear that the Old Town remained a popular location for street prostitution.[8]

Despite the movement of some prostitution to these New Town areas by 1911, the Old Town remained the area with the most prostitution offences.

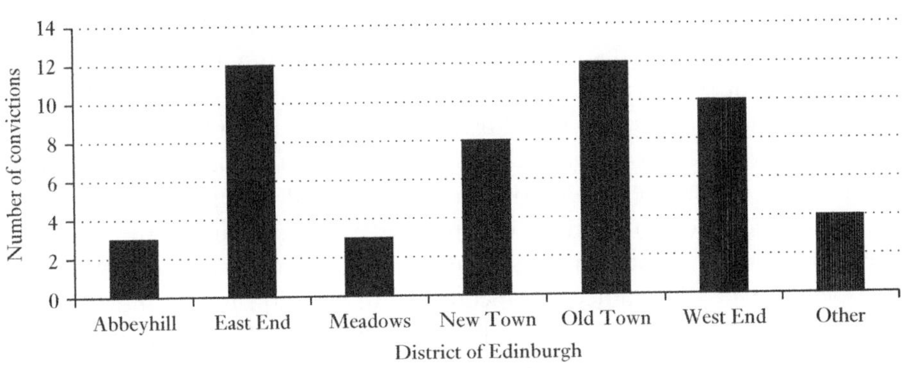

Figure 3.1 Importuning Convictions, Edinburgh Districts, 1903.

Source: Edinburgh Burgh Court Records, Jan–Oct 1903.[9]

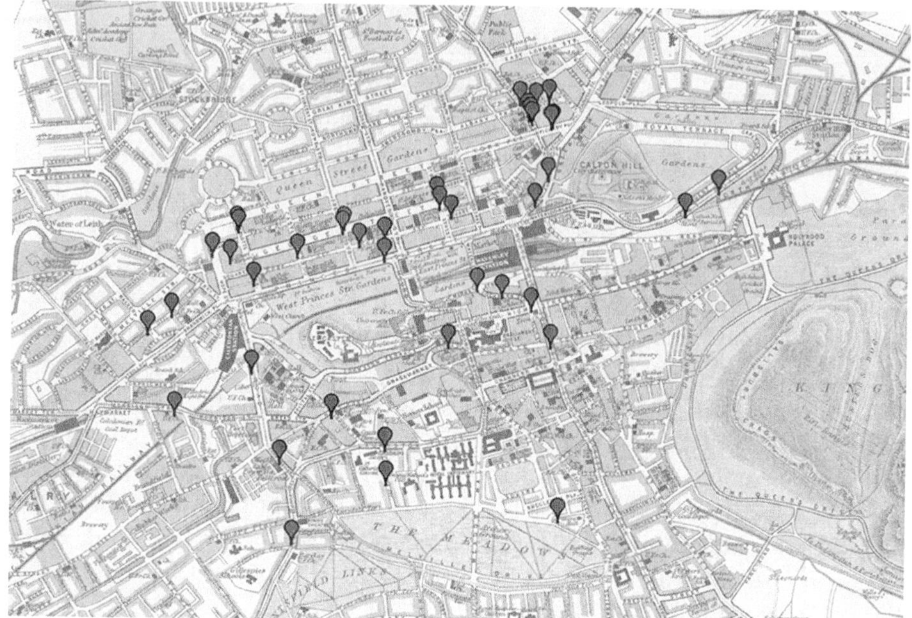

Figure 3.2 Location of Importuning Convictions on Edinburgh Map, 1903.
Source: Edinburgh Burgh Court Records, Jan–Oct 1903 http://geo.nls.uk/urbhist

For example, in 1911 thirty per cent of all prostitution offences occurred on the High Street in the centre of the Old Town. When all of the offences from 1911 are divided up according to the districts of Edinburgh in which they were committed, the prominence of the Old Town as the main location for street prostitution becomes even clearer, with forty-four per cent of all importuning convictions recorded to have occurred there. The district with the second highest amount of offences was the Central New Town, with fourteen per cent. The district with the third highest number of offences was the South Side, with twelve per cent of the importuning offences occurring there. This area borders the Old Town, and many of the streets closest to the Old Town were also well-known locations for prostitution. Therefore, when the number of offences which occurred in the Old Town and South Side are combined, they collectively equate to fifty per cent of all the offences. Nevertheless, the East and West End of the New Town had eleven and five per cent of the offences, respectively. In addition to the fourteen per cent which occurred in the Central New Town area, this means that thirty per cent of the offences took place in the New Town – an area which had previously not been commonly associated with prostitution. The remaining fourteen per cent were distributed among a variety of different districts, such

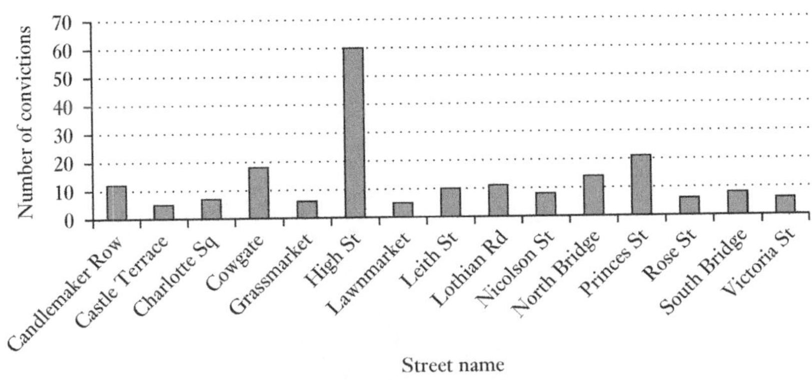

Figure 3.3 Importuning Convictions, Edinburgh Streets, 1911.
Source: Edinburgh Burgh Court Records, Jan–Oct 1911.[10]

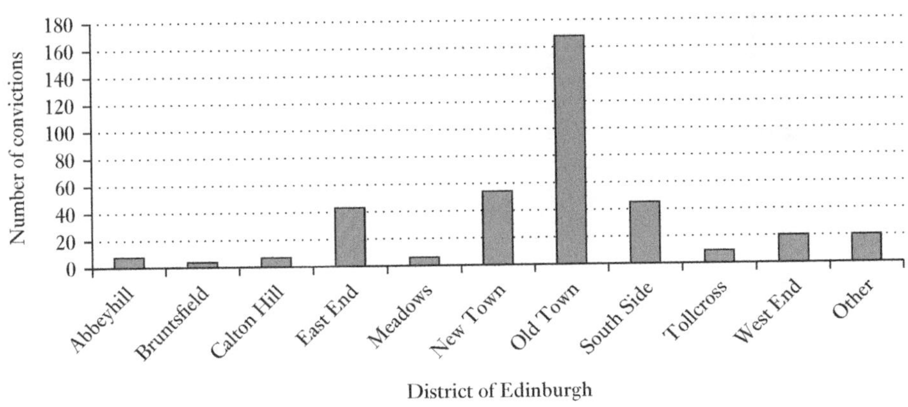

Figure 3.4 Importuning Convictions, Edinburgh Districts, 1911.
Source: Edinburgh Burgh Court Records, Jan–Oct 1911.

as Abbeymount, Bruntsfield and Tollcross. The evidence, therefore, shows that in 1911 the majority of offences still occurred in the Old Town, but the presence of offences in the Central, East and West End of the New Town suggests that by 1911 a considerable minority of prostitution was firmly established in the New Town.

By 1921 there had been a significant change in the location of prostitution offences.[11] The movement towards the New Town which was hinted at in 1911 had fully materialised by then. Leith Street had replaced the High Street as the main location for importuning offences, followed by Princes Street and Greenside Place. These streets are in the centre of the city, particularly in the East End of the New Town. The significance of this can be

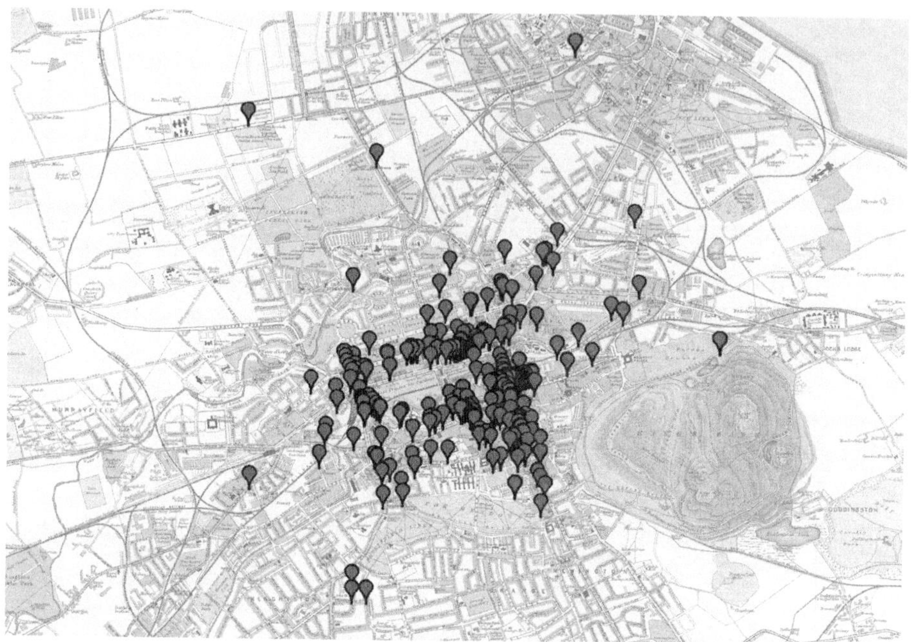

Figure 3.5 Location of Importuning Convictions on Edinburgh Map, 1911.
Source: Edinburgh Burgh Court Records, January–October 1911 http://geo.nls.uk/urbhist/

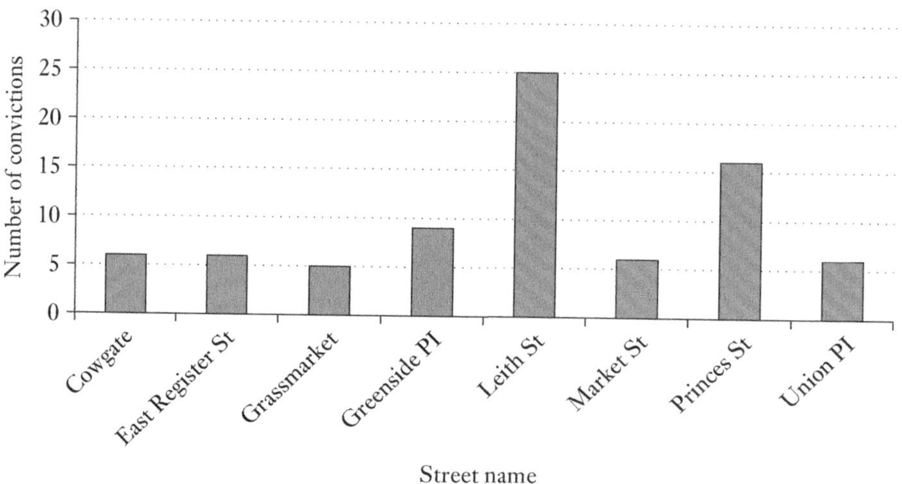

Figure 3.6 Importuning Convictions, Edinburgh Streets, 1921.
Source: Edinburgh Burgh Court Records, Jan–Oct 1921.

Figure 3.7 Importuning Convictions, Edinburgh Districts, 1921.

Source: Edinburgh Burgh Court Records, Jan–Oct 1921.

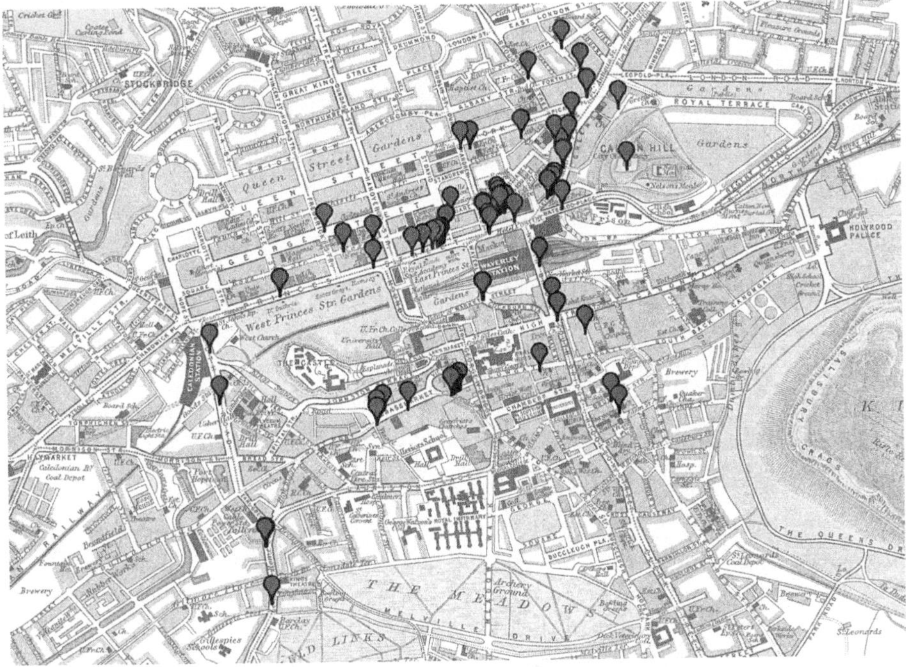

Figure 3.8 Location of Importuning Convictions on Edinburgh Map, 1921.

Source: Edinburgh Burgh Court Records, Jan–Oct 1921 http://geo.nls.uk/urbhist/

seen more sharply by focusing again on the districts. Figure 3.7 shows that seventy per cent of all offences in the 1921 sample were in the East End of the New Town and that twenty-three per cent were in the Central New Town area, whereas all of the other remaining districts added together represented

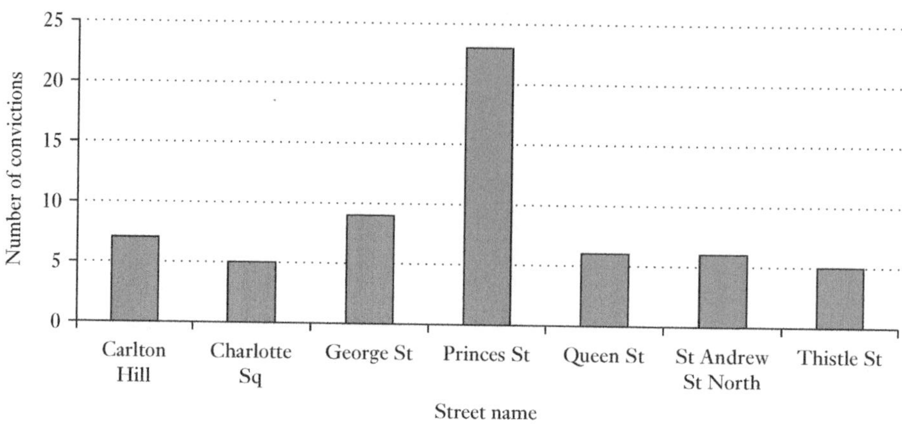

Figure 3.9 Importuning Convictions, Edinburgh Streets, 1931.
Source: Edinburgh Burgh Court Records, Jan–Oct 1931.

Figure 3.10 Importuning Convictions, Edinburgh Districts, 1931.
Source: Edinburgh Burgh Court Records, Jan–Oct 1931.

only seven per cent. This evidence clearly demonstrates that by 1921 the majority of prostitution offences occurred in the East End and Central New Town areas, and no longer in the Old Town.

An examination of the 1931 court data reveals a similar pattern. As in 1921, a large majority (eighty-eight per cent) of the offences occurred in the East End and Central areas of the New Town. Furthermore, by 1931 fifty-three per cent of the offences occurred in the central New Town areas, such as Princes Street, George Street and Thistle Street, in comparison to the thirty-seven per cent of offences that occurred in the East End areas of the New Town. Therefore, although the New Town as a whole remained the area with the most offences, by 1931 the central New Town areas had more offences than

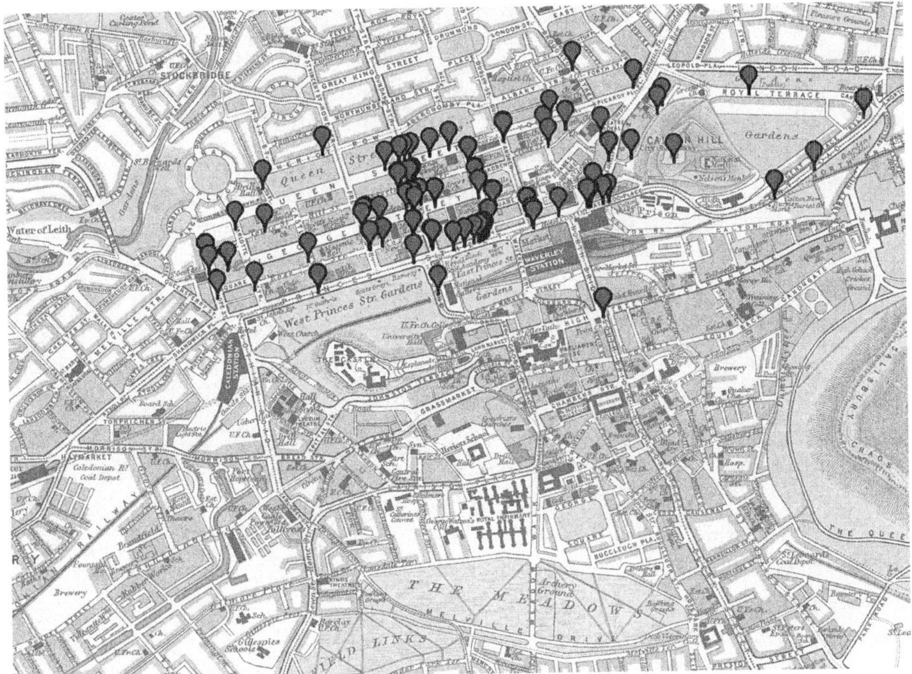

Figure 3.11 Location of Importuning Convictions on Edinburgh Map, 1931.
Source: Edinburgh Burgh Court Records, Jan–Oct 1931 http://geo.nls.uk/urbhist/

the East End. Interestingly, another ten per cent of the offences were recorded to have occurred in the West End district of the New Town – a relatively more wealthy area and one which previously had shown little evidence that street prostitution occurred there. In comparison, only two per cent of offences were recorded in the Old Town. This shift in the location of offences towards the more 'respectable', wealthier areas of the Central and West End of the New Town suggests that street prostitution during this period was moving further towards the centre of the city, both geographically and socially.

However, the use of criminal statistics alone to prove where street prostitution was located can be problematic, as it could be argued that criminal conviction statistics actually reveal more about policing policies than about the criminal activity itself.[12] Rather than showing the areas in which prostitution was most common, the court records may actually indicate where the police chose to enforce the solicitation laws. Considering that arrests for prostitution were usually initiated by the police rather than by a witness or victim, the criminal statistics relating to prostitution are particularly vulnerable to changes in police policy.[13] Consequently, if the police were turning their attention towards prosecuting women soliciting in 'respectable' areas, that may account for why there appeared to be a sharp decline in the amount of offences in the Old Town. Indeed, a more tolerant attitude towards prostitution in the working-class areas of the Old Town corresponds with the previous chapter's argument that police officers often turned a blind eye towards women's activities as long as they were not causing noticeable disturbance. However, regardless of whether or not the statistics are particularly low in the Old Town and high in the New Town due to increased police surveillance in the latter area, the relatively large number of women witnessed soliciting in these central New Town locations proves that a lot of solicitation did occur there. This suggests that the police's attempt to deter women from working in the central New Town areas was not successful, and the threat of police persecution was not a large-enough deterrent to stop women from working in these more profitable locations.

In addition to the crime statistics, the numerous police reports from the late 1910s, the 1920s and the 1930s confirm that the women routinely walked along routes which included some of the most important streets in Edinburgh, such as Princes Street, George Street and Frederick Street. For example, the following two separate extracts from police witness testimony, from the years 1920 and 1937, respectively, could represent any number of the vast amount of statements which described the very prominent routes the women took through the city centre;

> 1. At 10.40pm on date of charge, I saw the two accused accost two sailors in Princes Street. They left them and then went down Leith Street where they loitered about and accosted a civilian.[14]
> 2. At 11.10pm on the date charged she came under their notice loitering in St. Andrew Square . . . [she] proceeded westwards to George Street opposite number 52, there she spoke to a man who was seated in a stationary motor car for a few seconds then continued west to Frederick Street. On reaching there she loitered about for about 5 minutes or so, then proceeded southwards in Frederick Street and turned east in Princes Street.[15]

In addition, coffee stalls in central locations, such as the Mound, were well known as popular solicitation sites, and social workers commented on the 'depravity' of women who 'parade Princes Street night after night, making open advances to soldiers'.[16] It would appear, therefore, that any attempt to stop the majority of these women from soliciting in the respectable central areas of the city was unsuccessful. Perhaps the opportunities available in these areas were attractive enough to risk potential arrest.

Soliciting on the busy thoroughfares of the New Town's Central and

East End areas meant that the women had better access to potential customers and therefore a much higher chance of successfully importuning. They were also close to the main railway station at Waverley. Railway stations have long been recognised as places where prostitution occurs due to the large amount of people who pass through.[17] The railway station as a site for solicitation was particularly important during the First World War because soldiers were moved across the country by train. The court records show that it was not just the popular imagination or the military authorities' fear of venereal disease which linked soldiers and prostitution. In the witness testimonies, a large majority of the men whom the women solicited were described as 'soldiers', 'naval seamen', or other members of the armed forces. For example, in 1919 the police described how Mary Thomson and Mary Gibbons:

> . . . accosted an Australian soldier who spoke to them for a minute or two then left. On leaving the soldier, they accosted two naval seamen with a similar result. They then continued westwards and at the Palace Picture House they stopped two Canadian soldiers.[18]

Descriptions of women soliciting men from the armed forces may have been so numerous because it would have been easier for the police to recognise activity considered to be 'importuning' when a woman was standing with a group of soldiers rather than talking to civilians, especially considering the emphasis which had been placed on the dangers of prostitutes spreading venereal disease to members of the armed forces.[19] Nevertheless, the exceptionally large numbers of witness statements which described solicitation between prostitutes and soldiers suggest that the location of soldiers around the main railway station during the First World War clearly played a role in the movement of street prostitution from Edinburgh's Old Town to the New Town.

However, the importance of the First World War must not be overstated. The war ended in 1918, yet in 1921 most prostitution continued to occur in these same Central and East End districts of the New Town. Clearly there were more long-term factors influencing the location of prostitution. One of the most important of these was the location of entertainment and other commercial businesses. Elaine McKewon, for example, states that:

> Prostitution finds locational stability in night-life districts . . . despite its relatively high visibility, because these are areas where 'dissident' activities are widely known to thrive . . . and traditional social norms are relatively broken down.[20]

Edinburgh's East End had been associated with the theatre since the early nineteenth century, and by the 1920s there was a wide variety of new types of entertainment venues located in the area.[21] Many of the new dance halls and cinemas which were opened during this period, such as the Playhouse on Greenside Row and Fairley's dance hall on Leith Street, were situated in the East End of the New Town. The area was also well known for its pubs, fish-and-chip restaurants and ice-cream parlours – so much so that the locals described it as the place to get 'alcohol and ice' – a description justified by the fact that in 1911 there were twenty-two pubs in the small triangle between Leith Street and York Place.[22] It is likely, therefore, that this would have been a good catchment area for women to solicit the men who headed towards this area for entertainment, especially the soldiers who left Waverley railway station and headed to the New Town to enjoy their leave. Additionally, if sailors who were stationed in Leith wanted to go to Edinburgh's city centre for entertainment, then the East End, and in particular Gayfield Square at the top of Leith Walk, provided a perfect location for importuning the sailors who passed this area on their way to and from the port and the various entertainment venues in the city centre.

The location of entertainment venues was not only relevant during wartime. Throughout the whole period, the witness statements routinely described how the women often solicited in front of cinemas, theatres, dance halls, restaurants and pubs. For example, one witness found in a brothel described how he had met the accused at the 'Empire Theatre and accompanied them home to spend the night.'[23] Another report described how the police had found the accused 'with another prostitute in the shebeen at 3a Greenside Place known as the "dug out". . . Opposite the K.B. Hotel she accosted a navy petty officer, [and] entered the fish and potato restaurant.'[24] It was not only outside these venues that the women worked. 'Chuckers-out' were often employed in cinemas to make sure that prostitution did not occur inside, and the screening rooms were never fully dark for the same reason.[25]

As well as offering a high concentration of potential clients, the East End area was also close to low-rent indoor premises where the sex acts could take place. By the late nineteenth century, several buildings located in the East End of the New Town on streets such as Leith Street, Greenside Place, and St James Square had been 'made down'. This effectively meant that the large, attractive buildings originally designed for middle-class inhabitants had been converted into small tenement flats which housed working-class families, often in overcrowded conditions. This is especially true of the East End areas surrounding St. James Square and Gayfield Square, which had become notorious for their slum-like residences.[26] One of the main methods used by women once they had solicited a man on the street was to take him back to

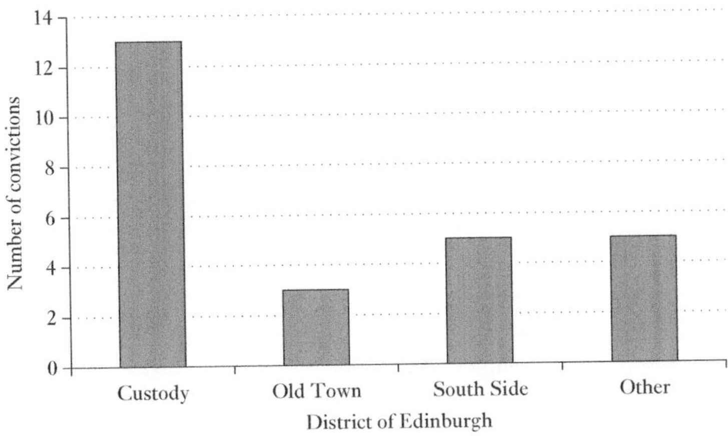

Figure 3.12 Home Addresses of Women Convicted for Importuning in Edinburgh, 1903.
Source: Edinburgh Burgh Court Records, Jan–Oct 1903.[29]

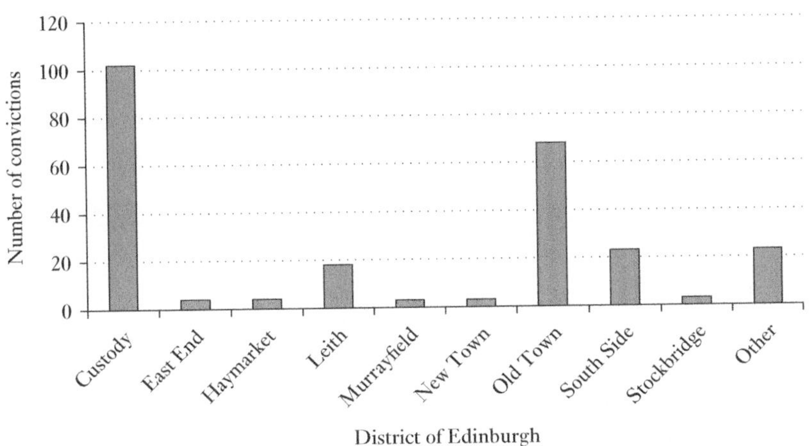

Figure 3.13 Home Addresses of Women Convicted for Importuning in Edinburgh, 1911.
Source: Edinburgh Burgh Court Records, Jan–Oct 1911.

either a privately rented 'short time flat' (rented only for an hour or two) or a brothel of varying descriptions. For example, in a case in 1928 a witness in a brothel case described how 'they had been accosted by the prostitutes Miller and Ryan, on the street, and after having a few drinks in a public house they had been taken back by them to the house for immoral purposes'.[27] Another man found in a brothel at 5 Prospect Terrace explained that he had 'met the accused and her sister in one of the main thoroughfares'.[28] This method therefore meant that it was necessary for women to live in, or have access

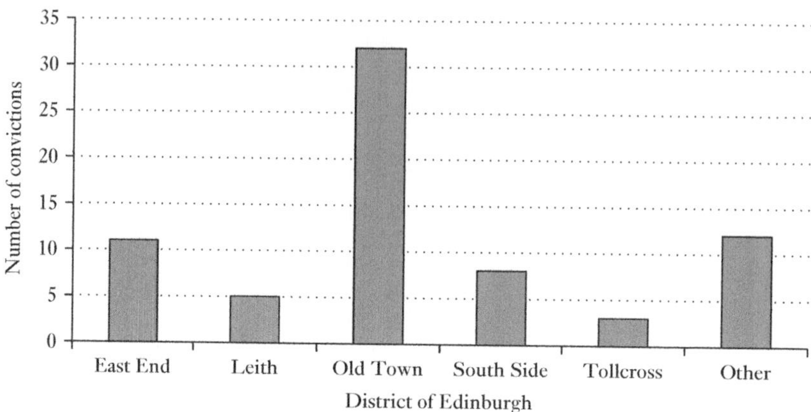

Figure 3.14 Home Addresses of Women Convicted for Importuning in Edinburgh, 1921.
Source: Edinburgh Burgh Court Records Jan–Oct 1921.

Figure 3.15 Home Addresses of Women Convicted for Importuning in Edinburgh, 1931.
Source: Edinburgh Burgh Court Records, Jan–Oct 1931.

to, accommodation around the city centre areas in which they solicited – something which the East End could provide.

The home addresses recorded in the Burgh Court records support the trend that by the 1920s and 1930s it became increasingly possible and desirable to work from flats closer to the more profitable areas in the New Town. Nevertheless, the higher rents in the central New Town would have meant that the women could only move as far as the East End of the New Town, and many still remained in the cheaper areas in the Old Town and the South Side through choice or necessity. It appears, therefore, that Muir was accurate in his depiction of the prostitutes in Edinburgh being able to cross the 'invisible barrier' between working-class and middle-class areas of the city. Although the women lived in the Old Town and the less expensive areas of the East End, they managed to cross class and gender boundaries by soliciting on some of the most prominent streets in Edinburgh.

It is clear from the above evidence that although women were more likely to be arrested in the New Town areas, the operational advantages associated with this area made the risk worth taking. What is more, the findings from chapter two show that the police were often apathetic towards policing prostitution and did not prioritise the policing of this seemingly 'victimless' offence. The relatively lenient sentences that women convicted of prostitution were typically given, such as cautions, fines or short prison sentences, were often insufficient to deter them from working in these more profitable areas. Whilst the middle classes may have wanted to ostracise 'deviant' women from the centre of the city as part of a wider project to forcibly map middle-class notions of respectability onto particular public spaces, in practice the implementation of such policies was unfeasible.[30]

Even when the police did try harder to implement the solicitation laws, the women had many tactics to avoid arrest. The cautioning system implemented in Edinburgh meant that women had to be cautioned for soliciting three times before they could be arrested and charged. This gave women plenty of warning, something which many used to their advantage. If women feared they were receiving too much police attention, they could move to different areas in the city, or to another nearby city, such as Glasgow.[31] For example, in 1919 twenty-two-year-old Sarah Montgomery was seen 'frequently on the streets accosting men' and was cautioned three times. However, shortly after this 'she disappeared for a month or so'.[32] Similarly, Mary Bradshaw also 'disappeared for a time' between her initial cautions in 1923 and her eventual arrest in 1925 after a further three cautions.[33]

Phil Hubbard and Teela Sanders' study of the red-light district in 1990s Birmingham used Michel de Certeau's analysis of everyday life in the city and Henri Lefebvre's notions of space as a 'socially-produced phenomenon' to highlight the ways in which women who engaged in prostitution 'used space to their own ends' in order to escape the 'ordering and disciplining processes that make distinctions between the normal and deviant'.[34] The evidence above, therefore, suggests that Hubbard and Sanders' argument that prostitutes are sometimes capable of tactically 'exceeding their socio-spatial confinement' and 'undermin[ing] the strategies of the strong by misusing spaces' is also applicable to Edinburgh.[35] This again demonstrates the police's inability effectively to control prostitution and the fact that prostitution in Edinburgh was not increasingly criminalised during this period.

If the women had no indoor location they could go to once they had solicited a man, some women would use secluded outdoor spaces. The

Burgh Court witness testimonies show the parks, doorways and alleyways around the Central and East End of the New Town offered opportunities for *al fresco* commercial sex. For example, a case in 1919 described how officers had found 'the prostitute Cecelia Wood' and a sailor 'having carnal connection' in the public stair at '38b New Street'.[36] Another case, this time from 1925, described how Mary Bradshaw (a 'suspected prostitute') 'entered the common stair there. About three minutes later both came out of the stair and proceeded to the top of Leith Street where the sailor left.'[37] There were also many references made to Calton Hill and Holyrood Park as common locations for importuning and sexual intercourse. The location of two large open park spaces only a few minutes' walk from the East End of Princes Street provided a convenient location for those women without access to indoor spaces. For example, in 1921 Elizabeth Young was found 'importuning male passers-by for the purposes of prostitution on the Calton Hill',[38] and in 1918 the police described how they saw Daisy Moor 'leave the Calton Hill with two sailors who left her in Leith Street after paying her some money.'[39]

The records which describe women having sex outside are quite rare, possibly because most of the reports do not describe where the sex act took place. However, by the 1920s an increasing number of separate cases were being heard in the Edinburgh Burgh Court of couples having 'carnal connection' in a public place. These cases were not necessarily related to prostitution, as anyone having sexual intercourse outdoors in public was liable for prosecution. However, in certain cases it is possible to match up the names of women prosecuted for prostitution with the names of women also prosecuted for having sex outdoors in public. For example, Elizabeth Winter was caught having sex in a doorway on the 'bye lane next to George Street' in June 1935, and in June 1937 she was convicted of importuning for the purposes of prostitution, also on George Street.[40] On both occasions she had previous offences for each crime.

In addition to concerns of space and place, it is also important to think about time. In particular, the time of day that the women solicited and whether it was light or dark is interesting. The police witness reports show that the women were arrested from as early as 5pm until as late as 3am, with the majority between 10pm and 1am. This inevitably reflected the times that the police chose to undertake surveillance; nevertheless, it is likely that the police would have chosen these times because they knew that most of the soliciting would take place then. This suggests that a majority of the solicitation took place after dark, and it is likely that the women used the cover of darkness to avoid detection from the police. On the one hand, this could mean that prostitutes were often restricted to working in the darkness, emphasising their outcast status and making their work more dangerous. On the other hand, the women who solicited after dark were able to break the gender boundaries which dictated that women should not to be outside at night-time, especially if unaccompanied.[41] In one sense, therefore, these women had more freedom than most other women to move throughout the city at any time of the day or night. They could also use this period in the night to cross class boundaries by soliciting in middle and upper-class areas. For example, a newspaper report in 1903 described how prostitutes were taking advantage of the poor lighting in the West End to solicit on streets inhabited by the upper classes.[42]

As the century continued, however, more women began to be seen out after dark enjoying the increasing nightlife entertainment opportunities the city had to offer.[43] Although many of these women were still accompanied by men, the increased presence of young women in the city centre after dark began to make it more difficult to differentiate between women who were soliciting and women who were returning from an evening's entertainment at the cinema or the dance hall. Moreover, not all of the arrests occurred during darkness. There are several arrests which occurred in the early evening and others that took place in the summer time when it remained light in Scotland until 11pm. It appears, therefore, that rather than being increasingly ostracised, women involved in prostitution were becoming less visibly segregated.[44]

In addition to the changes that occurred on a daily basis, it is also useful to think about change over a longer time span. For example, Neil Larry Shumsky and Larry M. Springer demonstrate that in San Francisco during the period from 1880 to 1934 the location of prostitution altered, depending on particular economic developments within the city, changing attitudes towards prostitution and how the police responded to those pressures.[45] Although many of the factors involved, such as disputes over land use, can be seen as more general issues associated with prostitution, the way in which these factors interacted at different points in time uniquely shaped the nature of prostitution in each city. Therefore, whilst Philip Howell's argument that prostitution in nineteenth-century Oxford and Liverpool was regulated by forcing it into specific locations away from respectable society does not apply to Edinburgh in the early twentieth century; it is likely that this type of regulation occurred later in the century.[46] Roger Davidson and Gayle Davis' examination of prostitution in mid-twentieth-century Scotland has shown that this type of 'informal regulation' or 'tolerance zone' did emerge in Leith after the Second World War.[47] The informal toleration of prostitution in Leith meant that women were free to work there without the fear of persecution from the police which they faced in the city centre. However, there is little evidence to indicate that such a policy existed in Edinburgh before the Second World War.

Leith was officially a separate town until 1920, when it was incorporated into the city of Edinburgh. This meant that before 1920 Leith had its own separate police force and court where the women would have been tried. Without the cooperation of the Leith police force, the Edinburgh police could not have actively pursued a policy which forced prostitution into Leith. Unfortunately, the Leith Burgh Court records from this period have not survived, and it is therefore difficult to know more about their policy or how many women were convicted for prostitution in Leith before 1920. Nevertheless, it is unlikely that the Leith police would have cooperated with a policy that redirected prostitution from Edinburgh to Leith. After 1920 crimes in Leith were prosecuted in the Edinburgh Burgh Court, but very few cases relating to Leith appear in the records. From the court records alone it is difficult to know whether this meant that there was relatively little prostitution in Leith, or whether the police had developed an informal tolerance policy in this area. The police records give no indication of the existence of any such policy; however, it is reasonable to assume that they would not have wanted to leave behind any related records, even if such a policy had existed.

Leith is a port town which principally developed around the harbour of Leith and the shipping business it generated. Considering that there is a long-established connection between prostitution and seafaring, it is likely that the high concentration of sailors in the port meant that a considerable amount of prostitution did occur there. Nevertheless, the fact that so many witness statements described sailors in the centre of Edinburgh indicates that they were not confined solely to the harbour area, suggesting that the street prostitution which took place in Edinburgh occurred independently alongside that in Leith. Moreover, the large number of offences recorded in Edinburgh's city centre suggests this was a good location to solicit the men who had no involvement with the port of Leith. Even though the police were employing the solicitation laws in these areas, the law was not an effective enough deterrent to force the women out of the area. It appears, therefore, that the benefits gained from working in the most advantageous catchment areas were worth risking possible arrest. Consequently, although legislation and policing policy undoubtedly had an important effect on where and how women solicited, it is clear that other factors, such as the sites of entertainment and other market forces, played an important role in the locating of prostitution in the centre of Edinburgh.

Location of Brothels in Edinburgh

There were considerably fewer convictions for brothel-keeping than importuning in Edinburgh during this period, which makes it harder to map the location of brothels as accurately as that of street offences. However, the data that is available offers some interesting trends to analyse. The Burgh Court records show that the brothels were distributed throughout the city and not restricted to one particular 'red-light' area. Although the East End often had a higher number of brothels than other districts, the distribution was far less concentrated than was the case for street solicitation. The brothels were spread across more districts than the importuning offences and included areas that were much further away from the city centre, such as Stockbridge, Murrayfield, Newington and the outskirts of Leith. For example, in 1915 twenty-two per cent of the brothel convictions were in the East End, seventeen per cent were located in Stockbridge and seventeen per cent in the outskirts of Leith. Similarly, in 1921, whilst thirty-eight per cent of convictions for brothel-keeping were in the East End, twenty-five per cent were located in Leith and twenty-five per cent in the South Side. One of the most likely causes for this was the increase in the number of car owners and users. Whereas women importuning on the street needed to be visible on the busy thoroughfares in the city centre, brothels could be located further away because men could travel there by car. The use of cars to transport the men, alone or in the company of the women, was reported in several witness statements, demonstrating how common it was becoming. For example, as early as 1917 a report described how a 'motor car drew up at Prospect Place and [they] observed the accused, her sister Jessie Watt . . . and a soldier leave the car and go into the stair.'[48]

The witness reports show that by the late 1920s and 1930s, when it was becoming more common for men to own cars, these vehicles increasingly played a role in importuning. There were several instances where a woman either walked up to a stationary car or tried to attract the attention of men passing by in their cars. For example, in 1937 police described how a suspected prostitute called Helen Stirling attempted to 'attract the attention of passing motorists by stepping to the edge of the pavement as they passed her' and, on another occasion, 'went up to a motor car which had drawn up on the south side of Princes Street, opened the door and spoke to the man who was driving it, and was in the act of entering the car when the witness approached.'[49] The car could then be used as a location for sex, or for transporting the couple to a particular indoor location. This type of importuning sounds very similar to what we today describe as 'kerb crawling', and it is quite possible that these cases were some of the earliest recorded examples of 'kerb crawling' in Edinburgh.

Clearly the distinction which has been made between indoor and outdoor prostitution is somewhat arbitrary, as in many cases street prostitution and brothel prostitution were closely linked. Women routinely solicited on the street and then went to an indoor location for the sex act. According to the law, these indoor spaces were technically brothels if more than one woman engaged in prostitution there. However, as we shall see, these brothels varied considerably in their size and nature and were often little more than private flats which had been adapted for the purpose of prostitution. The women who solicited on the street mainly chose to walk around busy areas in the centre of the city to increase their chances of importuning successfully. This would have also increased their chances of being arrested, but, unlike in brothels, the women could avoid detection by continuously moving around.[50] Subsequently, the brothels tended to be situated further away from the most prominent streets and distributed more widely throughout the city. If brothel owners wanted to situate their businesses in more central locations, then they had to be more clandestine about their operations.

The fact that women would solicit men on the street and then take them to a brothel meant that brothels could be placed in less visible locations. The witness statements show that once the men knew about a 'brothel', they would go back to the same place without needing to be solicited, another reason why brothels did not need to rely on being visible. For example, in the witness testimony given by a man found in a top-floor brothel flat at 205 Pleasance, the witness explained how 'they had been in the house on previous occasions and knew where to come for "a good girl"'.[51] The men would not necessarily come to the flat accompanied by the women; for example, a policeman described how he had 'watched a colonial soldier leave and a few minutes later two soldiers went up to the house and were admitted.'[52] Considering that brothel-keeping was illegal and could warrant a much higher fine or prison sentence than importuning, it was in the interest of the owners to draw as little attention to themselves as possible.

The higher rents in the most central New Town areas would also have deterred many 'brothel-keepers' from locating their businesses in these more expensive areas. Whilst it was free for women to solicit in the busy central New Town areas, once they had successfully importuned a man, they returned to the less expensive areas of the city to find an indoor location for sex. The brothels in the city centre therefore tended to remain in the Old Town and South Side areas, with some appearing in the less expensive areas of the East End and New Town. Furthermore, the indoor spaces that some women used for prostitution were their own homes, which were usually situated in less expensive areas, such as the Old Town, South Side or Leith. Nevertheless, there were a few brothels in the more central New Town areas, presumably providing services for more wealthy clients. Therefore, whilst most prosecutions for brothel-keeping occurred in the less respectable areas around the Old Town, the location of brothels throughout the city shows that they were not restricted to any particular area. In this respect, Edinburgh was similar to London and New York, which also did not have one particular 'red-light' zone during this period.[53]

'From floor to ceiling – just "rookeries"': The Geography of Prostitution in Glasgow

There are no surviving Burgh Court records for Glasgow, which means that it is not possible to gain the level of detailed information about the location of prostitution in Glasgow that would be needed for a 'like-for-like' comparison with Edinburgh; however, there are some sources available which can give an indication of where soliciting occurred and where brothels were located. In particular, brothel cases and Immoral Traffic Act cases that were heard in the Sheriff and High Court in Glasgow provide some useful information. For example, a case in 1919 against Alfred Joseph Vaughn for brothel-keeping provides interesting details about a brothel that was located at 68 Saint George's Road in the central St. George's area of Glasgow.[54] The house consisted of seven rooms and a kitchen, with four rooms on one floor, and three rooms in an attic above. The rent was £48 per year. A woman was employed to run the brothel but Alfred Vaughn was described as the main manager. Another witness report from a case in 1912 against William Thomson for harbouring prostitutes described the brothel he managed at the central location of 6 West Russell Street as being 'one stair up, and consist[ing] of 2 rooms and kitchen.'[55]

The Duke Street Prison Registers also prove some further information. For example, many of the brothels that appeared in the register were in very central areas, such as the brothel run by Margaret Brennet at 13 Cambridge Street, and the brothel at 86 Dundas Street run by Catherine Mclean. Other very central addresses of brothels included 54 Bell Street, Brown Street and 19 Wilson Street. Areas in and around the Cowcaddens were also reported to have had many brothels. For example, 163 Cowcaddens as well as 11 and 46 Milton Lane were all described as brothels. The 1911 'Memorandum on Social Evil in Glasgow' also described how there were 'numerous brothels in the northern district'.[56] Whilst these areas are quite central, they also included districts which had developed into 'slums'. In a similar way to what occurred in Edinburgh, the upper and middle classes in Glasgow increasingly left the central areas of the city as new housing was developed in the suburbs during the nineteenth century. As a result, the working classes moved into these former grand buildings and 'made them down' into much smaller dwellings, so that they could house the rapidly increasing number of urban workers.[57] In particular, areas such as Calton, Cowcaddens, Bridgeton,

Maryhill and the Gorbals attracted large numbers of migrants, which increased the overcrowding.[58] These areas became notorious for crime and prostitution. However, prostitution was not confined to them; instead, as was the case in Edinburgh, by the start of the twentieth century prostitution was also commonly occurring in the central business and entertainment districts.

A 1902 dispute over public house licensing hours provides one of the most detailed descriptions of the location of prostitution in Glasgow during this early part of the century. In 1902 the Glasgow council wanted to shorten the licensing hours so that pubs in the Broomielaw district would shut at 10pm. The area was predominantly working class, and its location directly next to the river Clyde meant that it was heavily influenced by the shipping industry. Indeed, during the nineteenth century the area was known for its large amount of pubs and prostitution. *The Scotsman* newspaper described the hearing and gave extracts from the witness statements given by pub owners and policemen. Alexander McIntosh, the former Superintendent of the Western District Police, explained how over the past thirty-five years the Broomielaw had greatly improved. He stated that:

> Previously you would get ten or twenty loose women in the district for one now. [I] could point out tenements that had been houses of ill fame, from floor to ceiling – just 'rookeries' . . . now [I] could point out more prostitutes in Sauchiehall Street in one night than in the district in question in one week, or even a fortnight.[59]

Peter Stewart, a private investigator, made a similar statement confirming that prostitution was more commonly occurring on central commercial streets such as Sauchiehall Street, rather than the Broomielaw area. He first described how he was instructed to take the detective with him and patrol the Broomielaw district between nine and twelve o'clock on the previous night. He then described how:

> from nine to twelve, all the women he saw, of any description, would number about twenty. So far as he could see, only three of them were of loose character. If he had gone to Argyle Street or Bath Street or Sauchiehall Street, there would have been no comparison.[60]

When asked by the advocate, Mr Wilson, whether the prostitutes could be seen 'to swarm in these places' around Bath Street and Sauchiehall Street, Stewart readily agreed.[61]

Some of these reports were given by men who were against earlier closing hours (or were employed by someone who was), and it was in their interest to represent the Broomielaw area in a positive light. However, although their statements cannot be taken at face value, they are still very useful. The full extent to which prostitution had ceased to occur in the Broomielaw area may be uncertain, but the statements do suggest that although this area had been a well-known location of prostitution during the late nineteenth century, by the beginning of the twentieth century more prostitutes were now working on Sauchiehall Street, Argyle Street and Bath Street – perhaps some of the most prominent streets in the centre of Glasgow. Similar to areas in the Central and East End of the New Town in Edinburgh in which prostitution occurred, these streets in Glasgow were also close to the two main railway stations and were well known for having a variety of different entertainment venues located there. This would suggest, that, as was the case in Edinburgh, the principal location of prostitution in Glasgow moved from a less respectable (albeit still relatively central) working-class area to the busiest entertainment and commercial districts of the city centre. However, this did not mean that prostitution no longer occurred in the working-class districts, such as the Cowcaddens and the Gorbals in Glasgow or the Old Town and South Side in Edinburgh; rather, it was not restricted to these 'less respectable' locations.

This comparison is also supported by the criminal statistics for Glasgow. For the years 1892–1908 the Chief Constables in Glasgow recorded how many times officers had visited brothels in particular areas. These figures do not relate to the actual number of brothels in that particular area, and, as with street offences, it could be argued that they reveal more about police policy than about the prevalence of brothels. Nevertheless, they do give some indication of where brothels were located, even if it is difficult to know the location of brothels that were not visited by the police. Table 3.1 shows that between 1892 and 1900 District A (Central District) had a large majority of the brothel visits and that district B (Western District) had the second largest amount of brothel visits. The other districts had relatively few visits, and most districts apart from E (Northern District) and C (Eastern District) received no visits at all. After 1900 the location of brothel visits began to change. They became more spread out between the A, B, C and E districts, and the difference between the number of visits to each of these districts declined. The district with the most visits varied slightly from year-to-year, but in general, although A district remained predominant, visits to districts C and E became more frequent. Although the Glasgow brothels appear to have been more centrally located than brothels in Edinburgh during the nineteenth century, by 1900 the locations began to diversify, and if the police annual reports of brothel visits had continued further, it is fair to hypothesise that this trend might have continued.

Table 3.1 Percentage of Visits to Brothels in each Police District of Glasgow.

Year	District A	District B	District C	District D	District E	District F	District G	District H	Marina
1892	80%	5%	0%	0%	15%	0%	0%	0%	0%
1893									
1894	78%	9%	1%	0%	0%	0%	0%	0%	0%
1895	82%	11%	0%	0%	7%	0%	0%	0%	0%
1896	85%	9%	0%	0%	6%	0%	0%	0%	0%
1897	85%	7%	0%	0%	7%	0%	0%	0%	1%
1898	80%	8%	7%	0%	3%	2%	0%	0%	0%
1899	70%	12%	14%	0%	2%	2%	0%	0%	0%
1900	51%	26%	18%	1%	3%	0%	1%	0%	0%
1901	27%	36%	27%	3%	3%	0%	3%	1%	0%
1902	32%	40%	19%	0%	7%	1%	0%	1%	0%
1903									
1904	31%	5%	44%	11%	2%	0%	1%	0%	6%
1905	0%	10%	16%	2%	56%	0%	3%	0%	0%
1906	30%	13%	27%	0%	27%	0%	3%	0%	0%
1907	4%	17%	58%	6%	2%	6%	2%	0%	0%
1908	21%	8%	25%	4%	25%	4%	12%	0%	0%

Source: Glasgow Annual Reports, 1892–1908.

Although the different range of sources available for Edinburgh and Glasgow means that it is difficult to compare the two cities over the whole time period, it is nevertheless possible to make useful comparisons. In both Edinburgh and Glasgow there was no single vice district located on the peripheries of society. Instead, prostitution coexisted among a variety of businesses and entertainment venues in the heart of the city centre. Therefore, if 'people's identities are in part constructed through the spatial locations they inhabit and frequent', as Hart has claimed, then the location of prostitution in the city centre would have had an important influence on the women who worked there.[62] Rather than being outcasts from society, the women who were involved in prostitution moved between districts, living and working in the centre of the city. Chapter five will further explore the ways in which a woman's engagement in prostitution did not necessarily mean her exclusion from working-class society. It will also examine how space and place shaped women's experiences of prostitution.

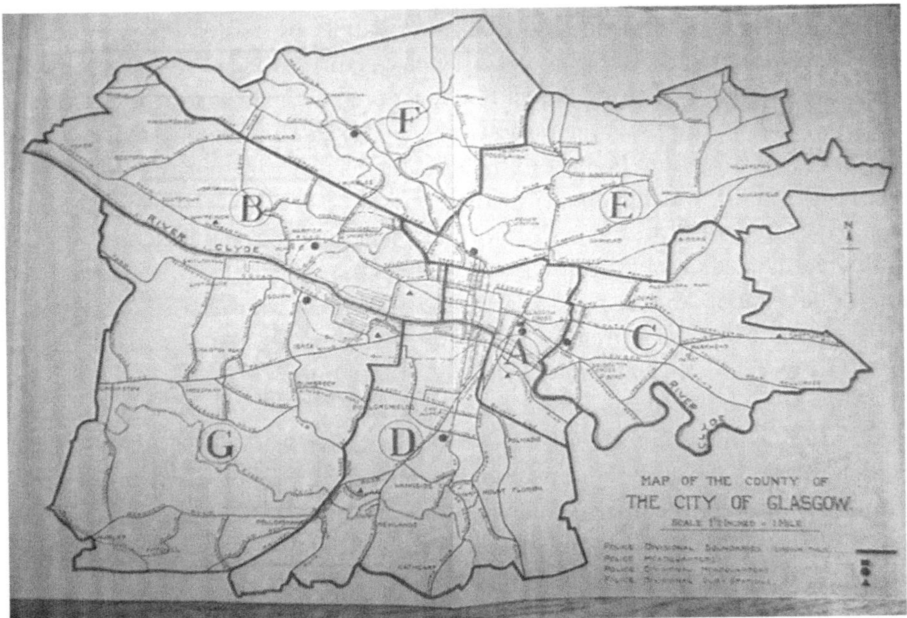

Figure 3.16 Map of Police Districts in Glasgow in 1933.
Source: Glasgow Police Annual Reports.

Conclusion

Ashworth's study of red-light districts in Western Europe established that the main factors which determined the location of prostitution were 'accessibility, opportunity and constraint'.[63] This chapter has focused on the first two factors and found that during the early twentieth century the location of street prostitution in Edinburgh moved further towards the centre of the business and entertainment districts, because these busy areas provided the best 'accessibility and opportunity' for the women who relied on visibility for their solicitation to be successful. Although there is not the same quantity of detailed source material available for Glasgow, the evidence suggests that street prostitution in Glasgow also occurred in the very centre of the city.

However, the location of brothels in both cities varied slightly from this pattern. Whereas women who solicited on the street used central locations to maximise their visibility and to enhance their 'accessibility' and 'opportunity', those working in brothels could depend on other methods. Due to brothels' stationary nature, brothel-keepers could rely on the fact that once men knew the location, they could return again without needing to be solicited. Alternatively, new customers could be solicited on the street in central locations and then directed to the brothel in a more remote area. This meant that brothels in Edinburgh could be more widely dispersed throughout the city and not necessarily restricted to the city centre. In Glasgow, the brothels were mainly situated in more central locations at the start of the twentieth century, but by the interwar period they also began to become more widely dispersed throughout the city. This chapter has shown that the distinction between indoor and outdoor prostitution was often blurred. Whilst some women solicited and engaged in the act of prostitution outdoors, on the public streets, stairways and parks, other women solicited on the street and then went indoors for the sex act. Alternatively, some women worked primarily from a brothel, or in more clandestine environments, such as dance halls, but they were not necessarily restricted to these indoor spaces.

The third and final important factor identified by Ashworth was 'restriction'. This is most commonly associated with legislation and police action which restricts the activities and movements of the women involved in prostitution (although it can also refer to more informal 'restriction' through the work of reformers, or pressures from commercial business interests). Whilst in London an increase in the criminalisation of street prostitution during the early twentieth century forced women off the streets and into using alternative clandestine indoor methods, this chapter has shown that in Edinburgh and Glasgow prostitution still occurred in the very centre of the city well into the twentieth century, suggesting that commercial factors were more influential in shaping the location of prostitution than any police attempts to control it.[64] By taking advantage of the opportunities in the busy central and middle-class districts of the city, the women not only crossed boundaries of respectable femininity, but also transgressed borders of gender and class.

Notes

1. This chapter was developed from an original article published by the *Journal of Scottish Historical Studies*: Louise Settle, 'The Social Geography of Prostitution in Edinburgh, 1900–1939', *Journal of Scottish Historical Studies*, 33, 2 (2013), pp. 234–59.
2. Edwin Muir, *Scottish Journey* (London: Heinemann/Gollancz, 1935), p. 12.
3. Susan Varga, *Edinburgh New Town* (Stroud: Tempus, 2007).
4. William Tait, *Magdalenism. An Inquiry into the Extent, Causes and Consequences of Prostitution in Edinburgh* (Edinburgh, 1840).
5. Ibid.
6. *Leith Walk and Greenside, A Social History*, Leith Walk Research Group (University of Edinburgh, 1978–1979), p. 16.
7. All graphs relating to importuning offences in Edinburgh are compiled

from the Edinburgh Burgh Court Records, held at Edinburgh City Archives. The court records are not digitised, and therefore to make the manual data collection more manageable I took a sample from these records for the years 1903, 1911, 1921, 1931 (the 1901 records are missing). From each year, I collected data relating only to the months of January, April, July and December.

8. Edinburgh City Archives (hereafter ECA), Edinburgh Burgh Court Records (hereafter EBCR).
9. For the purposes of this study the city has been divided into eight main geographical districts: West New Town, Central New Town, East New Town, Abbey Hill, Old Town, South Side, Tollcross and Haymarket. It is not possible to use parishes or electoral constituencies to divide the city because the latter are too small and the former too large. Instead, I have divided the city in a way which makes the process of change over time most visible. Ascribing streets to districts is only intended as a device to help the reader visualise how the location of prostitution has changed and is, therefore, meant to be indicative of general patterns. Figures 3.1, 3.2, 3.4, 3.5, 3.7, 3.8, 3.10 and 3.11 only include regions which had three or more convictions for importuning. Those with less than three are included in the 'other' section.
10. All graphs relating to importuning offences in Edinburgh are compiled from the Edinburgh Burgh Court Records, held at Edinburgh City Archives.
11. See Figures 3.6, 3.7 and 3.8.
12. See, for example, Howard Taylor, 'Rationing Crime: The Political Economy of Criminal Statistics since the 1850s', *Economic History Review*, 3 (1998) pp. 569–90.
13. Carol Smart, 'Law and the Control of Women's Sexuality: The case of the 1950s', in P. Hutter and G. Williams (eds), *Controlling Women: The Normal and the Deviant* (London: Croom Helm, 1981).
14. ECA, EBCR, case of Gwendoline Jones or Fletcher and Agnes Pryce, 31 December 1920.
15. ECA, EBCR, case of May Henderson, 13 May 1937.
16. NRS, HH16/1 Press Reports, *The Evening Dispatches*, 23 March 1919.
17. G. Ashworth, P. White and H. Winchester, 'The Red-Light District in the West European City: A Neglected Aspect of the Urban Landscape', *Geoforum*, 19 (1988) pp. 201–12.
18. ECA, EBCR, case of Mary Thomson and Mary Gibbons, 19 May 1919.
19. See, for example, Roger Davidson, *Dangerous Liaisons: A Social History of Venereal Disease in Twentieth-Century Scotland* (Amsterdam: Rodopi, 2000); Angela Woollacott, '"Khaki Fever" and its Control:

Gender, Class, Age and Sexual Morality on the British Home front in the First World War', *Journal of Contemporary History*, 29 (1994) pp. 325–47.

20. Elaine McKewon, 'The Historical Geography of Prostitution in Perth, Western Australia', *Australian Geographer*, 34, 3 (2003) pp. 297–310, p. 298.
21. *Leith Walk and Greenside*, p. 21.
22. Ibid, p. 22.
23. ECA, EBCR, case of Elizabeth Houghton, 15 October 1919.
24. ECA, EBCR, case of Marjory Milner, 4 February 1921.
25. Brendon Thomas, *The Last Picture Shows, Edinburgh: Ninety Years of Cinema Entertainment in Scotland's Capital City* (Edinburgh: Moorfoot, 1984).
26. *Leith Walk and Greenside*.
27. ECA, EBCR, case of George Ritchie, 15 February 1928.
28. ECA, EBCR, case of Mary Watt, 8 March 1917.
29. Before 1921 the police used the category 'in custody' for those women who were currently in custody and had not given another address. However, by 1921 this practice had changed so that they recorded the woman's last known address and the category of 'in custody' was removed.
30. Judith Walkowitz, 'Going Public: Shopping, Street Harassment, and Streetwalking in Late Victorian London', *Representation*, 62 (1998) pp. 1–30; Paula Bartley, *Prostitution: Prevention and Reform in England, 1860–1914* (London: Routledge, 2000).
31. See, for example, Jennifer James, 'Mobility as an Adaptive Strategy', *Urban Anthropology*, 4 (1975) pp. 349–64.
32. ECA, EBCR, case of Sarah Montgomery, 24 June 1919.
33. ECA, EBCR, case of Mary Bradshaw, 28 November 1925.
34. Phil Hubbard and Teela Sanders, 'Making Space for Sex Work: Female Street Prostitution and the Production of Urban Space', *International Journal of Urban and Regional Research*, 27, 1 (2003) pp. 75–89; Henri Lefebvre, *The Production of Space* (Oxford: Basil Blackwell, 1991); Michel de Certeau, *The Practice of Everyday Life* (London: California University Press, 1984).
35. Hubbard and Sanders, 'Making Space for Sex Work', p. 83.
36. ECA, EBCR, case of May McArthur, 2 December 1919.
37. ECA, EBCR, case of Mary Bradshaw, 30 November 1925.
38. ECA, EBCR, case of Elizabeth Young, 31 January 1921.
39. ECA, EBCR, case of Daisy Moore, 27 March 1918.
40. ECA, EBCR, case of Elizabeth Winter, 29 June 1935 and 5 January 1937.

41. See, for example, Judith Walkowitz, *City of Dreadful Delight: Narratives of Sexual Danger in Late-Victorian London* (London: Virago, 1992).
42. *The Scotsman*, 1 October 1903, p. 7.
43. For more information on night-life entertainment during this period see, for example, Marek Kohn, *Dope Girls: The Birth of British Drug Underground* (London: Granta, 1992); Judith Walkowitz, *Nights Out: Life in Cosmopolitan London* (London: Yale University Press, 2012); Billie Melman, *Flappers and Nymphs: Women and the Popular Imagination in the Twenties* (Basingstoke: Palgrave Macmillan, 1998).
44. For more on the changing role of women in the public sphere see, for example, Walkowitz, 'Going Public', *Representation*, pp. 1–30.
45. N. Shumsky and L. Springer, 'San Francisco's Zone of Prostitution, 1880–1934', *Journal of Historical Geography*, 1 (1981) pp. 71–89.
46. Howell, Philip, *Geographies of Regulation: Policing Prostitution in Nineteenth Century Britain and the Empire* (Cambridge: Cambridge University Press, 2009) p. 11.
47. Roger Davidson and Gayle Davis, '"A Festering Sore on the Body of Society": The Wolfenden Committee and Female Prostitution in Mid-Twentieth-Century Scotland', *Journal of Scottish Historical Studies*, 24, (2005) pp. 80–98, p. 88.
48. ECA, EBCR, case of Mary Watt, 8 February 1917.
49. ECA, EBCR, case of Helen Stirling, 13 October 1937.
50. Jennifer James, 'Mobility as an Adaptive Strategy'.
51. ECA, EBCR, case of Elizabeth Houghton, 12 October 1919.
52. Ibid.
53. Julia Laite, *Common Prostitutes and Ordinary Citizens, Commercial Sex in London 1885–1960* (Basingstoke: Palgrave Macmillan, 2012); Timothy J. Gilfoyle, *City of Eros: New York City, Prostitution, and the Commercialization of Sex, 1790–1920* (London: W. W. Norton, 1992).
54. NRS, JC31/1919/7, Bill of suspension and liberation by Alfred Joseph Vaughn, Ivy Vaughn, 68 Saint Georges Road, Glasgow, v. George Smith, Interim P. F. Glasgow, 1919.
55. NRS, JC31/1912/10, 'Judiciary appeal by John James McIntyre, P. F. Glasgow v. William Thomson', 6 West Russell Street, Glasgow, 1912.
56. GCA, T. PAR 1.16, *Memorandum on the Social Evil in Glasgow*, 1911, p. 6.
57. For first-hand descriptions of tenement life in Glasgow see, Jean Faley, *Up oor close: Memories of Domestic Life in Glasgow Tenements, 1910–1945* (Wendlebury: White Cockade, 1994).
58. Michael Pacione, *Glasgow: the Socio-Spatial Development of the City* (Chichester: John Wiley and Sons, 1995).

59. *The Scotsman*, 12 April 1902, p. 11.
60. Ibid, p. 11.
61. Ibid, p. 11.
62. Hart, '(Re)Constructing a Spanish Red-Light District: Prostitution, Space and Power' p. 215, in D. Bell and G. Valentine (eds), *Mapping Desire* (London: Routledge, 1995), pp. 195–207.
63. Ashworth, White and Winchester, 'The Red-Light District in the West European City'.
64. Julia Laite, 'Prostitution in London, 1885–1930', PhD Thesis (University of Cambridge, 2008).

CHAPTER 4

Reforming the 'Fallen': Voluntary Organisations, Probation and the Informal Regulation of Prostitution

The role that voluntary religious and philanthropic organisations played in the policing of prostitution in Britain during the nineteenth century is relatively well documented, but less is known about the role that these institutions continued to play in the twentieth century.[1] The early twentieth century is often seen as a period characterised by the movement away from philanthropy in favour of a more modern, scientific approach towards social work. However, in Scotland the development of the probation service in close association with voluntary organisations formally enshrined in law a system of regulating prostitution that had previously been more informal. Rather than punishing all women who were accused of prostitution offences with fines and short prison sentences, magistrates in Edinburgh and Glasgow increasingly opted to give some women probation sentences instead. This penal-welfare approach towards the regulation of prostitution therefore relied on and encouraged the close cooperation between the police and magistrates on the one hand and the voluntary organisations involved in probation on the other. However, not all of the women convicted of prostitution were given the option of probation and not all of them necessarily appreciated or complied with this new penal-welfare approach.

The first half of this chapter will outline the ways in which probation sentences were used to police women who committed prostitution offences and examine the close links that existed between the new probation service and voluntary institutions. The second section will look more closely at the daily activities of these voluntary organisations, focusing particularly on the Magdalene Asylums, the Scottish National Vigilance Association (SNVA) and the Women Patrols. These case studies will allow us to examine how the collaborations that were established between these voluntary organisations and the probation service influenced the regulation of prostitution and women's experiences of the criminal justice system.

The Probation Service

Chapter two has shown how, rather than attempting to criminalise the women involved in prostitution, the police in early-twentieth-century Scotland were often apathetic or tried to employ a more welfare-oriented approach. One of the most important ways in which this penal-welfare approach was implemented in Scotland during the first half of the twentieth century was through the probation service. In 1907 the Probation of Offenders Act officially introduced probation as an alternative means of rehabilitating people who had committed petty offences.[2] The Act made it possible for cases tried under summary law to be dismissed and the accused to be placed under the supervision of a probation officer for a maximum period of three years.[3] The conditions of probation stipulated that the offender must be of good behaviour, while also allowing for other conditions, such as prohibiting offenders from associating with undesirable characters and requiring them to remain in employment or to abstain from consuming intoxicating liquor. After the Criminal Justice Administration Act of 1914, magistrates could also stipulate where a probationer must reside for the duration of the probation period.[4] The magistrate chose which conditions the probationer had to follow according to the nature of the offence and the 'character' of the offender. They could also stipulate whether the probationer would be put under the supervision of a probation officer or under their 'own bond', with a set monetary penalty as a security, a sum usually between one and five pounds. If the bond was broken or the probationer committed another offence, the offender was sent back to court, where the original offence could be resurrected and a sentenced passed.[5] Therefore, whether or not a probationer was sent back to court for sentencing was not necessarily dependent on whether he or she broke the law, but on a list of factors designed to assess whether he or she was living according to middle-class notions of respectable behaviour.

During the nineteenth century the reformation of offenders was carried out solely by religious voluntary organisations, such as the Police Court Missionaries, who have been credited for first establishing a system of probation in Britain.[6] However, during the twentieth century the state increasingly took over this responsibility. Initially, the responsibility was primarily monetary, with the central government offering to pay for half of the salaries of the probation officers, whilst the local government in each area would pay the remaining half. It was hoped that this would encourage the councils to employ professionally trained full-time officers. However, in many situations the same people who had previously been working to reform offenders in a voluntary capacity now took up the new roles as probation officers. This is exactly what happened in Edinburgh. Rather than the local council paying the probation officers directly, the officers continued to work for their various voluntary organisations and the council instead paid the voluntary agency a fee according to how many probation cases they supervised. Even after the 1931 Probation of Offenders (Scotland) Act introduced probation committees and stipulated that each committee area should have at least one salaried probation officer, Edinburgh Council used a loophole in the law to continue using the officers from voluntary organisations up until the end of the Second World War.[7] In Glasgow between 1905 and 1931 plain-clothed police officers were used as probation officers, alongside a small number of female probation officers who were employed to supervise women and children. These female probation officers were selected according to their previous experience working with women and children, primarily in a voluntary setting. In 1931 the Probation of Offenders (Scotland) Act prohibited the use of police as probation officers and the council instead hired salaried probation officers. The female probation officers, however, continued in their previous roles.

The passing of the Criminal Justice Administration Act in 1914 meant that it was possible to stipulate where probationers must reside, and in Edinburgh and Glasgow this meant that the women who were considered in need of close supervision were sent to institutions run by religious voluntary organisations. In particular, both the Glasgow and Edinburgh Magdalene Asylums worked closely with the local magistrates to ensure that women on probation for prostitution offences would be sent to their institutions.[8] For example, in 1913 Miss Paterson, the matron at the Glasgow Magdalene Institute since 1909, was licensed to care for Robina Stewart for three years. During this period, Stewart was to reside at the Magdalene Institute, and the Juvenile Delinquency Board would pay a maintenance allowance of five shillings per week.[9] Whilst the Magdalene Asylums in Edinburgh and Glasgow were the most common destinations, female probationers were also sent to the House of Mercy at Horbury in Wakefield, the Salvation Army house on the Grassmarket in Edinburgh, the Lochee Rescue Home in Dundee, the Church of Scotland Home in Paisley, the Lochburn Home in Maryhill in Glasgow and the Woodfield House in Colinton. The majority of these organisations were either directly run by particular Christian denominations, or had strong affiliations and associations with religious organisations. Moreover, it was generally agreed that it was important for the probationers to be supervised by someone of their own denomination, as they could provide the appropriate moral guidance. Therefore, although the probation service was in theory secular, and it is often associated with a move towards a more modern social work approach to rehabilitation, the considerable connections it had with various religious voluntary organisations meant that religious reform ideology continued to exert a strong influence over the character of probation in Scotland.

Probation and Prostitution

The development of the probation system was at first uncertain and piecemeal, but by the First World War probation was increasingly being used to deal with women convicted of prostitution offences in Edinburgh and Glasgow. The women put on probation for prostitution offences were mainly placed under the supervision of probation officers associated with, or working for, voluntary organisations. For example, Miss Kiff from the Salvation Army, Miss Margaret Copeland from the Edinburgh Magdalene Asylum, Miss Stag from the National Vigilance Association and Miss Livingston from the Church of Scotland Shelter were frequently cited as probation officers tasked to supervise women convicted of prostitution offences. Most of the probation officers were women, as it was thought that they would be the most appropriate role models and mentors. However, some male probation officers were also assigned to supervise women, such as the Reverend MacKinnon and the Reverend Thomson.

The number of women put on probation for soliciting offences varied considerably throughout the period, but after probation reports first started to appear in 1913, the highest volume of reports occurred between 1916 and 1925. For example, in Edinburgh during 1916 thirty-two women were placed on probation for prostitution-related offences, while in 1921 there were twenty-nine similar cases. After 1925 the number of probation cases began to decrease, and by the late 1930s probation cases for those accused of soliciting had become rare, with only one or two in most years, and none in 1939. There were no fixed criteria to determine which women accused of prostitution offences should be placed on probation rather than given a short prison sentence or made to pay a fine. Although age did play an important role, the individual's character and other personal attributes were also likely to have influenced the magistrate's decision about who might benefit from probation. Previous conviction history was seen as a decisive indicator of a woman's character and her potential for reform, and a large number of the women who were put on probation did not have previous prison sentences, or at least not extensive ones.[10] However, that was not the only qualifying criterion, as several women placed on probation did have previous convictions, and some had even previously received the full sixty days allowed for a soliciting offence. For example, Isabella Thompson, who in 1921 was sent to the Magdalene Asylum as a condition of her probation, had previously been in prison for twenty days for a solicitation offence.[11] Similarly, Margaret Leonard, who was described by police officers as a 'convicted prostitute', was at first given another chance 'on account of the time that had elapsed since her last conviction', but was later placed on probation for six months.[12] Marjory Milner, who was described as 'conducting herself as a prostitute almost nightly' and as being 'always more or less drunk', was also given six months' probation and told to remain in the Magdalene Asylum for the said period.[13] However, although these women were 'convicted prostitutes', the case notes suggest that there were other reasons why these particular women may have been seen as potential good candidates for probation. Marjory Milner was described as a 'house wife . . . [with] four children under 16 years' and Molly Wilson as 'poor and single'.[14] These women were regarded not so much as hardened criminals, but as victims of circumstance who needed help rather than punishment. As we shall see, these selection criteria were very similar to those of the various voluntary organisations to which the women were sent.

Roughly a third of all the women put on probation for prostitution offences were sent to reform homes for the period of their probation. The others received regular visits from their probation officers and were expected to listen to their advice and to behave accordingly. This could involve them being sent to a new job arranged for them by the probation officer, or abstaining from alcohol and the company of 'immoral types'. Being placed on probation outside of the institutional setting did not necessarily mean that the women received less attention from the probation officers, most of whom were also associated with various voluntary organisations. The probation officer made detailed reports about the probationers' home life; their health and appearance, the cleanliness of their home, their behaviour and their relationships with friends and family. They also encouraged women to find appropriate forms of work and monitored their employment activities. Several letters written by probation officers detail the ways in which they attempted to control and reform the women under their charge by regularly visiting their homes and working with their parents to encourage them to discipline their daughters in accordance with their probation bonds. For example, in 1917, Reverend Mr MacKinnon (the probation officer for Isabella Shepard Armour) put considerable effort into tracking her down and attempted to make her leave Edinburgh and return to her parents' home in Blackburn. He worked in close connection with her parents, but they still could not force Armour to leave Edinburgh.[15]

The use of probation was intended as a more sympathetic and progressive approach towards dealing with prostitutes that would stop the vicious circle of recidivism that occurred when women were frequently given fines and short prison sentences. Many believed that prison only corrupted these women further and that their moral reformation was more likely to be successful under the guidance of a suitable female role model, the probation officer. However, whilst on the one hand a probation sentence meant that some women were spared a prison sentence, on the other hand these women had their freedom restricted in different ways and for periods that were potentially far longer than was allowed under legislation relating to prostitution offences. In comparison to the usual sentence of forty shillings or twenty days in prison in default of payment, a probation sentence could last between six months and three years. For those who were given residence orders and forbidden to leave the designated institution, it was a much more long-term and intrusive punishment than the maximum 60 days' gaol sentence allowed for prostitution offences. Therefore, although the use of probation was couched in terms of being a more modern, benevolent approach, it could be viewed as part of a much wider movement that saw the increased connection between punishment and welfare.

Drawing on the work of Jacques Donzelot and Michel Foucault, David Garland has shown how this increased preference for rehabilitation rather than punishment, which resulted in an overlap between the provision of welfare and the creation of penal policies during the early twentieth century, was part of a broader social project to create 'better' citizens and to control 'anti-social' behaviour.[16] This overlap was in part facilitated by the desire of members of voluntary philanthropic organisations to achieve professional status and to increase their influence. This ambition made voluntary social workers more willing to work closely with penal bodies, such as the police and magistrates. At the same time, rising prisoner numbers and prison overcrowding during this period meant that the government was increasingly keen to develop new ways to deal with problematic members of society without resorting to incarceration. The use of probation, reformatories and asylums therefore offered a cheaper, more effective way of 'normalising and correcting' people's behaviour. This was seen as a particularly useful approach for dealing with 'problematic' women, as it was thought that such institutions were more capable of reforming these women by training them to adopt 'appropriate' gender and class roles.[17]

Whether this connection between the criminal justice system and welfare was a positive or negative development is debatable. Maurice Vanstone argues that the development of probation in connection with voluntary organisations was not simply motivated by humanitarian and philanthropic concerns, but was a 'class based activity' that justified the existing social order.[18] In Scotland, the probation service's close alliance with Christian charities run by middle-class volunteers meant that their ideology regarding gender, class and sexuality was intertwined with the new probation system, both practically and ideologically. It was this link between the middle-class Christian voluntary organisations and the probation service that was vital in the establishment of the underlying notion that the successful reformation of women was dependent upon their adoption of respectable feminine behaviour. By classifying women according to whether or not they fitted this middle-class ideal of respectable femininity and labelling them accordingly as either 'victims' or 'criminals', the system turned its attention away from the underlying socio-economic reasons that lay behind why women engaged in prostitution and focused instead on the women's behaviour and 'character'. Therefore, rather than the introduction of probation leading to a more enlightened, modern method of reforming 'deviant women', as many idealistic penal reform enthusiasts hoped, it could be argued that it worked to further cement the previous methods of conditioning women to uphold traditional class and gender roles, enshrining in the law middle-class domestic sphere ideologies.

However, whilst the police and probation officers did have considerable powers to restrict and regulate the activities of 'prostitutes', many women found ways to evade the methods of surveillance and control that were employed by the probation officers. As in the cases of Jane Thomson, Jemima Boyle and Elizabeth Wallace, roughly fifty per cent of the probation reports ended with statements such as 'she has failed to observe the conditions of her bond in the respect that she has been behaving badly and refused to stay in a home.'[19] In some cases the probation officers gave up hope of reforming certain women. For example, Mrs Baxter, the probation officer for Helen Ramsay, insisted that she would 'have nothing more to do with this girl' because she had left the home to which she had been assigned and had 'been in hospital with some disease'.[20] Mary Butcher was equally determined not to remain in any of the institutions to which she was sent. After being convicted for theft and sent to the Dalry Reformatory on 27 January 1915 for three years, aged fifteen, by March 1917 she had already committed further offences and was this time placed on probation and sent to the Edinburgh Magdalene Asylum. However, on 19 June 1917 she ran away and was later arrested again for importuning on Princes Street. When arrested she explained that she had been earning her living on the streets for the past four months. Consequently she was again placed on probation, this time at the Seabank Home in Aberdeen where she was to reside under the supervision of Miss Stewart. Clearly, these women, and many others like them, were not willing to be subjected to the loss of freedom imposed on them by the probation bonds.[21]

This refusal to be locked up in asylums and to conform to external expectations of respectable working-class female behaviour certainly highlights these women's agency. Unfortunately, these defiant acts of resistance often ultimately ended in the women being sent to yet another institution or gaol. During the First World War there were some cases where women escaped and remained 'at large', but these cases remained few and were perhaps a result of the general disorganisation and confusion caused by the upheaval of war. In most cases, once the woman was found or the probation officer reported that the woman had broken any one of the conditions of her probation bond, she was sent to the Burgh Court where the magistrates would decide how to proceed. For example, Helen Gardiner, who 'failed to observe the conditions of her bond', was given a ten-day prison sentence, and Margaret Wilson, who had 'gone away without leaving any address', was later found and given a ten-day prison sentence.[22] Similarly, in 1921, Isabella M'Gregor and Jane McKenzie who had run away from the Magdalene Asylum were given sixty-days' and thirty-days' prison sentences, respectively.[23] Although the probation officers may not have wanted the women to be sent to prison, the threat of such action would have been useful when trying to encourage women to obey the rules. Nonetheless, the fact that so many women would risk imprisonment and abscond from reform homes or break the probation bonds shows just how unwilling they were to submit to this type of reformatory discipline and demonstrates the lengths to which they would go to regain their independence.

However, not all of the women broke their bonds and some women did benefit from probation. As problematic as this link between domestic sphere ideology and probation was, it was arguably less harmful than an extended period in prison. For most women, the opportunity to be supervised in their own home would have been far preferable to being incarcerated in prison, and even for those women forced to reside in institutions, the living standards in such reform homes had risen considerably since the nineteenth century and were certainly higher than those in gaol. More importantly, the help that these women were given to find new forms of employment whilst on probation meant that they had a far greater chance of leaving prostitution than the women who were given prison sentences. From the probation reports alone, it is difficult to discern more about these women's experiences of probation or what happened to them afterwards. However, it is clear that not all the women rejected the welfare support and advice that the probation officers attempted to provide. Several letters within the probation reports suggest that some of the women responded to probation positively (or at least in the way the probation officers intended). For example, in 1911 twenty-year-old May Lindsay was described by her probation officer as doing 'remarkably good'[sic] and was pleased to report that May 'writes regularly' and has been working as 'a nurse in a good family'.[24] Similarly, in 1916 the probation officer for twenty-five-year-old Helen Mitchell described how 'her mother says that her conduct is quite satisfactory. I have seen her frequently and I can see she is a different girl. She has given up bad company'.[25] Similarly, in 1935 Elizabeth Mackinnlay's probation officer explained that Elizabeth 'behaved well' and that it was 'her desire to become a laundry maid.'[26] These women seem to have taken advantage of the opportunities that the probation officers provided and used them in order to avoid prison and to secure future employment. The next section of this chapter will look more closely at the realities of life for the probationers who were sent to institutions such as the Magdalene Asylums and question whether their experiences differed from those of women who were supervised at home or sent to more 'progressive' institutions, such as the Scottish National Vigilance Association.

Rescuing 'Unfortunate Girls': The Edinburgh and Glasgow Magdalene Asylums

The Edinburgh Magdalene Asylum was first opened in 1797 and was situated on the Canongate in the centre of the Old Town.[27] Its founders intended that through good instruction, religious teaching, industrial training and hard work the asylum would rescue 'fallen women' and reform them into respectable members of society. In 1864 the asylum moved to the countryside to allow more seclusion and unpolluted space for drying laundry.[28] The Glasgow Magdalene Asylum opened in 1815 and, like its Edinburgh counterpart, it also aimed to promote 'the repression of vice and the reformation of penitent women'.[29] Unlike Edinburgh's asylum, Glasgow's asylum was located in the countryside throughout its existence, far from preying eyes and away from the sights and sounds of the city that might tempt the inmates to return to their former lives outside the institution's walls. In 1841 the Glasgow Asylum merged with the new home for 'female juvenile delinquents' and was renamed the 'House of Refuge for Females', only to be later renamed the Magdalene Institute once again.[30] Rather than rescuing 'professional prostitutes' with long criminal records, the asylums were intended for young, 'newly fallen' women who were 'neither pregnant nor diseased'.[31] It was hoped that those women who were 'truly repentant' would voluntarily enter the institution, with a genuine desire to be reformed. However, as we have seen, during the early twentieth century the police, magistrates and probation service increasingly used the asylums as alternative locations for women who had been convicted of prostitution offences.

The women who came to the Asylums voluntarily were expected to stay in the institution for two years, and the women sent there on probation had to remain there for as long as their probation bond stipulated, usually one year.

During this time the 'inmates' were to be reformed through adherence to religious moral training, alongside discipline and hard work. This work mainly involved washing, sewing and other types of domestic chores. In Edinburgh, the women were expected to work six and a half days per week and were only given six days of holiday per year.[32] In neither institution were the women paid wages for their labour. The institutes had no state funding and so relied on charitable donations and the profits made from the women's laundry work, although after the introduction of probation in 1907, the local government did pay them a small maintenance fee for each probationer they accepted. In Edinburgh the women were given some of their earnings according to how productive and well-behaved they were perceived to be. In Glasgow the women instead received clothes on a similar basis. The Glasgow Institute justified not paying the women wages by explaining that the women 'do not receive wages, but they are lodged, boarded, clothed, taught and generally cared for.'[33] This system was intended, in theory, to encourage the women to appreciate the value of hard work and, perhaps more importantly, to increase the overall productivity of the institutions.

In addition to work, prayer and education constituted an important part of their daily routines. The Asylums originated during a period of widespread religious revival, and the evangelical focus on spreading the word of Jesus by caring for and reforming individuals in a 'Christ like' manner was an important motivating factor behind their establishment.[34] It was hoped that through regular church attendance, religious instruction and Bible reading, the women would repent their sins and learn how to live virtuously. In Glasgow one hour per day was dedicated to teaching literacy so that every inmate could read the Bible and, once this was accomplished, the women were given their own Bibles. In addition to religious education, some secular education was also provided, such as geography, maths and music.[35]

Linda Mahood's research on the Glasgow Magdalene Institute during the nineteenth century has shown that the daily routines of hard work, religious instruction and education were intended to help reform women according to middle-class notions of respectable feminine behaviour. An important aspect of this was the notion that women belonged in the domestic sphere. The majority of the women who entered the Magdalene Asylum were from working-class backgrounds and, therefore, the domestic sphere ideology had different implications for them than it did for the middle classes. In the Magdalene Asylums, this ideology was incorporated into the type of work and training that the women were expected to undertake, primarily laundry and other domestic tasks.

The committee minutes for both the Glasgow and Edinburgh Magdalene homes show that domestic labour, particularly laundry, remained the main form of work and training during the early twentieth century. In 1905 the Edinburgh Magdalene Asylum Ladies' Committee Minutes described how the home should be open to 'girls' who were willing to be taught 'household duties' which would make them 'more eligible for domestic service'.[36] In 1907 the Glasgow Magdalene's annual report described how the committee members were 'especially grateful to the friends who favoured the laundries with their washing, without which their labours would be in vain, as the moral and physical training of the inmates can only be accomplished by steady employment'.[37] Similarly, in 1910 and 1913 the annual reports assured their readers that 'the directors are grateful to those who helped them over the "idle time" by sending their work to the laundry' and that 'steady and regular employment is . . . essential to the training of all who come'.[38] In 1919 the annual report again described how laundry work was important to the 'inmates' because it taught them 'a skilled employment by the exercise of which they become able to earn a living in a respectable way.'[39] Furthermore, the importance of the laundry as a source of income for the home can be seen in the institutes' financial accounts throughout the period. For example, in 1909 the 'earnings from inmates' made up forty-two per cent of the Glasgow Magdalene Institute's annual income.[40] Consequently, the institution was keen to ensure that they made the highest possible profits from the inmates' work and continued to enlarge and modernise their laundry facilities. For example, the 1916 report described how 'the directors have in view the necessity of remodelling the washing house and laundry in order to enable more efficient work to be turned out, and to meet the competition of modern and highly organized laundries.'[41]

It was not only whilst they resided in the Institute that the women were expected to conform to the domestic ideal. After two years in the asylum, it was expected that the women would be fully reformed and equipped with the necessary skills to enable them to find employment. The training they had received, however, meant that they were primarily qualified only for domestic service or similar jobs, such as washing or sewing. For example, in 1907 the Glasgow Institute's annual report described how 'classes for cooking, sewing, mending, and outfit-making have recently been organised . . . It is hoped that the systematic instruction given . . . will fit the girls more fully for the domestic duties to which they may be called.'[42] Not only would teaching the women skills in domestic work help them find employment; the training of new domestic servants would also help to solve the 'servant problem' that was ongoing during this period due to the increasing number of women who were reluctant to enter domestic service in light of new employment opportunities elsewhere.[43] There was no mention of women successfully finding 'situations' outside traditional types of domestic or factory work, and at no point were the women given any training that might have equipped them to work in the newly emerging 'white collar' occupations, such as retail or office work, which were becoming available to some women during this period.[44] The prospects of former 'inmates' therefore remained limited by the traditional class and gender expectations of the Asylums well into the twentieth century.

Another option available to some women was emigration. In the minutes of both the Edinburgh and Glasgow Asylums, there is reference to women who emigrated to countries such as Canada, Australia and the United States. For example, in 1909 the Edinburgh Magdalene Asylum minutes described that the committee 'heard some letters from Canada' which described that the girls were 'happy in their situations' and that four other girls were doing their time 'to enable them to go to Canada'.[45] Similarly, in 1911 more letters were read from 'inmates who had gone to Canada'.[46] In 1927 the minutes explained that the Edinburgh Magdalene Asylum had previously worked together with the Salvation Army to help women emigrate and that the Salvation Army had been 'very useful' in helping them gain information from the emigration office.[47] In Glasgow there was also mention of women going abroad: for example, in 1898 Kitty Monclif[48] was sent to South Africa after spending two years in the Institution, and in 1906 the annual report recorded that two 'inmates' had gone to America.[49] However, unlike the Edinburgh minutes, in the Glasgow records there was less reference to women being sent abroad after the first decade of the twentieth century, and after 1906 the annual reports contained fewer detailed explanations of where the women went after leaving the institution. It is unclear whether this was because the Edinburgh Asylum was keener to help women emigrate, or simply because the Edinburgh Asylum kept more detailed records of the movement of the women after they left.

Whilst emigration may have offered new opportunities for some women, they were still hindered by their lack of necessary training required to obtain jobs outside domestic labour. The Edinburgh Magdalene Asylum's 1927 minutes suggest that the women who went abroad were still expected to enter the same types of domestic employment abroad as those who stayed in Britain. One report described how 'one of the inmates whose period of residence expired shortly had expressed the desire to go to Canada. She is a good laundress, and would probably do well if she could begin again away from friends here'.[50] It appears, therefore, that a 'new start' did not necessarily mean new job opportunities but was instead a chance for the women to escape their previous lives and reputations. Although the committee members of these institutions believed that women could be reformed, their encouragement of women to move abroad in order to have a 'fresh start' suggests that the members remained sceptical about the women's ability to continue their 'reformed' way of life if they returned to the same social environment in which they had lived before entering the institution.

If the women did not enter paid employment once they left the Magdalene Asylum, they were either sent to another type of institution, such as an infirmary or a poorhouse, or returned to family and friends. Therefore, these women were again expected to remain in a domestic environment under the protection of their families or other institutions. In cases where their families and friends were considered to be potentially harmful or likely to lead the 'inmates' astray, the women were encouraged to break all ties with them. However, the committee members wanted to compensate for this by making the environment inside the asylum like that of a substitute family. For example, in 1909, the Glasgow annual report described how the 'girls' saw the institution as 'a home', and looked to the matron 'as indeed a mother.'[51] Once they had left the institution, the women were encouraged to keep in contact, and the minutes describe several cases of women who wrote letters and returned to visit the institution.

It is clear, therefore, that the Magdalene Asylums continued to be run according to domestic sphere ideology well into the twentieth century. However, this domestic ideology remained prominent in most areas of society during the early twentieth century, and all women during this period, regardless of whether they had been inmates at the Magdalene Asylums, would have had their home and work life shaped by this ideology to some extent. Whilst the Magdalene Asylums may have been more enthusiastic proponents of domestic service than some other sectors of society, it would be unfair to judge the Asylums too harshly for not being more progressive during a time when many of these women would have also seen marriage, motherhood and domestic labour as a natural role for working-class women.

The Magdalenes

As in the nineteenth century, the Magdalene Asylums remained primarily interested in 'saving' those women who they thought would respond well to reforming discipline and hard work, a requirement that was sustained well into the interwar period.[52] The Glasgow annual reports for the years 1906, 1907, 1909, 1910 and 1915 give detailed information about the background of the inmates. The majority of the women were between sixteen and twenty-four years of age and an average of fifty-nine per cent of them were under twenty-four years.[53] It was assumed that younger women were more susceptible to reforming influences and were less likely to have been fully 'corrupted'. The naivety and vulnerability associated with youth was often seen as one of the main causes of their 'fall', and therefore these 'victims' of inexperience were seen as more worthy of the Institute's benevolent reforming influence. Nevertheless, few were under sixteen, as the directors worried that having 'children' in the institution would cause complications due to the stipulations of the 1908 Children Charter which set out guidelines and rules that had to be followed in institutions catering for children. Therefore, in 1909 the directors agreed that 'no persons under 16 years be admitted into the home so as to avoid the responsibility of the act', although there were several exceptions to this rule when 'special case[s]' arose.[54] In the same year, another motion was passed which stipulated that 'women of 40 years of age and upwards should not be admitted except in very exceptional cases.'[55] Nevertheless, when the numbers of 'inmates' began to dwindle in the 1930s, the committee proposed that 'the limit be extended to 45 years instead of 40'.[56]

The records show that the majority of the women were not what the Institute's committee members would have described as 'hardened prostitutes'. These 'habitual criminals' were thought to be too set in their immoral ways for reformation to be successful. One indication of this policy is the fact that most of the women had never been admitted to a lock hospital for the treatment of venereal diseases. For example, in 1909 eighty-two per cent of the women were recorded as never having been admitted to a lock hospital.[57] In 1910 the equivalent percentage was eighty-five and in 1915 it was eighty-seven.[58] Upon entering the Institute, the women were examined fully and anyone infected with venereal disease was sent to the lock hospital for treatment.[59] This would suggest that the majority of the women did not suffer from venereal disease, as it was difficult for them to hide any illness (although successful diagnosis was not always guaranteed).[60] It is possible that some of the women may have lied about their previous medical history, although in view of the close association between the lock hospital and the Magdalene Asylum, it is likely that the Asylum would have been able to double-check this information.[61]

The Magdalene Asylums also did not admit sick or pregnant women. In 1894 the Glasgow Magdalene Institute minutes included a letter which explained that 'surely you can understand the distinction between a reformatory and a hospital. This institution can only admit those who are in good bodily health, the hospital is the place for those who are otherwise.'[62] In Edinburgh, a 'medical examination by the doctor' was similarly required before the girls could be admitted into the Asylum.[63] The institutions saw themselves as 'moral hospitals', but those women who needed physical medical treatment were referred to the infirmary. Sick women could not work; therefore they could neither learn a trade nor contribute to the running of the institution. In 1909 the Glasgow Institution passed a motion that stipulated that 'in admissions, preference should be given to strong healthy women and those women whose feeble health or drunken habits had unfitted them for work should be declined.'[64]

The Glasgow Institute's annual report statistics also show that the majority of the women had never been in prison. In 1909 the percentage of the women that were recorded as 'never having been in prison' was seventy-seven per cent;[65] in 1910 the percentage was seventy-six; and in 1915 it was eighty-one.[66] The Glasgow Magdalene Institute was clearly reluctant to accept women who had been in prison (or, alternatively, women who had been in prison were less likely to want to enter the reform Institute). These figures support the arguments put forward by Linda Mahood and Viviene Cree that women were categorised according to their presumed capability to reform and that this served as a new method of controlling women's sexuality.[67] Once a woman had been labelled as a 'hardened criminal' and sent to prison, she was less likely to be deemed a good candidate for reform. However, for the years 1909, 1910 and 1915 (those years with reports which included data on the penal history of the women), on average seventeen per cent had previously been in prison.[68] This suggests that there was some flexibility in the Institute's approach and that some women were given a second chance. However, of those women who were listed as having previously been imprisoned, on average only nine per cent were recorded as having been in prison 'frequently'. It appears that, on the one hand, although the institution was prepared to give some women who had been in prison a 'second chance', they were less sympathetic to 'habitual criminals'. On the other hand, although the number of 'habituals' may have been low, the fact that the institution did accept some women who had 'frequently' been in prison suggests that they were willing to evaluate the situation on a case-by-case basis.

Whilst the majority of the women had never been to prison, many had previously resided in other types of institutions. The Glasgow Institute's annual reports for 1909, 1910 and 1915 show that on average fifty-two per cent of the women had previously resided in a reformation institution and, of these, several had been in 'other' similar institutions, such as industrial schools. There is no detailed information about exactly which institutions the women had been to, but the data suggest that different organisations worked together to place women in particular institutions according to their specific needs at different points throughout their lives. The large number of women who went to other institutions, such as hospitals, poorhouses and church-based hostels after they left the Magdalene Institute, also supports this argument.[69] For example, in 1914 the Glasgow Magdalene Institute directors 'agreed to take back a former inmate who in February last was taken out of Lochburn home and taken to Aberdeen by Mr Watson, a director of the Aberdeen Ladies Mission Committee'.[70] Similarly, in 1911 and 1927, the minutes mentioned correspondences with the National Vigilance Association of Scotland (NVASED) and described how the Salvation Army had been 'very useful'.[71] If a woman ran away or left the Magdalene Institute voluntarily before she had successfully completed her two years, the rules stipulated that she was not meant to be allowed to return to the Institute. However, the records show that this rule was not always adhered to and women were often given a second chance. For example, in 1896 after Sarah McLaughlin 'ran away and misconducted herself', she was later 'taken back . . . [and] restored to her place in the washing house'.[72]

Mahood's research on the Glasgow Magdalene Institute during the nineteenth century found that the 'inmates' were primarily from working-class backgrounds.[73] The Glasgow Magdalene Asylum's annual reports suggest that this was also true in the twentieth century. The two most common types of previous employment undertaken by the women were domestic service, which accounted for twenty-seven per cent, and factory work, which accounted for twenty-five per cent.[74] Other common types of employment included laundry work, farm service and hotel work. The reports also include information about the women's 'fathers' employment', which also mainly included working-class occupations. The most common type of paternal employment recorded in the years 1906, 1907, 1909 and 1910 reports was 'labourer', with an average of twenty per cent of the fathers listed under that occupation.[75] Overall, there was a wide variety of different paternal occupations, such as blacksmiths, carpenters, engineers, farmers, masons, miners, painters, policemen, sailors, soldiers, shoemakers and shopkeepers.[76] Although many of these occupations can be categorised as working-class, the women came from a wider range of family environments. Several of these occupations could be classed as skilled working class or lower middle class, and therefore if the women's fathers were in regular employment, the families were likely to have had a sufficient income to support themselves.

On the one hand this evidence suggests that not all of the women who entered the Magdalene Asylums were from poverty-stricken families. On the other hand, in 1909 the Directors of the Glasgow Institute described how a large proportion of the 'inmates' were 'drawn from the most hapless and helpless of their sex – orphan girls, motherless girls, ill-used step-daughters, and girls of weak intellect'.[77] The Institute's statistics back this assertion, showing that the majority of the women did not have both parents. For example, in the years 1906, 1907, 1909, 1910 and 1915, on average forty-one per cent of the women were described as orphans and only twenty-five per cent had both parents alive.[78] The loss of one parent would have had considerable consequences for families, both economically and emotionally. Therefore, whilst absolute poverty may not have been the primary reason why these women entered into prostitution, an unstable family life was an important factor. It could be argued, therefore, that the focus that had been placed on assessing women's' 'character' – whether they held 'victim' or 'criminal' status – was detracting attention from the underlying family problems and socio-economic inequality that caused women to resort to prostitution.

The Magdalene Institutes were not only concerned with the conduct of women during their stay in the Institute but also about their lives before and after they entered. For example, in 1919 the importance of obtaining knowledge about the women was reiterated by the Ladies' Committee who recommended that 'in order to obtain a reliable record of the women who have been under our care for one year and over, the matron, assisted by the outside agent, shall keep a record of such in a ledger dorm, devoting a page to each person'.[79] The outside agent, who was employed to attend the 'police courts daily' and distributed 'invitation cards for fallen women' to encourage them to enter the institution, was also expected to devote 'part of her time . . . to the aftercare of former inmates'.[80] This gathering of information about the women allowed for the increased surveillance and control of individuals' private lives, based on the premise that welfare was to be provided.

David Garland has argued that 'through the services of the various voluntary agencies, probation officers, after-care agents, etc., the range of knowledge available to the authorities [was] extended to encompass not only the offender, but also his family and home'.[81] Therefore, the penal-welfare complex created an 'extended basis for disciplinary intervention and regulation' so that attention was shifted from the offence to the offender.[82] In the Magdalene Asylums, it was ultimately the woman's ability to adopt 'normal' notions of 'correct' gendered and sexual behaviour that was being judged. If women were to receive 'welfare' in the form of 'benevolent reform', rather than being sent to prison for punishment, they had to submit to these forms of surveillance and behave according to their rules. The use of Magdalene Asylums for the reformation of women on probation therefore resulted in the state sanctioning these methods of reforming women according to middle-class Christian ideas about how working-class women should behave. Frank Mort has similarly argued that institutions such as the Magdalene Asylums were part of a middle-class 'onslaught on the culture of the poor', which attempted to influence the behaviour and moral sensibilities of the working classes so that they would conform to bourgeois ideals.[83] However, there are some problems with this analysis of the Asylums during this period. Firstly, the considerable number of women who chose to run away from the Magdalene Asylums rather than to submit to this type of control shows that the Asylums were not capable of making all of the women conform to these middle-class standards of femininity. Secondly, it could be argued that those women who did follow the rules did so in order to benefit from the training and employment opportunities on offer that would allow them to leave prostitution. Whilst these opportunities were limited to domestic employment, they were at least preferable to prison. Moreover, the next section will outline the ways in which the living conditions within the Magdalene Asylums improved considerably by the 1920s.

Daily Life in the Magdalene Asylums

During the nineteenth century, discipline and hard work played a central role in the daily routine of the Magdalene Asylums. Mahood's study of the Glasgow Magdalene Institute found that the women often worked for over ten hours a day and that head shaving was used to discourage women from leaving the institution before their two years were over.[84] By the twentieth century head shaving was no longer practised and, as Mahood points out, disciplinary methods had already begun to change by the latter part of the nineteenth century. As the twentieth century continued, the disciplinary and penal aspect of the asylum slowly decreased and conditions within the Asylums improved considerably. Although there were still strict rules that had to be followed and working hours remained long, by the 1920s the institutions appear to have become less austere places. Both the Glasgow and Edinburgh Asylums even began to arrange 'special treats' for the women. For example, the Edinburgh minutes often referred to the annual New Year's Day treats – events which usually included a meal, gifts, music and other types of entertainment. In 1934 the Edinburgh minutes described 'how successful the picnic to Blackness had been' and that they 'all hope[ed] that perhaps it may become an annual event'.[85] Similarly, in June 1936 'Miss Hamilton . . . most kindly asked the young women and girls to her house for an afternoon picnic'.[86] There were also frequent references to different types of entertainment provided for the women at the Glasgow Magdalene Institute, such as the annual New Year's celebrations and the annual 'summer treat'.[87] This was all in stark contrast to the nineteenth-century efforts to hide the women away from respectable society.

It was not only during these 'special treats' that the women were offered entertainment. The Glasgow Magdalene Institute's annual reports often included a list of all the recreational activities that had taken place during the year, including concerts, musical evenings, talks by foreign missionaries, cinematography, readings and illustrated lectures on a wide variety of subjects.[88] In 1911 a 'special dinner was granted to the inmates on the coronation day'; in 1920 the women were each given small plots of land to grow flowers and vegetables; and in September 1921 they held a flower show with prizes for the best entries.[89] In 1922 it was proposed that 'part of the grounds' should be used as a 'play-ground for the girls' and that 'a set for the game of basketball be procured for their amusement'.[90] Music also appears to have played an important role in the institutions' entertainment. The Glasgow Institute, for instance, had a piano and an American organ and employed a singing teacher.[91] In the Edinburgh Magdalene Asylum there were similar types of entertainment, especially concerts.[92] The Edinburgh Asylum was also keen to improve the food given to the 'inmates'. For example, in January 1926 they put forward a proposal for 'improving the cooking, and the permitting of greater variety in the food', and in 1931 they made sure that the 'inmates were given a hot meal on Sundays'.[93] Although some of these activities would have been enjoyable for many of the women, they were mainly intended as forms of 'rational recreation' that would provide useful education, with a particular emphasis on lectures and readings.[94] For example, in January 1914 the minutes described a 'very successful' entertainment evening, including two illustrated lectures, one on 'Trips to Jerusalem' and the other on 'Switzerland and Venice'.[95]

The letters that the Edinburgh Magdalene Asylum received from former 'inmates' expressing gratitude 'for the help they got in the institution' and stressing their new 'desire to do well' clearly suggest that some women were thankful for a chance to 'reform' and did not necessarily feel that their time at the Institute had been an unwarranted hardship.[96] Nevertheless, the nature of the available sources, such as minutes and annual reports, means that it is difficult to escape a 'top down' perspective on how the 'inmates' actually experienced their time in these institutions. Not only is it unlikely that those who did not appreciate their time in the asylum would write to express this; the committee members would have been even less likely to want to write about those cases in their minutes or annual reports. The fact that several women were reported to have run away suggests that there were certainly some who strongly resented the rules, surveillance and loss of freedom that the Institute subjected them to.[97]

Overall, therefore, although living conditions did improve, and more emphasis was placed on the reformation of the women's character by 'gentle encouragement' rather than punishment, the basic principles that had existed during the nineteenth century remained similar in the twentieth. The women still worked long hours for little or no pay and were expected to be obedient and hard-working. Their employment remained centred around domestic labour, and successful reformation still translated into the successful adoption of middle-class notions of domesticity. Even when women were offered a chance to start a new life overseas, they were still expected to remain in the domestic sphere. Moreover, this institutional system essentially meant that the women had their freedom curtailed for up to two years and were subjected to more intrusive interference into their private home lives than they would have in prisons. Although the Magdalene Asylum may have become more attractive on the surface, these changes merely represented a more pleasant and acceptable way of controlling women rather than sending them to prison. Nonetheless, this emphasis on reforming women so that they adhered to domestic sphere ideologies was far from unique, as domestic sphere ideology continued to shape the lives of women both inside and outside the Asylums. For those women who were arrested for prostitution offences, the asylum may well have been a more desirable destination than gaol, and some women may have benefited from the support they received in finding employment, even if their choices were limited to domestic occupations.

The Magdalene Asylums were not the only voluntary organisations that engaged in the surveillance of women in an attempt to reform and control their behaviour. The next section will therefore use case studies of the National Vigilance Association of Scotland (Eastern Division) and the Women Patrols, which were set up during the First World War, to further explore the involvement of voluntary organisations in the regulation of prostitution.

The National Vigilance Association of Scotland, Eastern Division

The National Vigilance Association (NVA) was set up in 1885 in order to help enforce the 1885 Criminal Law Amendment Act. The Act aimed to facilitate a 'crackdown' on prostitution, to protect women from abduction, seduction and rape, raised the age of consent to sixteen and made gross indecency between males a crime. The NVA in Edinburgh was established in 1911 and was named the National Vigilance Association of Scotland, Eastern Division (NVASED). It undertook similar activities as the other NVA branches, such as investigating suspected brothels, immoral dance halls, obscene literature and films, and campaigning against pornography. Aside from their campaigning activities, their primary concern was to protect women who were perceived to be in moral danger by patrolling the streets, removing young people from places where they were thought to be at risk, and then providing them with help and advice.[98]

The NVASED worked together with many other organisations such as the Salvation Army, the Scottish Girls' Friendly Society, the National Union of Women Workers and the Magdalene Asylums. Initially, the NVASED referred some of the women that they 'rescued' to reform homes run by these organisations, including the Magdalene Asylums, or placed women into domestic jobs or tried to return them to their families. For example, in 1913 Katie Maxwell was found a situation as a tailor maid, and in 1914

Bethany Blair's child was 'taken into a shelter on condition that [she] went into service'.[99] In the same year, Ada Paterson, who had run away from home, was sent back to her mother.[100] Similarly, the NVASED also involved the women's families when trying to control those they thought were in moral danger. For example, in 1914 when Jemina Dickson 'refused to go to any home outside Edinburgh', the NVASED decided it was necessary to 'see the girl's father and induce him to use his authority in the matter'.[101] Not only was the NVASED trying to control where Dickson would be sent; it also wanted to persuade her father to use his traditional patriarchal power to control his daughter. The importance of influencing the girls' home life can also be seen in the fact that in 1913 the NVASED held a 'mothers meeting' which aimed to 'reach the mothers of the girls'.[102]

The women that the NVASED sought to help were primarily from working-class backgrounds. For example, seventeen-year-old Ruby Thompson (referred to above) was found work at the 'Gaigaide factory.'[103] Other similar cases include Mary Anderson (a girl in service), Ida List (a nurse who was pregnant), Priscilla (a seventeen-year-old who was dismissed from Rubben Works owing to her 'condition'), Charlotte Lee (a sixteen-year-old looking for work), Annie Riley (an eighteen-year-old who had lost her job because she got into 'bad company'), Maggie McLeachy (a sixteen-year-old girl from an industrial school), and Rachael Brown (who previously had been a domestic servant and then tried factory work).[104] The fact that the NVASED routinely provided shelter and clothing for the girls suggests that they had little money.[105] Newspaper articles about the NVA also illustrate that the girls were mainly from working-class backgrounds; for example, on 14 March 1918 the *Evening Dispatch* wrote that the girls whom the NVASED sought to help were 'usually from domestic service or other employment.'[106] As in the Magdalene Asylum minutes, the young women in the NVASED minutes were mainly referred to as 'girls', even when describing women in their late twenties.[107] This use of the word 'girls' to describe unmarried women in their late teens and twenties was not uncommon during this period; however, it clearly demonstrates an unequal power balance between those being helped and those in control and implies that this power imbalance was rooted in class and not simply in generational difference.

Like the Magdalene Asylum, the NVASED was also less interested in women who were considered 'hardened prostitutes'. The majority of the women described in the minutes were young girls who were behaving promiscuously or were in 'danger of being led astray'. For example, in 1913 they placed Nina Smith in a Glasgow reform home because it was feared that she was 'living in dangerous surroundings'.[108] In November 1913 they placed nineteen-year-old Mabel Brown, who had been 'on the streets for three weeks', into a reform home in Dundee.[109] The June 1916 minutes described how fifteen-year-old Annie McCormack, who had been 'running absolutely wild, [and] in with a bad set of girls', was sent to a convent in Dalkeith.[110] However, some cases did include women who had clearly been engaging in prostitution. For example, the May 1916 minutes described how the NVASED had placed Agnes Wilson into the Friendless Girls' Home because she had been 'decoyed into a house of bad fame', and an 'Irish girl' was sent to a convent after she had been in prison for three days for a prostitution offence. Nevertheless, although they had engaged in prostitution, these women were far from being seen as 'hardened prostitutes'. Wilson was labelled as being 'of weak intellect', and the 'Irish girl' was described as 'deeply repentant'.[111] Their vulnerability and eagerness to be reformed meant that they were seen as victims who were willing to be reformed rather than as 'hardened criminals'.

By the 1920s it appears that the NVASED members' attitudes and approach towards reforming and rehabilitating had changed and they had become particularly critical of what they saw as out-dated institutional methods. In 1924 the NVASED Ladies' Committee received a letter from the Edinburgh Magdalene Asylum asking why they had stopped sending women to the asylum. The Ladies' Committee members replied by sending a letter to explain that they had done so for the previous two years because:

1) There was no classification of cases.
2) No proper medical examination.
3) No recreational or educational side.
4) The commercial side developed to the almost utter exclusion of the moral and spiritual.
5) The training in the home does not properly equip the girls for future work.[112]

The NVASED was clearly very critical of the Magdalene Asylum's methods. It felt that the Asylum did not cater for the educational or vocational needs of the women and focused too heavily on making profits from laundry work. The NVASED wanted instead to pursue 'modern methods' and to break their association with more outmoded reform homes. The Edinburgh Magdalene Asylum minutes show that prior to the 1920s many aspects of the NVASED's criticisms were warranted, and these criticisms may have been a motivating factor behind the positive changes that were introduced at the Asylum during the 1920s. Regardless of the improvements, however, in 1928 members of the Magdalene Asylum's Ladies' Committee remained concerned about the negative connotations associated with the Asylum and in 1928 committee member Miss Hamilton proposed that the institution should change its name.

There was general agreement and 'sympathy with the change proposed', but the committee decided against it because of the 'costly legal proceedings' and the danger of losing endowments, gifts and legacies.[113]

The NVASED did not run a reform home, and the members were critical of this institutional approach in general, not only in reference to the Magdalene Asylums. Their promotion material described how 'modern social reformers have abandoned the fiercely retributive form of discipline as purely sterile; the new lines of efforts are regenerative, positive, and constructive'.[114] Instead of institutionalising women, the NVASED preferred to embrace the new 'professional' and scientific social work methods that focused on women as individuals. This diagnostic 'case-work' approach meant that the needs of each woman could be assessed and appropriate action taken accordingly. The NVASED worked with several organisations to ensure that they could provide the necessary help the women needed. This often included working with hospitals, the police, probation officers, voluntary workers, religious organisations, possible employers and family members. For example, in May 1916 the NVASED minutes described the case of seventeen-year-old Ruby Thompson, who, having just left the Royal Infirmary Lock Ward, was given temporary accommodation and assisted in finding suitable employment:

> Her mother refuses to have any more to do with her and Ruby is very anxious to make a fresh start and keep away from the bad girls who have influenced her . . . She is staying at the flat until a suitable home is found for her. Work has been obtained for her at Craigside Envelope factory.[115]

Although the NVASED's case-work approach was in many respects quite different to the Magdalene Asylums' institutional methods, it nevertheless followed a similar approach concerning what constituted 'saving' women.

The NVASED also worked closely with the police, especially regarding street solicitation and the suppression of brothels. The NVASED frequently informed the police about suspected brothels in the hope that the house could be placed under surveillance. For example, in May 1927 the minutes describe how 'communications were held with the Chief Constable' about patrolling the Princes Street Gardens in order to form a report on their condition. In December 1916 there were concerns raised in the Ladies' Committee meetings about 'the houses of ill fame', and it was noted that women working for the NVASED watched these houses and requested 'to see if the special constable could help in the matter.'[116] The Ladies' Committee also asked a solicitor to help them decide whether they could confront the landlady of a suspected brothel. The NVASED clearly became directly involved in the policing of what they understood to be immoral activity, and they were prepared to interfere directly in the lives of these women, employing surveillance, the police, or the traditional authority of 'the father' in order to make sure that young women behaved according to their notion of respectable femininity.

Women Patrols during the First World War

Women patrols were implemented shortly after the start of the First World War, in response to what became known as 'khaki fever', a term used to describe the moral laxity and increased sexual misconduct supposedly caused by the war.[117] It was believed that young women were particularly at risk because they bore 'the crest of this emotional experience' and hence were especially affected by the increased presence of soldiers.[118] Although the early twentieth century saw growing opportunities for women's independence, these new freedoms were 'accompanied by new restrictions, and new forms of regulation'.[119] In particular, the fear of the independent 'modern girl' remained strong because they posed a wider threat to society through their future role as the mothers of the next generation.[120] This was particularly important during the First World War when the sexual behaviour of women came to be regarded as a matter of national importance. The National Union of Women Workers (NUWW) was one of several organisations that responded to this increasing concern by creating women patrols. In 1914 the Scottish Union of Women Workers (SUWW) established the Scottish women patrols that would be independent of the central committee based in England.

The records of the Edinburgh women patrols show that the role of these patrols was mainly to tour streets and parks in an attempt to prevent immorality between young men and women. The members of the patrols were told that they should engage in the 'friendly surveillance of girls' near army camps and in the local parks.[121] During 1917 and 1919 the patrols also assisted as 'part-time Park-Keepers from 6:30 to sunset during 3 ¼ summer months in Holyrood Park . . . [and] were granted all the powers of park-keepers'.[122] The patrols also established clubs 'so as to form a centre for the girls' in order to distract them from fraternising with soldiers.[123] However, a letter sent to the Edinburgh Chief Constable explained that the role of the women patrols was 'mainly preventative' and it was intended that they should take 'care of girls and women who would not ordinarily come under the notice of the police.'[124] Patrol members were told to 'avoid speaking to a girl accompanied by a man' because their 'main aim' was to 'cause interruption' of any immoral activity by making their 'silent presence known.'[125] This was thought possible because it was presumed that the women patrols had moral superiority and therefore the right to become involved in the private lives of other women. Therefore, although the patrols did not often physically intervene, they did aim to regulate the behaviour of women using other methods.

One of the main reasons causing the government to support the patrols was concern about the increasing rates of sexually transmitted infection within the armed forces.[126] Angela Woollacott, Lesley Hall and Lucy Bland have shown that it was widely believed during the First World War that a major reason for the rapid spread of venereal disease was 'amateur prostitutes' and 'good time girls' having sex with the soldiers.[127] These women were supposedly not as careful as 'professional prostitutes', and the soldiers were less worried about having sex with them because they wrongly assumed that they were less likely to be infected with venereal disease than 'professional prostitutes'.[128] This prompted a legislative proposal to control the activities of these women. In March 1918, Regulation 40D under the Defence of the Realm Act (DORA) made it an offence for any woman with venereal disease to either have sex with, or solicit, a member of the armed forces.[129] Woollacott explains that the issue of 'khaki fever' became so important precisely because it was affecting all classes of society. This was equally true in Edinburgh. For example, a contemporary newspaper article stated that 'nearly every class and age of the community' was affected by 'khaki fever'.[130] Nevertheless, as was the case in the Magdalene Asylums and the NVASED, it was generally only young working-class women who were targeted for surveillance. For example, one article states that the patrols aimed to 'speak to girls who are with soldiers' and to make the 'young girls realise the foolishness of their behaviour.'[131] If middle-class women were also targeted, it was because they were thought to be temporarily lacking in proper bourgeois morals (due to the extraordinary circumstances of war) and therefore in need of the same instruction as working-class women. This can be seen most clearly in those newspaper articles which explained the problem of 'khaki fever' as caused by a temporary 'loss of self-control.'[132]

Lucy Bland argues that although the patrols were designed to protect women and girls, this protection often 'tended to slip into surveillance.'[133] It is clear that in Edinburgh, too, the women patrols provided another example of how voluntary organisations worked together with the state to control the behaviour of those women who did not adhere to middle-class notions of respectable feminine behaviour. Each organisation sought to distinguish between different women according to whether they were considered 'unfortunate girls' or 'hardened prostitutes' and tailored their response to them accordingly. Pamela Cox has argued that 'the drawing of differences between groups and the shaping of policies appropriate to these groups was certainly a key feature of the new governmentality'.[134] However, as was the case in

England, these 'new techniques of social regulation' in Scotland were also based on previous philanthropic methods, which meant that the perceived 'differences' between groups of women were based on 'old social visions, filtered through a lens of class, gender, ethnicity, religion and sexuality'.[135]

Conclusion

During the first half of the twentieth century the police, magistrates, probation officers and voluntary organisations in Edinburgh and Glasgow worked together to control and regulate prostitution. Instead of punishing women who were caught soliciting by sending them to prison, the police and magistrates increasingly turned to probation and voluntary organisations in an attempt to rehabilitate these women. Whilst in theory this approach was intended as part of a wider modernisation movement that gave preference to the individual diagnosis and reformation of offenders, in reality it retained many of its earlier characteristics. The newly developing probation service relied heavily on members of voluntary organisations, such as the Magdalene Asylums and the NVASED, to work as probation officers, and the women on probation for prostitution offences were frequently sent to these voluntary reform homes as part of their probation. Whether women were sent to institutions or allowed to remain in the community under the supervision of probation officers, they had their freedom restricted for much longer periods than women who were sent to prison. However, for some women, probation offered an alternative to gaol and a more realistic opportunity of leaving prostitution and finding alternative employment.

The study of the Edinburgh and Glasgow Magdalene Asylums has shown that there were some improvements in both institutions after the nineteenth century. By the 1920s the women received a much wider range of recreational activities and 'treats' and there were also improvements in the food and the accommodation. However, although the Asylums may have developed a more sympathetic approach to reforming these women, the 'inmates' were still expected to work very hard for little or no money, and their freedom was restricted for up to two years. More importantly, the basic underlying principle of training women to adopt middle-class notions of domesticity that had prevailed in the nineteenth century continued well into the twentieth. Furthermore, whilst some of the voluntary organisations, such as the NVASED, followed a more modern scientific 'case-work' approach and were highly critical of the outmoded institutional methods used by the Magdalene Asylums, they nonetheless shared similar middle-class notions regarding women's role within the domestic sphere, meaning this approach and ideology was adopted as part of the official method for regulating prostitution. Perhaps most crucially, this trend ingrained into the new probation system the assumption that whilst some women could be 'saved' through lengthy interference in their personal lives aimed at reshaping their character to fit 'normal' middle-class expectations of femininity, others were 'beyond the pale'. The 'hardened prostitutes' who rejected this reforming framework were therefore treated by the reform institutes, probation workers and the police as women not worthy of help or sympathy and instead sent to prison for punishment. This profiling and categorising of women according to their perceived 'character' therefore had far-reaching consequences and the impact that this system had on women's experiences of prostitution will be examined further in the subsequent chapters.

Notes

1. See, for example: Linda Mahood, *The Magdalenes: Prostitution in the Nineteenth Century* (London: Routledge, 1990); Paula Bartley, *Prostitution, Prevention and Reform in England, 1860–1914* (London: Routledge, 2000); Susan Mumm, '"Not worse than other girls": The Convent-based Rehabilitation of Fallen Women in Victorian Britain', *Journal of Social History* 29, 3 (1996) pp. 527–47; Amanda Anderson, *Tainted Souls and Painted Faces: the Rhetoric of Fallenness in Victorian Culture* (Cornell University Press,1993).
2. Probation of Offenders Act 1907 (3 Edw. 7, c. 25).
3. Fergus McNeill, 'Remembering Probation in Scotland', *Probation Journal*, 52, 1 (2005) pp. 23–38.
4. Criminal Justice Administration Act 1914 (4 & 5 Geo.5. c. 58).
5. Anthony Osler, *Introduction to the Probation Service* (Winchester: Waterside, 1995).
6. Maurice Vanstone, *Supervising Offenders in the Community: A History of Probation Theory and Practice* (Aldershot: Ashgate, 2004).
7. Probation of Offenders (Scotland) Act (21 & 22 Geo.5. c. 30).
8. Glasgow City Archive (hereafter GCA), TD1776/1 GMIHC, 11 November 1921.
9. GCA, TD1776/1 GMIHC, 14 October 1913.
10. Edinburgh City Archive (hereafter ECA), (Edinburgh Court Records (hereafter EBCR).
11. ECA, EBCR, 21 July 1921.
12. ECA, EBCR, 21 April 1921.
13. ECA, EBCR, 5 February 1921.
14. ECA, EBCR, 21 April 1921.
15. ECA, EBCR, 4 April 1917.

16. David Garland, *Punishment and Welfare: A History of Penal Strategies* (Aldershot: Gower, 1985); Jacques Donzelot, *The Policing of Families* (Baltimore, 1997); Michel Foucault, *Discipline and Punish: The Birth of the Prison* (London: Penguin, 1979) (Harmondsworth, 1991).
17. See, for example, Bartley, *Prostitution, Prevention and Reform in England*; Lucia Zedner, *Women, Crime and Custody in Victorian England* (Oxford: Clarendon, 1991).
18. Ibid. p. viii.
19. ECA, EBCR, 10 February 1920; 3 March 1922; 24 November 1921.
20. ECA, EBCR, 1 April 1921.
21. ECA, EBCR, 21 September 1921.
22. ECA, EBCR, 26 April 1921; ECA, EBCR, 2 June 1921.
23. ECA, EBCR, 22 November 1921; ECA, EBCR, 23 November 1921.
24. ECA, EBCR, 9 October 1916.
25. ECA, EBCR, 9 May 1916.
26. ECA, EBCR, 23 August 1935.
27. Mahood, *The Magdalenes*, p. 75.
28. Ibid, p. 90.
29. GCA T-PAR 1.6 p. 625, Glasgow Magdalene Institute Annual Report (hereafter GMIAR), 1906.
30. Mahood, *The Magdalenes*, p. 76.
31. Ibid, p. 77.
32. ECA SL237/2/3 Edinburgh Magdalene Asylum Ladies' Committee Minutes (hereafter EMALC), 29 October 1908.
33. GCA T-PAR 1.31 p. 913, GMIAR, 1919.
34. GCA, PA11/2/8 *The Origins and Development of the Glasgow Magdalene Institute*, Glasgow, 1905, p. 4.
35. ECA, SL237/2/3 EMALC, 1900–1937.
36. ECA, SL237/2/3 EMALC, 13 October 1905.
37. GCA, T-PAR 1.16 p. 721, GMIAR, 1907, p. 10.
38. GCA, T-PAR 1.16 p. 721, GMIAR, 1910, p. 7; GCA, T-PAR, GMIAR, 1913, p. 8.
39. GCA, T-PAR 1.31 p. 913, GMIAR, 1919, p. 2.
40. GCA, T-PAR 1.13 p. 957, GMIAR, 1909, p. 16.
41. GCA, T-PAR 1.27, GMIAR, 1916, p. 4.
42. GCA, T-PAR 1.8 p. 625, GMIAR, 1907, p. 3.
43. See, for example, Leonore Davidoff, 'Mastered for Life: Servant and Wife in Victorian and Edwardian England', *Journal of Social History*, 7, 4 (1974) pp. 406–28; Anne E. Bowler, Chrysanthi S. Leon, Terry G. Lilley '"What Shall We Do with the Young Prostitute? Reform Her or Neglect Her? ": Domestication as Reform at the New York

State Reformatory for Women at Bedford, 1901–1913', *Journal of Social History* 47, 2 (2013) pp. 458–81; Lucy Delap, *Knowing Their Place: Domestic Service in Twentieth Century Britain* (Oxford: Oxford University Press, 2011).

44. See, for example, M. Arnot, E. Bartels, V. Beechey, L. Birke, S. Himmelweit, E. Hitelegg, D. Leonard, S. Ruehl and M. A. Speakman (eds), *The Changing Experience of Women* (Oxford: Robertson, 1982); Ina Zweiniger-Bargielowska, *Women in Twentieth-Century Britain* (Harlow: Longman, 2001).
45. ECA, SL237/2/3 EMALC, 15 April 1909.
46. ECA, SL237/2/3 EMALC, 11 October 1906; 15 April 1909.
47. ECA, SL237/2/3 EMALC, 12 January 1927.
48. GCA, TD1776/1 Glasgow Magdalene Institute Homes Committee Minute Book (hereafter GMIHC) 1898, 10 May 1898.
49. GCA, T-PAR 1.6, p. 625, GMIAR, 1906, p. 7.
50. ECA, SL237/2/3 EMALC, 12 January 1927.
51. GCA, T-PAR 1.13 p. 957; GMIAR, 1909, p. 7.
52. Mahood, *The Magdalenes*, p. 75.
53. GCA, GMIAR, 1906, 1907, 1909, 1910, 1915.
54. GCA, TD1776/1 GMIHC, 11 May 1909; GCA, TD1776/1 GMIHC, 9 June 1909.
55. GCA, TD1776/1 GMIHC, 4 December 1909.
56. GCA, TD1776/1 GMIHC, 4 April 1934.
57. GCA, T-PAR 1.13 p. 957, GMIAR 1909, p. 14.
58. GCA, T-PAR 1.16 p. 721, GMIAR, 1910.
59. GCA, TD1776/1 GMIHC, 13 March 1894.
60. For further discussion on the connection between prostitution and venereal disease see Roger Davidson and Lesley Hall (eds), *Sex Sin and Suffering: Venereal Disease and European Society Since 1870* (London: Routledge, 2001); Mary Spongberg, *Feminizing Venereal Disease: The Body of the Prostitute in Nineteenth-Century Medical Discourse* (London: Macmillan, 1997).
61. Pamela Cox, 'Compulsion, Voluntarism, and Venereal Disease: Governing Sexual Health in England after the Contagious Diseases Acts', *Journal of British Studies*, 46, 1 (2007) pp. 91–115.
62. GCA, TD1776/1 GMIHC, 13 March 1894.
63. ECA, SL237/2/3 EMALC, 31, January 1907; ECA, SL237/2/3 EMALC, 8 January 1914.
64. GCA, TD1776/1 GMIHC, 4 December 1909.
65. GCA, T-PAR 1.13 p. 957, GMIAR, 1909, p. 14.

66. GCA, T-PAR 1.16, GMIAR, 1910, p. 13; GCA, T-PAR 1.26 p. 747, GMIAR 1915, p. 14.
67. Viviene Cree, *From Public Streets to Private Lives: The Changing Task of Social Work* (Aldershot: Avebury, 1995), p. 18.
68. GCA, GMIAR 1909, 1910, 1915.
69. CCA, T-PAR 1.13 p. 957, GMIAR, 1909, p. 13.
70. GCA, TD1776/1 GMIHC, 9 June 1914.
71. ECA, SL237/2/3 EMALC, 17 March 1892; 19 October 1911; 12 January 1927.
72. GCA, TD1776/1 GMIHC, 8 December 1896.
73. Mahood, *The Magdalenes*, p. 3.
74. GCA, GMIAR, 1906, 1907, 1909, 1910, 1915.
75. GCA, GMIAR 1906, 1907, 1909, 1910.
76. Ibid.
77. GCA, T-PAR 1.13 p. 957, GMIAR, 1909, p. 7.
78. GCA, GMIAR, 1906, 1907, 1909, 1910, 1915.
79. GCA, TD1776/1 GMIHC, 11 November 1919.
80. GCA, TD1776/1 GMIHC, 11 November 1921; GCA, TD1776/1 GMIHC, 12 June 1917.
81. David Garland, *Punishment and Welfare*, p. 236.
82. Ibid, pp. 104–5.
83. Linda Mahood, *The Magdalenes*; Judith Walkowitz, *Prostitution and Victorian Society: Women, Class, and the State* (Cambridge: Cambridge University Press, 1980); Frank Mort, *Dangerous Sexualities: Medico-Moral Politics in England since 1830* (London: Routledge, 1987), p. 29; Paula Bartley, *Prostitution, Prevention and Reform in England.*
84. Mahood, *The Magdalenes*, p. 80.
85. ECA, SL237/2/3 EMALC, 17 October 1934.
86. ECA, SL237/2/3 EMALC, 26 June 1936.
87. GCA, TD1776/1 GMIHC, 13 June 1893.
88. GCA, T-PAR 1.16 p. 721, GMIAR, 1910, p. 11.
89. GCA, TD1776/1 GMIHC, 9 May 1911; 2 October 1920; 9 September 1924.
90. GCA, TD1776/1 GMIHC, 13 June 1922.
91. GCA, TD1776/1 GMIHC, 14 October 1913.
92. ECA, SL237/2/3 EMALC, 14 October 1925.
93. ECA, SL237/2/3 EMALC, 13 January 1926; 15 April 1931.
94. For further discussion on leisure and rational recreation see, for example; Peter Bailey, *Leisure and Class in Victorian England: Rational Recreation and the Contest for Control, 1830–1885* (London: Routledge, 1978); Gary Cross, *A Social History of Leisure since 1600* (Venture,

1990); Andrew Davies, *Leisure, Gender and Poverty* (Milton Keynes: Open University Press, 1992).
95. ECA, SL237/2/3 EMALC, 8 January 1914.
96. ECA, SL237/2/3 EMALC, 8 October 1924; 1 March 1906.
97. GCA, TD1776/1 GMIHC, 14 September 1909.
98. Cree, *From Public Streets to Private Lives*, p. 28.
99. National Library of Scotland (hereafter NLS) Acc.11191/2 Minutes of the Ladies' Committee National Vigilance Association of Scotland (Eastern division) 1913–1926 (hereafter MLCNVASED) 2 April 1913; 29 July 1914, p. 137.
100. NLS, Acc.11191/2, MLCNVASED, 4 October 1914.
101. NLS, Acc.11191/2, MLCNVASED, 19 July 1914.
102. NLS, Acc.11191/2, MLCNVASED, 19 February 1913.
103. NLS, Acc.11191/2, MLCNVASED, 18 May 1916.
104. NLS, Acc.11191/2, MLCNVASED, 29 July 1914; 13 September 1914; 4 October 1914; 6 January 1915; 2 December 1914; 16 December 1917; 19 April 1917.
105. NLS, Acc.11191/2, MLCNVASED, 6 January 1915; 21 February 1918.
106. NLS, Acc.11191 Family Care Papers, Newspaper Cuttings 1912–1928, p. 35, *The Evening Dispatch*, 14 March 1918.
107. NLS, Acc.11191/2, MLCNVASED, 20 January 1915.
108. NLS, Acc.11191/2, MLCNVASED, 30 April 1913.
109. NLS, Acc.11191/2, MLCNVASED, 4 November 1913.
110. NLS, Acc.11191/2, MLCNVASED, 1 June 1916.
111. Ibid.
112. NLS, Acc.11191/2, MLCNVASED, 4 January 1924.
113. NLS, Acc.11191/2, MLCNVASED, 9 November 1928.
114. NLS, Acc.11191 Family Care Papers, Newspaper Cuttings 1912–1928, p. 41.
115. NLS, Acc.11191/2, MLCNVASED, 18 May 1916.
116. NLS, Acc.11191/2, MLCNVASED, 12 December 1916.
117. See, for example, Angela Woollacott, '"Khaki Fever" and its Control: Gender, Class, Age and Sexual Morality on the British Home Front in the First World War', *Journal of Contemporary History*, 29 (1994) pp. 325–47.
118. *The Scotsman*, 6 October 1916, p. 4.
119. Pamela Cox, *Gender, Justice and Welfare: Bad Girls in Britain, 1900–1950* (Basingstoke: Palgrave Macmillan, 2003), p. 12.
120. Ibid, p. 12.
121. NLS, HH31/16/13: First World War: Women Patrols Papers, p. 2.

122. Imperial War Museum (hereafter IWM), EMP 42/3: Women's Work Collection, Report on Women Patrols for Scotland 1914–1920, p. 4.
123. IWM, EMP 42/3: Women's Work Collection, Report on Women Patrols For Scotland 1914–1920, p. 3.
124. NLS, HH31/16/13: First World War: Women Patrols Papers, p. 3.
125. NLS, HH31/16/13: Papers of the Women Patrols; HH31/16/13: First World War: Women Patrols Papers.
126. Roger Davidson, *Dangerous Liaisons, a Social History of Venereal Disease in Twentieth-Century Scotland* (Amsterdam: Rodopi, 2000).
127. Lesley Hall, 'War always brings it on': War, STD's, the Military, and the Civilian Population in Britain, 1850–1950', in *Medicine and Modern Warfare*, Roger Cooter, Mark Harrison and Steve Sturdy (eds) (Amsterdam: Atlanta, 1999); Lucy Bland, 'In the Name of Protection: The Policing of Women in the First World War', in Julia Brophy and Carol Smart (eds), *Women in Law: Explorations in Law, Family and Sexuality* (London: Routledge, 1985) pp. 23–49; Angela Woollacott, 'Khaki Fever and its Control'.
128. Ibid.
129. Woollacott, 'Khaki Fever', p. 333.
130. *The Scotsman*, 6 October, 1916, p. 4.
131. Ibid.
132. NLS, HH31/16/13: First World War: Women Patrols Papers, p. 5.
133. Bland, 'In the Name of Protection', p. 23.
134. Cox, *Gender, Justice and Welfare*, p. 13.
135. Ibid, p. 13.

CHAPTER 5

Women's Experiences of Prostitution

> I am a prostitute although I have never been convicted, and for several months past accused has been living with me at 38 New Street. Since he has lived with me he has never done any work and during the period charged he forced me out on the streets to earn money by prostitution in order to keep him. I have frequently complained to the police, both uniformed men and plain clothed men, regarding accused forcing me to go on to the streets and I have called the police up to the house in New Street where we reside. Accused does not get any pension or out of work donation and has been living entirely on the earnings of my prostitution.[1]

The above witness statement, made by May McArthur on 16 May 1919, was taken during the trial against James Clinton, who was charged and convicted under the Immoral Traffic Act for living off the earnings of prostitution. This evidence fits with the common understanding of prostitutes as the victims of vicious pimps. However, the fact that McArthur was able to complain to the police frequently, testify in court, and ultimately help to secure the conviction of Clinton suggests that she was not powerless and that the relationship between these individuals was more complex than is sometimes assumed. We shall return to McArthur's story in more detail later, but, for now, McArthur's case stands as an example of how women's experiences of prostitution were varied and complex, and certainly worthy of further investigation.

Historical research on women's experiences of prostitution is especially pertinent considering that their experiences, although central to our understanding of commercial sex, have typically not been the main focus of historical studies. This omission is especially problematic, considering that their experiences are fundamental to feminist and policy debates concerning the nature and position of prostitution in society.[2] Those historians who do examine prostitutes' experiences primarily focus on the nineteenth century, or on countries other than Britain.[3] The difficulties of finding sources that provide accounts of women's experiences of prostitution are in part responsible for this dearth in research. Most of the sources that are available, such as police, court, poor law, census and voluntary organisations' records, were not written by the women themselves and are heavily mediated. However, despite the limitations of these types of sources, they can provide some important insights. By using data relating to over 800 women, alongside in-depth case studies of individuals, this chapter will use a collective biography approach to examine the major themes that shaped the lives of women involved in prostitution in Scotland during the early twentieth century; the various reasons why they entered or exited prostitution at certain stages during their lives; and the different types of relationships that existed among 'prostitutes', 'pimps' and 'brothel-keepers'. Importantly, this evidence will begin to reveal a level of women's historical agency that has often been difficult for historians to ascertain.

'Disreputable behaviour': Mary Muirhead and Mabel Jamieson

Mary Muirhead was born in September 1874 in Saltcoats, North Ayrshire, to parents Joseph and Isabella Muirhead.[4] Her father was described as an iron-moulder but less is known about her mother, other than the fact that she died prior to 1905 and that Mary's father subsequently remarried. On 1 January 1900, twenty-six-year-old Mary married twenty-year-old David Johnstone, a labourer from Castle Finn, Ireland. Mary was two months pregnant on her wedding day, and on 5 July 1900 her first daughter, Elizabeth, was born. In January 1902 Mary delivered a still-born baby. On 10 January 1903, her first son, David, was born, and on 17 June 1905 she gave birth to her second son, Robert. During this period she moved every few months between different addresses in Govan and Glasgow.[5]

By 1905 Mary was described as 'separated' from her husband and working as a cleaner; however, her earnings must not have been sufficient to provide for the family, as they were periodically in the poorhouse throughout 1905 and 1906.[6] During this period, her husband's parents, David Johnstone and Elizabeth Osborne, came from Ireland to encourage their son to return with them. They were willing to take the children but would have 'nothing whatsoever to do with [Mary]' due to her 'disreputable behaviour'.[7] David and the eldest child moved to Ireland but Mary stayed in Scotland with the two younger children. In 1907 Mary was sentenced to seven days' imprisonment for theft and in 1911 for importuning for the purposes of prostitution.[8] Over the next six years, David was convicted three times for the desertion of his wife, receiving sentences ranging from forty days to four months. Meanwhile, Mary and the children returned frequently to the poorhouse. On 31 January 1912, Mary was sent to the infirmary wing at Barnhill poorhouse, suffering from bronchitis, and was again described as 'mak[ing] a livelihood by immoral earnings'.[9] By the end of 1912, Mary's seven-year-old son Robert had died in hospital, and in 1917 Mary's absent husband died in a Liverpool hospital. In 1925, aged 50, Mary died from 'natural causes' at her home address in Glasgow.

Mabel Jamieson was born in 1898 in Rothesay, to parents George and Annie Jamieson. Her father worked in the jute industry and by the 1911 census the family of five was living at 135 Alexander Street, Dundee. On 2 February 1917 Mabel, aged eighteen, was arrested for importuning and placed on probation for twelve months. During her probation period, she was required to reside at the Dundee Rescue Home on Ferry Road, under the supervision of Mrs Pearche. By September that year, however, Mabel had been transferred to the Salvation Army's Women's Home due to her 'bad behaviour' in the previous institution. The Ferry Road home reported that Mabel was a 'lazy girl who frequently misbehaved, making her a bad influence on the other girls within the home'.[10] She had also managed to escape on various occasions, once persuading another girl to leave with her. On 14 September 1917 the Salvation Army Home received a letter from Mabel's father pleading with them to let his daughter return home. The letter explained that his wife had passed away three years ago and that he needed Mabel to return to care for two younger siblings. Mabel was allowed to return home under the condition that she would remain under the supervision of a probation officer. There are no more records relating to Mabel after this point.

Mary Muirhead's and Mabel Jamieson's stories highlight important themes relating to women's involvement in prostitution. Whilst both women faced considerable difficulties, Mary's life tells us more about the poverty, illness and hardship many women endured, whereas from Mabel's story we learn more about the various institutions that tried to reform 'fallen women'. In part, these differences illustrate how responses to prostitution changed over the period, especially in terms of the new opportunities given to younger women to enter probation and reform homes rather than prison, but they also remind us that each woman's life course was unique. The chapter will explore these themes in more depth by examining women's collective and individual experiences and life courses. Whilst the nature of sources means that they can only provide us with a partial insight into the lives of people involved in prostitution, by placing these stories together to form a collective biography, they do allow us to begin to piece together fragments of women's experiences of prostitution.

Women's Family Circumstances, Occupation and Employment Patterns

Like Mary Muirhead and Mable Jamieson, a large majority of the women convicted of prostitution offences came from working-class backgrounds. Their parents were commonly described as non-skilled or semi-skilled workers, such as labourers, colliers and factory workers.[11] However, like Mary Muirhead's father, who was an iron-moulder, a considerable minority were also described as skilled workers.[12] Additionally, some of the women, such as Peggy Drummond and Margaret Ross, were described as coming from 'very respectable people.'[13] The rise in wages and the reduction in primary poverty during the early twentieth century meant that for women with parents in regular employment it was unlikely that their families' poverty alone was the reason they entered prostitution. Nonetheless, irregular or seasonal work, along with high unemployment in some industries during the interwar years, meant that many families experienced extreme hardship during this period, meaning poverty and the lack of alternative economic opportunities remained an important factor behind why many of these women chose to enter prostitution.[14] Moreover, when the police wrote something in the section of the Burgh Court report that asked for the accused's 'financial circumstances' (which, admittedly, was not very often), it mainly described them as 'poor' or 'unemployed'.

The death or desertion of one parent or both was not uncommon during this period, and like Mary and Mabel who both lost their mothers whilst they were young, many of the women engaged in prostitution were orphans or half orphans. For the years 1906, 1907, 1909, 1910, and 1915, the Glasgow Magdalene Asylum records show that on average forty-one per cent of the women were described as orphans and only twenty-five per cent had both parents alive.[15] Not only did this mean low economic security for the women; the emotional impact and lack of family support networks may also have contributed to their move into prostitution. However, having both parents alive did not necessarily result in a safe and secure upbringing and there were several cases of women who came from abusive homes. For example, twenty-year-old Isabella Shepard claimed that she originally left her home in Blackburn 'on account of her father's harshness'.[16] However, the probation worker reported that she did not think that this was a fair assessment of the situation and described how:

> The father was at home when I called and expressed great indignation at such a charge being made against him. The other members of the family support the father, and my own personal observation bears out the truth of his statement. The parents are doing everything in their power to save their daughter from a life of misery.[17]

Exactly why Isabella ran away from home is uncertain; however, it is clear that unhappiness at home played an important role. Whether due to physical or emotional abuse, the death or desertion of parents, or a desire to leave an unhappy family situation in search of new opportunities, it is clear that the women often came from difficult home situations.

Even for those women with more stable early years, the choice of husband could massively change their chances of future prosperity. Women turning to prostitution after being left alone to support themselves and their children is a common theme in the Poor Law and Burgh Court records. For example, it was the desertion of Mary Muirhead's husband that appears to have had a particularly detrimental impact on her life. Similarly, in 1902, thirty-six-year-old Margaret Douglas from Glasgow was described as 'destitute' and making her 'living on the streets'[18] due to the fact that her husband Robert Douglas had deserted her three years earlier whilst they were living in London.[19] Likewise, Agnes Fraser explained how after she married John Fraser they lived in a New Lanark Cooperative house for six years until he deserted her and moved in with another woman in Motherwell.[20] Later she explained that she had left him 'owing to his cruelty' because he had 'infected her with a venereal disease' and that she knew 'nothing of his whereabouts'.[21] Even the temporary absence of the husband due to illness, imprisonment or military service could have similarly dire consequences.

Caring for young children without support from the children's father was particularly problematic for many women. When twenty-year-old Bridget Tolland from Ireland was deserted by her husband James Tolland, she turned to prostitution because she was left to care for her two-year-old daughter, Hannah.[22] Similarly, after thirty-five-year-old Elizabeth Pretsell separated from her husband in 1919, 'owing to him carrying on with another woman', she had to use her earnings from prostitution to support three daughters: Florence, aged thirteen, Elsie, aged nine and Joan, aged four.[23] Although women's wages were rising during this period, there was still a strong emphasis on the role of the 'male breadwinner'.[24] Women earned considerably less than men and were often the first to be laid off when redundancies had to be made. Without the contributions of another adult wage earner, it would have been very difficult to support a young family whilst also providing the necessary child care.[25] To cope with this situation, many women relied on their friends and family, with both parents and siblings helping to provide childcare. For example, Margaret Mackie's 'fourteen-year-old daughter Bessie lived with her uncle', and Agnes McKenzie's daughter lived with her grandmother in New Lanark.[26] However, not all women had this kind of support readily available.

Even for those women who had childcare support from relatives, prostitution still offered much higher wages than any other typical working-class women's employment and necessitated far fewer hours of work, something especially helpful for women with children to support and care for. Exactly how much money a woman could earn varied significantly according to a variety of factors, such as the type of sexual act performed; where the act took place; the financial means and expectations of the men she solicited; her age, attractiveness and experience; and the unpredictable outcome of individual negotiations. Little evidence has survived which indicates the average prices of different sex acts. However, there are a small number of examples in the witness reports which provide a rough indicator of prices. For example, during a street solicitation case in 1914 one man stated that he had paid 4s, and on another occasion in 1914 a different man told the police that he paid 5s. By 1918 this amount had doubled to 10s.[27] In 1911 a report on 'the social evil' in Glasgow described how prices fluctuated and varied according to the individual and the sex act performed. The report explained how one girl received amounts ranging 'from between 1s to 31s' for each act of prostitution.[28] The report also describes how in 1907 a nineteen-year-old girl was given £2 for her first act of prostitution, which quickly reduced to 10s per transaction after that.[29] In another case, this time from 1919, Jane Swanson explained how 'she never took any payment until morning, and that she left it to the men to give her what they thought she was worth.'[30] This suggests that the man had an upper hand in deciding the terms of the contract; however, none of the other reports mention anything relating to how the women set or negotiated prices, and therefore it is difficult to tell whether this was a common practice. Nonetheless, even taking into account the wide variety of wages and the fact that some women were not necessarily earning substantial amounts, they still earned more for the number of hours they worked than was on offer in the alternative female occupations.

Tony Henderson's study of eighteenth-century prostitution showed that, in London, 'economies of makeshift' meant that women moved in and out of prostitution according to their economic circumstances.[31] The Glasgow Duke Street Prison records suggest that, as in the eighteenth century, many women who sold sex in the early part of the twentieth century continued to be involved in other types of work in a 'makeshift economy', only resorting to prostitution to top up their incomes during times of economic hardship

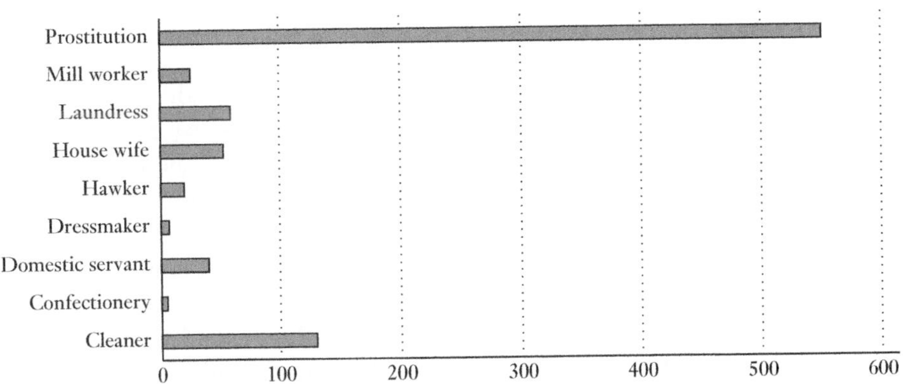

Figure 5.1 Occupations of Women Arrested for Importuning.
Source: National Records of Scotland (NRS), Glasgow Duke Street Prison Register, 1903, 1911, 1921, 1931. N = 888.

and leaving once they had secured more stable employment or marriage. Figure 5.1 shows that the women who were sent to Duke Street Prison for importuning offences had previously been employed mostly in working-class female occupations, such as cleaning, laundry, sewing, hawking, domestic service and textile work. Therefore, although the expanding upwardly mobile 'respectable working class' may have tried to keep their distance from prostitution, it is clear that in the twentieth century the 'makeshift' economy continued to play a significant role in the lives of women involved in prostitution, meaning they were not isolated from working-class communities.[32]

Interestingly, the number of women whose employment was described as 'prostitution' in the prison registers declined from fifty-eight per cent in 1903 to thirty-five per cent in 1931. This suggests that by the latter part of the period women arrested for importuning in Glasgow were increasingly involved in a variety of employment aside from prostitution and did not necessarily view prostitution as their primary occupation, instead affiliating themselves with women in other working-class occupations. Whilst the state may have classified women who sold sex according to their involvement in prostitution, the women themselves did not necessarily see their 'occupation' as their main source of identity. This was especially true for women involved in new forms of indoor clandestine prostitution. Chapter six will look more closely at how it became increasingly possible for women involved in prostitution to make distinctions among themselves and their work due to new clandestine methods that made it easier for them to hide their activities and to create new identities separate from those of the 'street walker' or the 'common prostitute'.

Migration and Immigration

Mary Muirhead was rarely listed as staying at the same address for more than three months and was constantly moving between Govan and Glasgow. Similarly, Mabel Jamieson frequently changed address, as she moved from one reform home to another. Like these two women, many of the other women involved in prostitution in early twentieth-century Scotland also appear to have led unsettled lives, with some moving much longer distances than Mary Muirhead or Mabel Jamieson. For example, in 1910, twenty-three-year-old Elizabeth Miller 'left her father's house in Liverpool to go to Glasgow' to work as a cleaner, but ended up importuning on the streets of Glasgow.[33] Similarly, in 1917, nineteen-year-old Ruby O'Connor was reported to have moved to London from Cork to work as a domestic servant, but after the birth of a son (who subsequently died), she moved to Glasgow where she worked as a prostitute.[34] For women who moved away from their families to find work in other areas, the loss of family support networks and of the stability they provided may have been a contributing factor behind

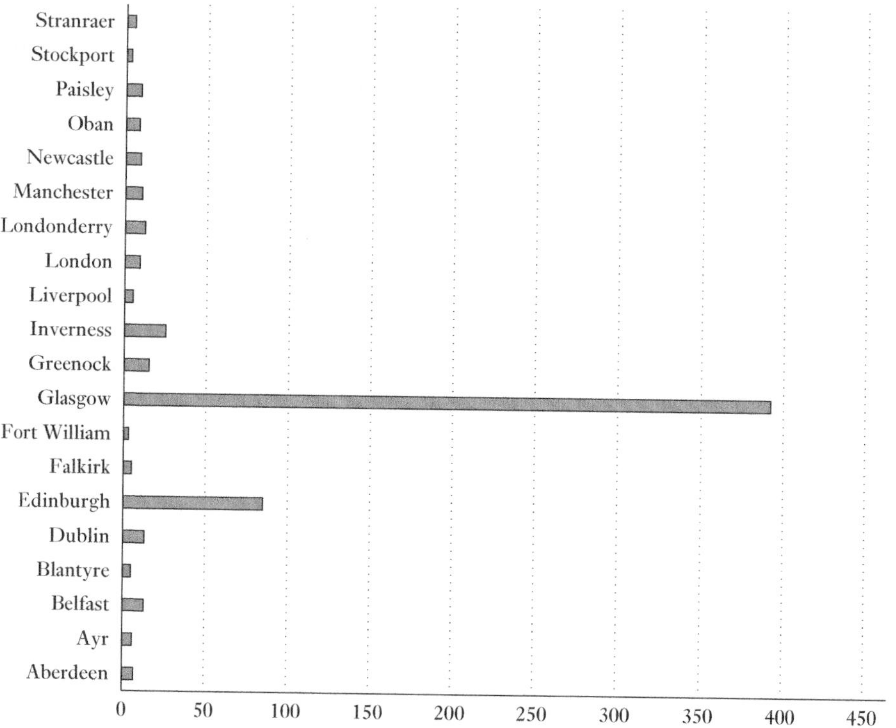

Figure 5.2 Birthplace of Women Convicted for Importuning.

Source: NRS, Duke Street Prison Registers, 1903, 1911, 1921, 1931 N = 585.

their resorting to prostitution in times of need. However, for some women their choice to migrate may have been due to a preference to work away from their local area in order to keep their involvement in prostitution secret from their families. Frequent movement between different towns and cities was also used as a method to find work according to local demand and to avoid police surveillance.

The Glasgow Duke Street Prison registers show that the women imprisoned for importuning offences there came from a wide range of towns, cities and even countries. Whilst at the start of the twentieth century the majority of women reported Glasgow as their place of birth, several other cities within Scotland, England and Ireland – such as Edinburgh, London and Dublin – were also commonly recorded. However, by 1911, although women continued to come from similar locations around Scotland, England and Ireland, there were considerably fewer women who were born outside Scotland, and outside Glasgow in particular. For instance, in both 1911 and 1931 all the birthplaces recorded were in Scotland, and in 1921 only three were outside Scotland. This suggests that migrant workers played a less significant role in the Scottish sex industry by the interwar period.

The Duke Street Prison's statistics on the nationality of women convicted for soliciting offences also show that a high percentage of the women involved in prostitution in Scotland after 1911 were Scottish. Whereas in 1903 forty-nine per cent were described as Scottish, forty-three per cent Irish and six per cent as English, by 1921 fifty-seven per cent were Scottish, thirty-five per cent Irish and eight per cent English. The reduction in the number of Irish women involved in prostitution in Scotland corresponds with a general decline in the rate of Irish immigration. Census statistics show that Irish immigration 'fell consistently after 1900, and that in the period 1920–31 it was probably out-weighed by those Irish who emigrated from Scotland'.[35] However, it is interesting to note that the number of women whose nationality was described as Irish was larger than the number of women described as having been born in Ireland. This is likely due to the fact that the prison officials classed women whose fathers were Irish to be of Irish nationality, regardless of their Scottish birthplace. This suggests that, rather than the upheaval of immigration, it may have been the prejudice they faced due to their association with the Irish community that contributed to their move into prostitution.[36] It is likely that the difficult economic plight of Irish men trying to find employment in sectors of the economy traditionally dominated by Scottish Protestants, who were hostile to Irish Catholics taking their jobs, may have also negatively affected female workers and wives.[37] If so, their difficulty in finding adequate employment may have disproportionately contributed to Irish women's movement into prostitution.

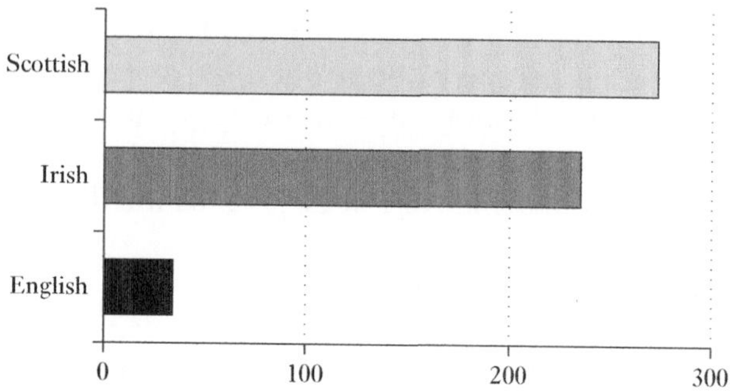

Figure 5.3 Nationality of the Women, 1903.
Source: NRS, Duke Street Prison Registers. N = 542.[38]

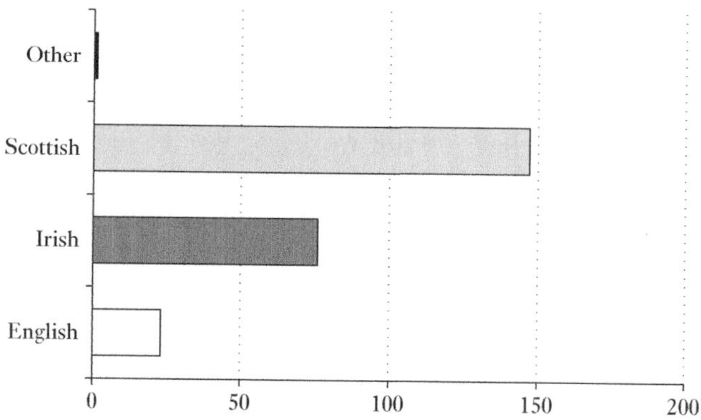

Figure 5.4 Nationality of the Women, 1911.
Source: NRS, Duke Street Prison Registers. N = 247.[39]

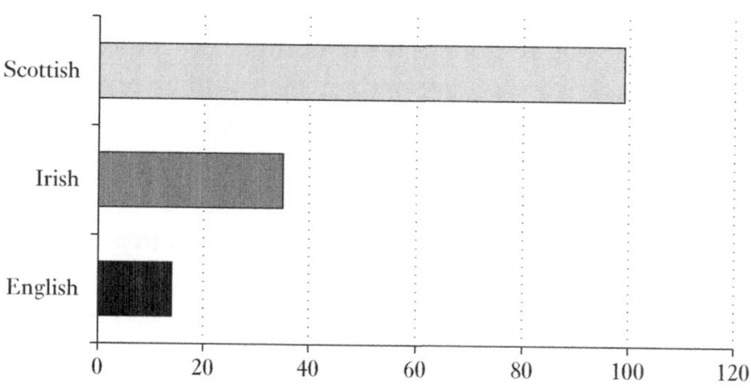

Figure 5.5 Nationality of the Women, 1921.
Source: NRS, Duke Street Prison Registers. N = 148.[40]

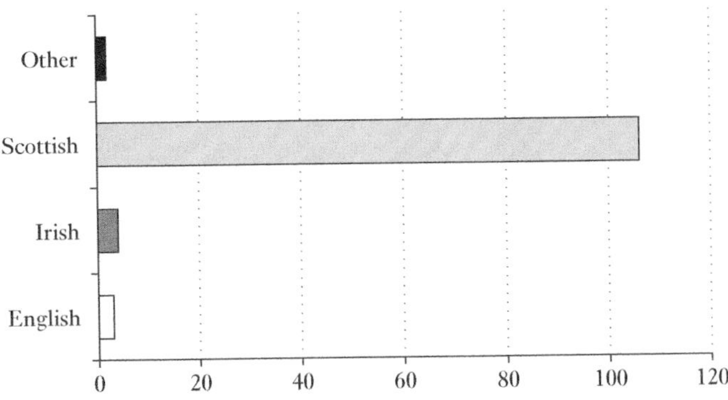

Figure 5.6 Nationality of the Women, 1931.
Source: NRS, Duke Street Prison Registers. N = 115.[41]

Women's Ages

Throughout the period from 1903 to 1931 the majority of women convicted of importuning in Glasgow were aged between twenty-one and thirty-five. Figures 5.7 to 5.10 show that by the 1920s and 1930s the age range had narrowed and the percentage of twenty-one to twenty-five-year-olds increased. Whereas in 1903 and 1911 there had been a notable number of women in their mid-to-late thirties and forties among those convicted of importuning, by 1931 this age group had declined. This suggests that prostitution was increasingly a temporary job that women engaged in whilst they were young and left when they grew older. Judith Walkowitz's research on nineteenth-century prostitution in England has shown that 'for practical and psychological reasons, most women were probably ill-equipped to endure the rigors of the "profession" for more than a few years'.[42] It would appear that the same was true in early twentieth-century Scotland and that prostitution was only a temporary stage in women's lives before they married or found new economic opportunities.[43] Thus, after a short period, the women re-joined the working-class community, if indeed they had ever left it in the first place. The continued lowering of the age range suggests that women involved in prostitution were not increasingly ostracised from working-class communities or necessarily labelled as 'prostitutes' for their entire lives, but were quite capable of entering or returning to other occupations once they left prostitution. Moreover, the reduction in the number of women at the lowest end of the age range reflects the fact that the younger women were increasingly given warnings or probation sentences, in accordance with the new penal-welfare approach that was being implemented.

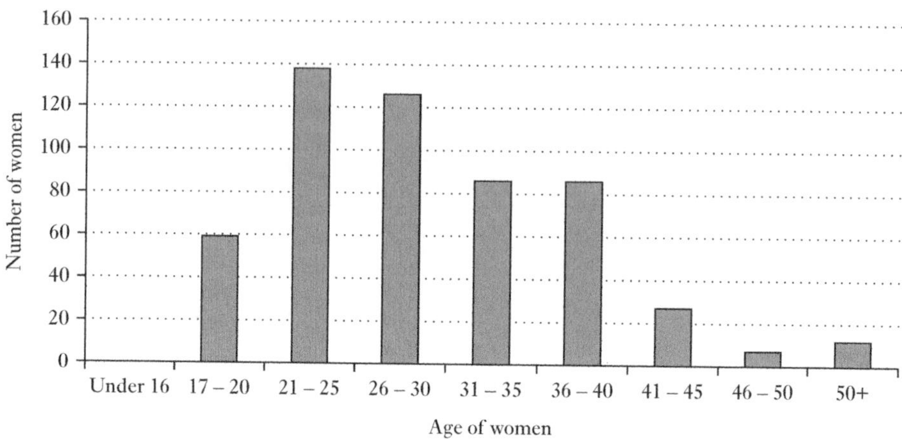

Figure 5.7 Age of the Women, 1903.
Source: NRS, Duke Street Prison Registers.

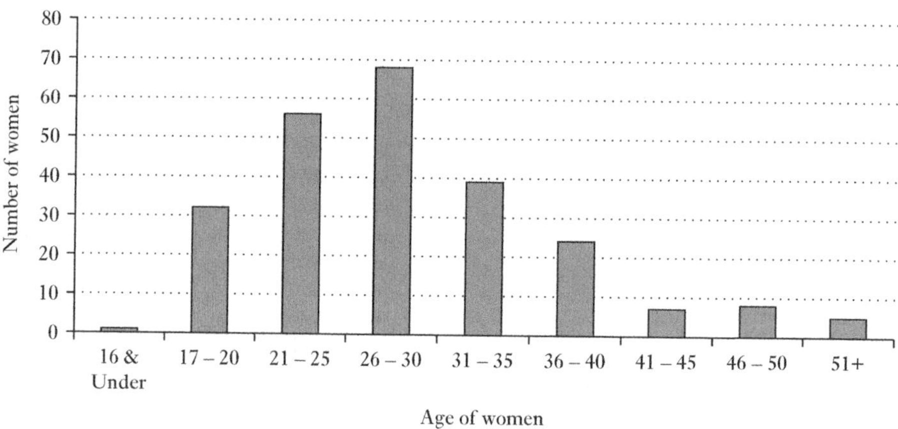

Figure 5.8 Age of the Women, 1911.[45]
Source: NRS, Duke Street Prison Registers.

Ill-health, Venereal Disease and Alcoholism

Social purity reformers during the nineteenth and early-twentieth centuries commonly emphasised the detrimental impact that prostitution had on women's health, and the image of the destitute 'fallen woman' lying helplessly close to death was a common motif used to stir sympathy. The reformers stressed not only the increased risk of catching venereal disease, but also the harm that resulted from the poverty and unsavoury lifestyle associated with the occupation. Whether or not prostitution really did increase the likelihood of a premature death, ill-health certainly was a common problem for many of the

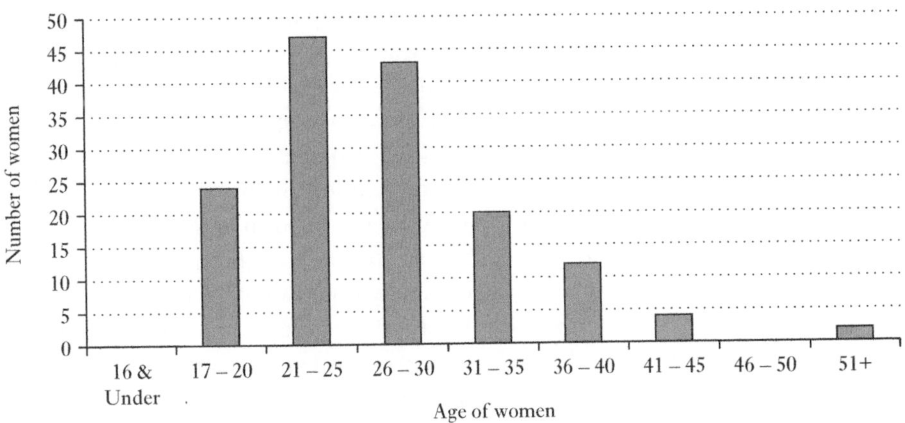

Figure 5.9 Age of the Women, 1921.[46]
Source: NRS, Duke Street Prison Registers.

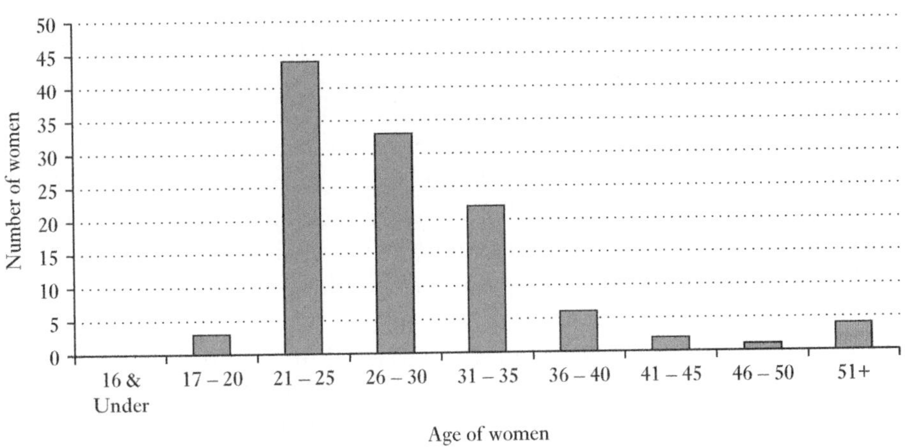

Figure 5.10 Age of the Women, 1931.[47]
Source: NRS, Duke Street Prison Registers.

women. For example, in 1912, Mary Muirhead was hospitalised with 'bronchitis' and subsequently was admitted to the infirmary on several more occasions; Elizabeth Erskine, a forty-eight-year-old widow from Greenock, had 'dropsy'; forty-year-old Isabella Thomson from Alloa was described as 'wholly disabled and destitute'; and thirty-six-year-old Mary McAllister from Ireland was noted to have 'headaches' that were 'probably due to syphilis'.[48] However, ill-health and disease was common among all sections of the population during this period, especially for members of the working classes who were often forced to survive on meagre diets and to live in poor-quality overcrowded accommodation. Therefore, to single out women who were involved in prostitution as being especially vulnerable to disease is perhaps misleading.

Whilst social purity and health campaigns unfairly focused on prostitutes as the main transmitters of venereal disease, an injustice that was part of a wider movement to stigmatise prostitutes and to rationalise controlling their activities, venereal disease did remain a common danger for the women involved in prostitution. Although the use of condoms was becoming more widespread by this point, not all of the women had easy access to them or knew how to use them effectively, and their customers may not always have been willing to use them either. Frequent exposure to infection therefore remained a dangerous occupational hazard and many of the women consequently spent time in lock hospitals. For example, Agnes McKenzie had been in a lock hospital on several occasions, and in 1935 twenty-one-year-old Peggy Drummond from Blackbridge in West Lothian was placed in a lock hospital for six months, where she subsequently gave birth to her baby.[49] By the first decades of the twentieth century, accurate diagnoses and effective treatments for venereal diseases were becoming available, thanks to the invention of the Wassermann test in 1906 and the discovery of Salvarsan. Nevertheless, these treatments were not necessarily easily available or reliable, and the Glasgow lock hospital continued to rely on painful mercurial therapies, leeches and urethral injections of salts long after 1900.[50] The lock hospitals or venereal disease wards of infirmaries and poorhouses could often be frightening and unpleasant places where patients were 'heavily regimented and stigmatized'.[51]

Alcohol abuse was another serious health problem that the women involved in prostitution often faced. There were many instances in which women were described as drunk at the time of their arrest. For example, in June 1920, twenty-year-old Marion Ferguson was described by the police as having recently 'taken to drinking heavily', and, in March of the same year, twenty-three-year-old Elizabeth Livingston was reported to have begun 'drinking pretty heavily' after she left her husband in New Zealand and returned to Scotland.[52] These two examples are only a small fraction of the cases which involved alcohol, and the Criminal Conviction Registers also show that the same women were charged on separate occasions for drunk and disorderly behaviour. By the 1920s there was even a specific section of the witness report dedicated to noting whether the accused was sober or drunk when arrested. From sampling these reports, it is possible to estimate that roughly half of all the women apprehended for importuning were reported as having been under the influence of alcohol at the time of their arrest.

Alcohol and prostitution have long been associated with each other, in part due to the fact that public houses were well known as common places for prostitutes to solicit men.[53] However, without access to the type of records that could provide detailed information about each woman's personal circumstances, it is hard to know whether the involvement in prostitution encouraged women to drink, or whether prostitution was used as a means to fund a pre-existing habit. Sociologists have shown that in some situations today women who are dependent on drugs turn to prostitution as a way to fund their addiction; it could be argued that a similar scenario applied to those women who were dependent on alcohol in the early twentieth century.[54] However, alcohol could also have been a coping mechanism once women had already turned to prostitution. The extent to which their alcohol consumption differed from other working-class women's drinking habits, or constituted 'alcoholism', is equally difficult to establish.[55] Firstly, the fact that up to fifty per cent of the women were described as 'sober' when they were arrested shows that alcohol did not necessarily play a regular part in all of the women's lives. Secondly, female alcohol consumption was increasingly accepted as a normal part of working-class women's leisure activities by this period. Temperance surveys at the end of the nineteenth and beginning of the twentieth century frequently showed that women made up between twenty-five and thirty per cent of all public house customers and a similar percentage of those arrested on charges of drunkenness.[56] The First World War was also widely noted to have facilitated a large increase in the number of respectable working-class and lower middle-class women patronising pubs, as the reduction in the male population, an increased female engagement in the public sphere and an effort on the part of the proprietors to attract women though the use of separate female drinking areas all made it more acceptable for women to drink in public.[57] Whilst this apparent increase in female drinking caused much concern among moral reformers and temperance advocates, the more general acceptance of female drinking meant that it was no longer assumed that only prostitutes were to be seen openly drinking in public.

Institutions

It was not only at the infirmary and the lock hospital that the women involved in prostitution were frequent visitors. Like Mabel Jamieson, who spent time on probation in various rescue homes, many of the women also spent considerable periods of time in a variety of different institutions, such as Magdalene Asylums, industrial schools, refuge shelters, poorhouses and prisons. For example, in 1919, eighteen-year-old Isabella McGregor was arrested for soliciting and placed on probation.[58] She was originally instructed to reside at St Andrew's House at Joppa in Midlothian under the care of the Sister in charge. However, when the Sister wrote to the magistrates to explain that the home was 'unable to keep the girl Isabella McGregor [because] she has been a bad influence over the girls in the house', Mcgregor was instead sent to 14 Dublin Street in Edinburgh, to be under the care of Jane Sibbald.[59] After failing to uphold her probation bonds due to her 'bad conduct', she was sentenced to thirty days in prison. Similarly, in 1918 nineteen-year-old Margaret Wilson, a married dairymaid who was caught importuning in July 1918 on Leith Street, and eighteen-year-old Mary McGravie, who was arrested for keeping a brothel at 10 Gifford Park, were both sent to reside at the Dalbeth Home in Glasgow.[60]

As we have seen in chapter four, the Magdalene Asylum offered women in search of food and shelter an alternative to the poorhouse, but only if they could prove that they desired to leave prostitution and to become a 'reformed', 'respectable' member of the working class. For those who did not qualify or want admission into reform homes, the poorhouse remained the place of last resort for women who had no other source of support. Whereas some women only appeared in the poor law records once or twice during particularly difficult periods, others needed more regular assistance. The case of Margaret Mackie provides a good example of a woman who spent time in the poorhouse on various different occasions throughout her life. After Margaret Mackie was abandoned by her husband in London, she came to her native Glasgow where she struggled to support herself via prostitution and spent several periods in the poorhouse. Her first entry into the poor house was in September 1893 and then again on two further occasions during August 1898 and April 1899. During these visits she was described as an alcoholic and suffering from a leg injury. After leaving the poorhouse, she then went back to London, only to return to the Glasgow poorhouse in July 1902 and November 1903. On this occasion she was still described as an alcoholic living off prostitution, but she was also described as a dressmaker. After 1903 she does not appear in the poor law records again for almost twenty years, and one might hope that this meant she was living in more comfortable circumstances, perhaps earning a living as a dressmaker. Unfortunately, the records reveal nothing about her life until she returns to the poorhouse in April 1924 and again in April 1925. After these admissions she was found work as a seamstress at the Salvation Army Home on London Street in Glasgow and received 15s weekly, but this employment did not last long and by April 1926 she was again in the poorhouse for a month until she received work as a seamstress at 10 Ball Street. In June 1927 she tried to gain admission to the Edinburgh Magdalene Asylum but she was sent again to the poorhouse because she was over the Asylum's age limit. Margaret died on 16 August 1927, aged sixty-two.[61] As the poor law records have been used to compile this example, the evidence to some extent highlights economic hardship. Nonetheless, these records show that poverty and reliance on the poor law continued to be a common experience for women involved in prostitution well into the twentieth century.

Prison was another experience shared by many of the women involved in prostitution. As we saw in chapter two, the majority of the women who committed soliciting offences were given fines, with the most common sentence being a fine of forty shillings. However, prison sentences were commonly given to repeat offenders, and the women who could not afford to pay their fines within the allotted timeframe were sent to prison in default of payment for a maximum of forty days (although many women managed to pay their fines before having to serve the full forty days). Therefore, whilst those women who earned higher amounts could avoid prison, those with lower and less reliable incomes ended up in prison more frequently. Nonetheless, even relatively well-off women could find themselves in prison on some occasions, especially if the judge decided to make an example of a particular woman by giving her a prison sentence without the option of a fine. Whilst the material conditions within women's prisons had slightly improved since the nineteenth century, they were still far from pleasant.[62] Long periods of cellular confinement and regular punishments remained common, and women who experienced prison during this period wrote of the 'joyless, monotonous, severe oppression of prison life'.[63]

Relationships between Prostitution and Other Forms of Crime

The Edinburgh Police Criminal Conviction Registers show that some women convicted of importuning had very long criminal histories that included over 200 offences in some cases. However, the majority of the women had a lower number of offences, with ranges of anywhere between five and fifty being more usual. The most common types of offences aside from importuning were theft, obscene behaviour, breach of the peace, drunk and disorderly behaviour or physical violence of varying types. For example, between 1902 and 1912 Madge Thomson, aged eighteen at the time of her first offence, was convicted of fifty-eight offences.[64] Whereas thirty-two of these were for importuning, the remaining twenty-six were for crimes such as theft, drunkenness and disorderly behaviour. Similarly, between 1900 and 1924 Agnes Duff, aged nineteen at the time of her first offence, was convicted on 118 occasions.[65] Thirty-five of these offences were prostitution-related but the remaining eighty-three included offences such as drunk and incapable and indecent behaviour. Several women were also convicted of crimes of a more violent nature. For instance, Janet Cranston was convicted of assaulting a woman and a boy, and Janet Mannock was convicted of assaulting a man and a girl.[66]

The majority of the women did not have prostitution recorded as their first crime; instead, it was usually a minor offence, such as disorderly behaviour or drunk and incapable. The Glasgow Duke Street Prison registers show that the average number of previous convictions for women convicted of importuning was 27.1 in 1903, 28.3 in 1911, 17.8 in 1921 and 24.6 in 1931.[67] On the one hand, this may suggest that it was only once women were already implicated in petty crime and 'anti-social' behaviour that they became involved in prostitution. Judith Walkowitz supports that assertion, arguing that in England during the nineteenth century women often became involved in prostitution slowly, once they had already been drawn into other types of crime and were thus gradually introduced to the environment and community surrounding prostitution.[68] The considerable number of women who had a high number of convictions for offences other than prostitution would suggest that this was also the case in Scotland during the early twentieth century. However, this does not explain the cases where women had no or very few previous convictions before being convicted for prostitution. In these cases, it is possible to infer that it was their involvement in prostitution that had led them to commit further crimes. For example, Frances Finnegan has shown that in York during the nineteenth century theft was a common side occupation for women who robbed the men they solicited.[69] Easy access to men's valuables whilst they were vulnerable and otherwise occupied gave women an opportunity to supplement their earnings from prostitution. The high number of women involved in prostitution who also had theft offences recorded in the Criminal Conviction Registers suggests that this continued to be the case in the twentieth century.

The Criminal Conviction Registers, however, primarily refer only to women who had been arrested and convicted frequently for prostitution and various other crimes. Firstly, this means that they do not include the women who were skilful at avoiding detection. Secondly, once women had come under the surveillance of the police, their likelihood of being 'caught' for crimes such as theft would have increased, meaning that the number of crimes committed by women involved in prostitution might have become over-represented in the registers. Thirdly, the registers tell us very little about the many women engaged in prostitution who may not have been involved in theft, or other crimes. For those women with only very short conviction histories, their previous convictions might simply have reflected the fact that until the police were certain that a woman was a 'common prostitute', they often charged her with other minor offences, such as breach of the peace, to ensure that they were not accused of falsely arresting women who were not 'common prostitutes'. Similarly, the number of violent crimes committed by women involved in prostitution may not necessarily have been any higher than those committed by other working-class women during this period.[70] Nonetheless, whether or not prostitution led to involvement in other crimes or vice versa, it is clear that many of the women who engaged in prostitution also committed various other types of offences throughout their involvement in prostitution. Court appearances and prison sentences therefore played a noticeable role in many of these women's lives.

Case Studies: Mary Mullaney, Jane Darroch and Edith Boyd

Despite their flaws, the Criminal Conviction Registers do offer more details about the women's lives other than simply their individual criminal histories. Several of the entries span the majority of the women's adult lives, and by examining these case files in more depth it is possible to begin to piece together the role that prostitution played throughout the course of their lives.

Mary Mullaney

Mary Mullaney was born in Midlothian in 1884 to parents James and Bridget Mullaney. Her father is described as a mason's labourer and her mother a housekeeper. By the time the 1901 census was taken, her father had died and the family were living in Edinburgh. Just one year later, on 18 July 1902, nineteen-year-old Mary married twenty-one-year-old William Nicolson, a mason's labourer. At this point, Mary was working as a bag maker and already had a considerable number of convictions. Mary's first run-in with the law occurred in 1899, aged fifteen, when she was arrested for assaulting a police officer.[71] This was followed by a series of other offences, mainly involving alcohol, disorderly behaviour and theft. In 1901 she was convicted for being drunk in charge of a child and for attempted suicide. In 1905 she was again convicted for attempted suicide. There were also several convictions for assault, one of which was for assaulting her husband, William Nicholson. Her first prostitution conviction did not occur until 1909, when she was aged twenty-five. Between 1909 and 1919 she was convicted of thirteen prostitution offences and of a wide range of other crimes, such as theft and assault. Mary died on 11 January 1920, aged just thirty-six.[72]

Jane Darroch

Jane Darroch was born in 1885 and was first convicted for disorderly behaviour in 1899, aged fourteen.[73] Between 1899 and her first prostitution offence in 1913, aged twenty-eight, she was convicted ninety-seven times for a variety of different offences, including breach of the peace, assault, theft and indecent behaviour; crimes which often resulted in her being sent to gaol. It is unclear whether her first prostitution offence reflects the date of her movement into prostitution, or simply the first time she was caught and prosecuted.

However, the substantial list of previous convictions would suggest that Jane was involved in other crimes from a young age and had gradually moved towards working in prostitution. In 1908, aged twenty-three, Jane was convicted for being drunk in charge of a child. Between 1913 and 1920, Jane was convicted for prostitution offences on sixteen different occasions, meaning it was likely that between the ages of at least twenty-eight and thirty-five, Jane continued to be involved in prostitution. It is uncertain whether Jane was employed in other occupations during this period; however, the disruption that would have resulted from the frequent convictions and prison sentences for importuning, theft, drunkenness and disorderly behaviour would have made it difficult to keep any steady form of 'respectable' employment. In 1922 she was charged with begging, and her final conviction in 1932 was for being drunk and incapable. Although Jane's convictions for prostitution ended in 1920, aged thirty-five, her subsequent convictions for begging and being incapable do not suggest that she left prostitution for more prosperous prospects. On 16 December 1932 she died, aged forty-seven.[74]

Edith Boyd

Edith Boyd was born in 1883 and was first convicted of stealing a petticoat in Glasgow in 1898, aged fifteen.[75] As punishment for this crime, she was sent to the Dalry Reformatory. However, she absconded from the reformatory on two occasions, after which she was sent to another reformatory in Aberdeen, where she again absconded. In May 1900 she was convicted of assaulting a man, followed by eight more convictions for offences such as breach of the peace and theft. In September 1901, aged eighteen, Edith was convicted of a prostitution offence for the first time and sent to prison for seven days. However, by this point prison would have become a familiar experience for Edith, as her previous convictions had carried sentences of up to thirty days. In April 1903 she was convicted for brothel-keeping and sentenced to sixty days in prison, followed by six further convictions for importuning offences during 1904 and 1905. From 1906 to 1915 she was continually convicted of importuning and other offences, such as theft and disorderly conduct, until her final prostitution offence on 7 December 1912. Several days later, on 19 December 1912, she was again arrested, but this time for being drunk in charge of a child. Over the next few years she was convicted of being drunk and incapable and of the theft of a fountain pen. Her last conviction was in December 1919 for the theft of money and the assault of a woman. At that point, Edith disappeared from the records, aged thirty-six.

From these case studies it is possible to see the emergence of common themes relating to women's involvement in crime and prostitution. The types of offences they committed highlight the fact that alcohol, violence, poverty and theft commonly featured in their lives and that a pattern of regular convictions and prison sentences would have made it difficult to uphold long-term 'respectable' employment. In the cases of Mary Mullaney and Jane Darroch, their long lists of convictions prior to the first prostitution conviction suggest that they were already involved in other crimes before they turned to prostitution. Edith Boyd also had several convictions prior to her first prostitution offence; however, her first conviction for prostitution happened at a much younger age than those of the other two women. Edith is also different from the other two women in that she was sent to various juvenile institutions and her case is a particularly good example of how these institutions were not necessarily successful in reforming juveniles or stopping reoffending. Nonetheless, this type of 'institutionalisation' was likely to have have had an impact upon her life, even if the institutions failed to provide the correctional influence they were designed to deliver.

The Criminal Conviction Registers also reveals details about the women's family lives, such as marital status or whether they had children. Whilst it can be misleading to infer too much from the women's conviction histories, the numerous drinking offences, assaults and attempted suicides do suggest that they all went through some personal difficulties during this period. Nonetheless, this tells us very little about their actual thoughts or feelings, and their own voices remain masked. Although offences such as attempted suicide might suggest that women felt depressed, it is misleading to view these women's emotions through our own understanding or expectations.

Whilst many of the cases in the Criminal Conviction Registers show a similar cycle of poverty, illness, crime and deprivation, not all of the women employed in prostitution had such long criminal records. Some women escaped conviction altogether and others had only very few minor convictions. For example, Mary Ann Clark was first convicted of disorderly conduct in 1902, aged twenty-four, and received her first prostitution conviction in 1903. During the next four years she was convicted of prostitution offences on nine more occasions and received four other sentences for being incapable and for the theft of whisky. The short criminal records of women such as Mary Ann Clark, and many others like her, suggest that these women only resorted to prostitution for a short time and left once other opportunities arose. Alternatively, in some cases their sudden absence from the records may reflect their successful avoidance of police surveillance by moving to other cities or working in a more clandestine environment. It is important to remember, therefore, that the Criminal Conviction Registers only represent the experiences of those women who had been 'caught' and whose convictions had been recorded. The Criminal Conviction Registers tell us little about the women who successfully avoided detection by the police and consequently had different experiences to those women who were frequently arrested. Chapter six will explore further the experiences of women who were involved in clandestine prostitution in dance clubs and were consequently less vulnerable to police persecution.

'Bullies' and 'Pimps'

During the late nineteenth and early-twentieth centuries there was mounting concern about the dangers of the 'vicious pimp'. As we have seen, fears about 'white slavery' were widespread and resulted in the setting up of international organisations and legislation to combat this danger. In Scotland between 1909 and 1912 social purity groups launched a major campaign to fight immoral traffic, resulting in the 1910 Immoral Traffic (Scotland) Amendment Bill being incorporated into the 1912 Criminal Law Amendment Act. The Act increased the punishment for men prosecuted under the Immoral Traffic Act and reintroduced flogging to Scotland. However, despite this moral panic, Judith Walkowitz and Edward Bristow have shown that the actual number of instances where women were drugged or tricked by pimps into travelling abroad and being forced into prostitution was relatively low.[76] Nonetheless, the hype generated by these fears led to a preoccupation with the activities of pimps and the creation of stereotypes, many of which were inherently racist and anti-Semitic.[77] Unfortunately, little concrete information is available about the actual lives of 'pimps' or their relationships with the women whom they exploited. However, the following case studies will begin to provide some insight into the lives of the men who lived off the earnings of prostitution and their relationships with the women they sought to exploit.

Thomas Gallacher, Henry Fair and Robert Ross

Thomas Gallacher was born in 1885 and, by 1899, aged fourteen, he was convicted of his first offence for malicious mischief.[78] Between 1889 and 1934 he was convicted of sixty-eight offences and the wide variety of different crimes he committed tells us more about his criminal and personal history. In May 1909 he was convicted under the Immoral Traffic Act for living off the immoral earnings of prostitution. His numerous convictions for theft and armed robbery suggest that he was also involved in a range of other crimes. Additionally, his desertion from the army in May 1915, his assault of a police officer and several convictions for disorderly behaviour and malicious mischief suggest that he held little respect for the law in general. His conviction history also confirms that he was a violent man who used violence to control and intimidate women. Overall, he was convicted of twenty-three different instances of assault, three of which were for assaulting his 'paramour', in 1916, 1918 and 1919, and a fourth for assaulting his wife in 1920. From the information known about Gallacher's violent and 'criminal' behaviour, it would appear that he certainly fitted the stereotype of the 'vicious' pimp.[79]

The conviction history of Henry Fair suggests that he, too, fitted the vicious pimp stereotype.[80] Born in 1880, Fair was described as a 'labourer' and was first convicted in 1898, aged eighteen, of desertion from the army and assaulting his wife. In March 1902 he was convicted under the Immoral Traffic Act, which happened again in January 1911 and November 1911. Between the time of his first conviction in 1898 and his last in 1914, he was convicted on thirty-six different occasions. The crimes he committed included stabbing his wife and several other assaults on women, assaulting a police officer, fraud, theft and embezzlement. Like Gallacher, Fair was a very violent man who was involved in a wide range of criminal activities, a fact that certainly supports the assertion that, at least in these two cases, there was truth behind the stereotype of pimps as abusive and dangerous men.

However, not all the men convicted of immoral traffic offences were as 'vicious' as Fair and Gallacher. Robert Ross, born in 1885, was described in the Criminal Conviction Registers as a 'waiter' and was first convicted of breach of the peace in 1900, aged fifteen.[81] In November 1908 he was convicted under the Immoral Traffic Act for living off the earnings of prostitution. Although Ross began to commit offences at an early age and continued to commit other minor offences, such as trespassing and the theft of a bicycle, eggs and some ink, he had far fewer convictions than either Fair or Gallacher and no convictions for more serious or violent crimes. Although this does not prove that Ross did not abuse the women off whose immoral earnings he lived (as much violence against women went unreported or undetected by the police), his criminal record at least suggests that he was generally less violent than Fair and Gallacher.

Whilst the role of the 'pimp' necessitated a certain level of exploitation, not all women entered into such a relationship unwillingly. There were many reasons why a woman may have chosen to live with a man and to support him from her earnings. Here, Victoria Harris's argument that in Germany not all 'pimp-prostitute' relationships were based solely on abuse and exploitation appears to be applicable to Scotland, too.[82] The presence of a man who could watch out for the police or provide protection from violent clients would have been beneficial for business and personal safety. What is more, relationships were often based on more than business alone, and the women were sometimes romantically involved with the men who acted as their 'pimps'. Whilst the seduction and emotional manipulation of women could be a tactic used by 'pimps' to control women, the wording of the Immoral Traffic Act meant that any man who lived with a prostitute and could not prove that he was financially independent was liable to be convicted. Therefore, even those men who were married to women involved in prostitution but did not necessarily encourage, manipulate or force them to sell sex, could be arrested under the Act. For instance, in 1902 twenty-eight-year-old Lewis Brash was sentenced to three months' imprisonment for living off the immoral earnings of his wife, twenty-five-year-old Ann Brash, a 'known prostitute'.[83] During the trial, Police Constable Cattanach described how 'he had known the accused and his wife for the past eighteen months. The latter was a convicted prostitute and the accused lived with her at a house in Earl Grey Street in Edinburgh which was conducted as a brothel.'[84] The Criminal Conviction Registers confirms that Ann had been involved in prostitution since 1899.[85] However, during her witness testimony, Ann explained that 'she never gave her husband any money, because he did not require it. He worked himself and supplied her with money. He also went the messages.'[86] Brash explained that he was a commercial traveller who sold watches and won money through gambling; however, when the magistrates pressed the matter further, it became apparent that he only had one watch to sell and little else. Brash was found guilty, but whether he actually forced his wife onto the streets to support him remains unclear. Whilst it is possible that Ann's testimony in support of her husband was given because she feared the consequences of testifying against him, there is no evidence to suggest that Brash was violent towards her, and it is entirely plausible that Ann genuinely wanted to prevent her husband from being convicted.

Another case which involved a married couple was that of Otto Hall and Nellie Hall. In March 1913 Hall, a sixty-year-old German 'general dealer and broker', was found guilty of living off the immoral earnings of his wife, Nellie Hall, a 'known prostitute'.[87] He was sentenced to six months' imprisonment and was to be deported to Berlin on completion of his sentence (which was later shortened to three months). Hall's appeal against his conviction was unsuccessful; however, his witness statement provides some interesting details about the couple's relationship. Firstly, Hall argued that he did not need the earnings of his wife because his general dealer and broker business in Edinburgh at 45 Thistle Street provided 'considerable income'.[88] Secondly, he contested his wife's evidence against him, stating that she had 'become antagonistic to him since she persuaded him recently to convey his whole fortune and effects *inter vivo* to her and also make his will in her favour absolutely.'[89] Hall also provided official legal documents and bank books to back up his statement. It is possible that Hall was lying to help his case for an appeal and the court documents alone tell us little about the complexities of the couple's relationship. Nevertheless, the will and the other documents do suggest that in this particular situation it may have been Hall who was the 'victim' rather than Nellie. Little is known about Nellie but the convenient imprisonment and deportation of her relatively elderly husband shortly after he had signed over his property to her certainly sounds suspicious. The judge did not think that this was sufficient grounds for Hall's release and sent him back to prison to serve the remainder of his sentence. The fact that he was a German man in 1913, during a time of high tension between Germany and Britain, may have had some influence on the judge's decision. This case in particular illustrates how it is not possible to classify all 'pimp' and 'prostitute' relationships according to black and white notions of 'victim' and 'abuser'. The following two case studies will shed further light on the lives of the men and women involved in prostitution and on the complexity of their relationships.

May McArthur and James Clinton

We shall now return to the case of May McArthur, whose story was briefly introduced at the start of the chapter. May was born in Alloa in May 1896 to parents Mary and Archibald McArthur, an iron-moulder from Glasgow. By the 1911 census May was working at a stocking factory and living at 421 Main Street, Alloa, in a two-room apartment with her aunt and uncle, fifty-seven-year-old letter collector John Irvine and sixty-four-year-old caretaker Jessie Irvine. Little else is recorded about May until her appearance in 1919 as a witness in the trial against James Clinton, who was accused under the Immoral Traffic Act of living off the immoral earnings of her prostitution. During the hearing, in addition to McArthur's witness statement which outlined how she had been forced into prostitution by James Clinton, an anonymous letter which had been received by the police in May 1919 was read aloud to the court:

> Dear Sirs,
>
> I write this note to let you know that there is a fellow in the Canongate if you caught him you would be catching a right scoundrel. He is un [sic] old timer at Rayants the prison, he takes the name of Clinton, I think his first name is James, he is living with a girl the name off McArthur . . . and she has a boy with him. Believe this letter to be genuine, you will catch him if you go down to New Street no. 38 the top flat and ask for McArthur, that is the girl's name. [sic]
>
> From a Canongate person who knows them both.[90]

The police then informed the court of the observations they had made whilst the couple had been under surveillance. They described how Clinton had:

> been living with the prostitute May Macarthur at 38 New St, and during that time I have not known him to do any work. I have frequently seen him loitering about the street during the day and in the company of the prostitute Macarthur. This prostitute has on two occasions, 5 May and 6 May, complained to me regarding accused forcing her to go onto the streets and earn money by prostitution in order to keep him as he would not go out to look for work. I have no doubt by what I have been told by the prostitute, and seen of accused myself, that he is living entirely on the earnings of her prostitution.[91]

Additional police statements described how on one occasion Clinton 'violently held her by the throat and compress[ed] her throat and with his fist did strike her one or more blows on the left eye whereby the said witness was hurt and her left eye discoloured.'[92]

Mary and John Kelly

On 23 July 1919, John Kelly was tried under the Immoral Traffic (Scotland) Act 1912 for living off the immoral earnings of his wife Mary Kelly.[93] During the trial, witness testimonies were given by several police officers but also by nineteen-year-old Mary Kelly and her fifty-two-year-old widowed neighbour, Jane Millar or Cunningham. The statements made by these two women describe their experiences in great detail and are worth quoting in full:

> **Mary Kelly**
> I married accused on 22 June 1918 in Edinburgh. He was then a private in the Royal Field Artillery and stationed at Redford barracks. I was a member of the Women's Army Auxiliary Corps and had only knew [sic] him for three weeks and only married him for the purpose of being discharged from the corps mentioned. I then left Edinburgh and returned about four months ago when accused was discharged, and we resided together in a furnished room at 4 Old Broughton. About 5 weeks ago we removed to a house of our own at 4 Simpson's Court Potterrow. Accused was discharged from the army about 5 months ago, since when he has never done any work, but has been in receipt of unemployment benefit to the extent of 29/-per week. About a month ago he forced me to go on the streets and act as a prostitute and I so conducted myself and handed over to him money which I had earned in that way. I usually frequented Princes Street and Tollcross district and accused followed me on the streets while I was accosting, the arrangement being that on my picking up a man he left and would

meet me at some pre-arranged spot later in the night or in the early morning. He was of drunken habits and frequently assaulted me and sneered at me for being of little use as a prostitute.[94]

Jane Millar
About 6 weeks ago the accused and his wife came to reside next door to me. During that time I am aware that he has never done any work but draws out work benefit. He is addicted to drink and I have frequently heard him assaulting her. About a week ago I heard thuds as if he was striking her and she was screaming and on going to the door of their house in order to assist her I found it locked. A little later she showed me marks all over her body which she said had been caused by accused because she would not go to the streets as often as he wished to act as a prostitute and bring in money . . . The accused would never allow his wife to go out of the house by herself and they both usually left the house together as darkness was coming down and returned together at various times after mid-night . . . I have repeatedly advised her to go away and leave him.[95]

Unfortunately there is little more recorded information about Mary Kelly, but the Edinburgh Burgh Court records do tell us more about John Kelly. In 1893 he was convicted of assault by stabbing, and in 1899 of assaulting a woman. During 1914 and 1917 he was again convicted of assault, this time for assaulting a woman and a policeman. The witness statements demonstrate how he violently attacked Mary on several occasions and would not let her leave the house without him. He not only abused her physically but also verbally insulted and 'sneered' at her. Like Fair and Gallacher, Kelly was clearly a violent man, and the use of violence was an important tactic in coercing women into handing over their earnings from prostitution. Even though her neighbour repeatedly encouraged Mary to leave, she was unable to do so.

Interestingly, John Kelly had already been brought before the Edinburgh Police Court for a similar offence in March 1912, and the records describe how he had evaded conviction 'on account of the prostitute with whom he was then living going back on her statement'.[96] The difficulty of assuring that women would testify against their 'bully' was something of which the police and magistrates were well aware. In many situations, fear of reprisal stopped women from coming forward or giving evidence. Alternatively, some women held strong personal affections and commitments to their 'bullies' and were reluctant to see them prosecuted. However, McArthur and Kelly's willingness to involve the police and testify in court suggests that some women used their knowledge of the immoral traffic laws to their advantage. Their ability to threaten the 'bullies' with informing the police about their illegal activities would have given the women some power. Whilst May McArthur and Mary Kelly were clearly subjected to violence and exploitation at the hands of men who forced them into prostitution and lived off their earnings, both women testified against these men and helped to secure their convictions under the Immoral Traffic Act. May McArthur's evidence was enough to secure a conviction, and James Clinton was given a fine of £5, or, in default of payment, a prison sentence of thirty days. Considering the violent behaviour of their 'bullies', this must have taken great courage, and although these women suffered violent abuse, their actions demonstrated considerable agency, even when their options were extremely limited. In the case of Nellie Hall, it is even possible that she used the Immoral Traffic Act to rid herself of a husband for whom she no longer had any use once she had taken legal ownership of his possessions.

If we continue to follow May McArthur's story further, we see that on 29 November 1919, McArthur was charged with keeping and managing her house at 38b New Street as a brothel and harbouring Cecelia Wood for the purposes of prostitution.[97] Her continued engagement in prostitution after the arrest of Clinton suggests that the policy of arresting 'bullies' on its own did not necessarily help women to exit prostitution. It is not clear why May and other women continued in prostitution; however, there are some likely reasons that might have made it difficult or undesirable for her to leave. Most crucially, the socio-economic factors that led women to enter prostitution in the first place did not change simply as a result of the arrest of their 'bullies'. As described earlier in the chapter, the low and irregular wages that women could expect to earn in most traditional female working-class occupations would have meant that the higher wages of prostitution remained attractive even after the arrest of their 'bullies'. In the case of May McArthur, it appears that remaining involved in prostitution offered an opportunity to improve her economic position, allowing her to earn money by renting a room to another woman. However, whether this represented a type of career progression or demonstrated the difficulty that women faced when trying to find other types of work once they had been involved in prostitution is uncertain and undoubtedly depended on the women's individual circumstances.

In the case of May McArthur, however, her continued involvement in prostitution during 1919 did not appear to have any long-lasting negative influence on her future ability to find work or a husband. On 14 November 1921, twenty-five-year-old May McArthur, now a letter press printer feeder, married thirty-three-year-old George Thomson, a widower journeyman. They lived together in Shettleston and had one daughter. May died in

Glasgow in 1961 from coronary artery thrombosis, aged sixty-five. Although we have few details about May's subsequent life, the fact that she was able to find respectable employment, marry and begin a family shows that an involvement in prostitution during her teenage years did not disqualify her from later securing all the traditional markers of success, such as marriage and motherhood, that were seen to distinguish a respectable working-class woman's life.

Brothels and Brothel-Keepers

During the early twentieth century the depictions of brothels in popular media were often quite contradictory. Those concerned about the dangers of immorality and the oppression of women portrayed brothels as depraved, dangerous places where women were sold into slavery and shadowy villains lurked around every corner. The discourses surrounding the 'white slave trade' panics during the late nineteenth and early-twentieth centuries enthusiastically embraced the stereotypes of 'vicious madams' and 'predatory bullies' entrapping young women in brothels and forcing them into a life of deprivation. Most infamously, W.T Stead's exposé of child prostitution in the series of articles published in the *Pall Mall Gazette*, entitled 'The Maiden Tribute of Modern Babylon', used the case of Eliza Armstrong to describe how poor young girls were being abducted and forced to work in foreign brothels.[98] It was later discovered that Stead had arranged the abduction and sale of Eliza into prostitution as a stunt to highlight the issue of child prostitution. However, although this particular example was fabricated, the image of the highly organised brothel dealing in the sale of child prostitutes remained influential. Conversely, during the same period, some popular literature represented brothels as exciting, titillating places populated by beautiful young women, who under the supervision of a 'madam' waited to be chosen by the wealthy patrons who arrived at the premises. For example, Evelyn Waugh's *Brideshead Revisited* and Oscar Wilde's *The Picture of Dorian Gray* focus on the men's enjoyment of these decadent surroundings and their potential to corrupt men, rather than on the oppression of women.[99]

These popular representations of brothels had little grounding in reality. The type of large, well-organised establishments which housed many women were more closely associated with a continental style of brothel than a British one. In countries such as France and Germany these types of brothels played an important part in the regulatory system which aimed to confine prostitution to a particular location and to limit the spread of venereal disease by medically inspecting the women and providing licenses accordingly.[100] Scotland, however, never had this type of regulation and none of these large 'continental style' brothels appear in the police or court records. In their place were a variety of different indoor premises.

In Scotland, local byelaws were used to legislate against brothels. In Edinburgh the keeping of brothels was forbidden under section 278 of the Edinburgh Municipal and Police Act of 1879 and, in Glasgow, section 137 of the Glasgow Police Act 1866 criminalised anyone who owned, managed or assisted the keeping of brothels. In addition to these local byelaws, the 1885 Criminal Law Amendment Act made brothel-keeping illegal at the national level. At first the definition of a 'brothel' was left uncertain; however, the 1895 case of *Singleton* v. *Ellison* ruled that a brothel should be defined as a house that was 'frequented and used for the purposes of prostitution by men and women other than the woman occupying the house'.[101] These loose criteria meant that small private flats or furnished rooms which housed more than one woman who was known to engage in prostitution could be legally defined as brothels and the occupants prosecuted as brothel-keepers.

The statements made by the police whilst compiling evidence against these 'brothels' provide very detailed accounts of the different types of establishments that existed. The size of these flats and the number of women who lived or worked in them varied considerably. They ranged from small one-room flats occupied by two women to larger premises with many rooms and several women. The latter example was quite rare, and a majority of the flats had only one or two rooms, occupied by two or three women. For example, the brothel at 5 Prospect Terrace, Edinburgh, consisted of 'a room, kitchen, and a small bed-room, and a shake-down in the room.'[102] A brothel at 40 Jamaica Street was described as a 'single apartment'[103] and another at Scott's Close was again described as consisting of only 'one apartment'.[104] Other brothels were slightly larger. For example, it was reported that four women, 'Evelyn Gibb, Margaret Robertson, Nellie Welsh and Margaret Muir', resided at the brothel at 47 St Stephen Street which was 'kept and managed' by Margaret Robertson. The brothel consisted of 'three apartments, kitchen, parlour and bedroom with a bed in each room'.[105]

Overall, the brothels described in the witness testimonies appear to have been little more than private homes or lodging houses which were used for prostitution and certainly not the large, well-organised businesses that existed on the continent. This is not necessarily to say that there were none of these establishments in Scotland; only that if there were, the police were not targeting them for prosecution. If they did exist, it is likely that they were more discreet in their operations and therefore fell outwith police surveillance. It is also possible that these types of brothels were frequented by rich and respected citizens, meaning it would not have been in the interests of the police to interfere. Similarly, it is possible to speculate that owners of more exclusive brothels had the money and influence to bribe the police, if necessary. However, as seen in chapter two, although there were rumours of bribery described in the autobiography of the former Edinburgh Chief Constable William Merrilees, there is no direct evidence to prove that bribery occurred in the Edinburgh police force.[106]

If the women could not afford to rent their own flats, they often lived in lodging houses. Lodging houses were originally designed for poor men, women and families to use as temporary accommodation when they could not afford to rent their own private lodgings. However, many of them gained a bad reputation and were associated with 'immoral activity', including prostitution. A significant number of the women arrested for importuning in Edinburgh and Glasgow were recorded as living in these types of premises. Two particular lodging houses which frequently appeared in the Edinburgh Burgh Court records were 17 James Court and 18 Blackfriars (both streets that lead off from the High Street in the Old Town). Although contemporaries certainly feared that these lodging houses were being used for prostitution, there is little evidence to prove the extent to which this actually happened. Instead, it is more likely that the women used other locations for work purposes and reserved the space at the lodging house for their private use. However, considering that it was common for women to solicit on the street and then bring the man to their place of residence, it is likely that at least some prostitution did occur there. The high number of women convicted of prostitution who lived at 17 James Court suggests that the owner (a woman called 'Cairns') must have known about the situation. Whether she was involved in engineering a situation that enabled her to profit from these

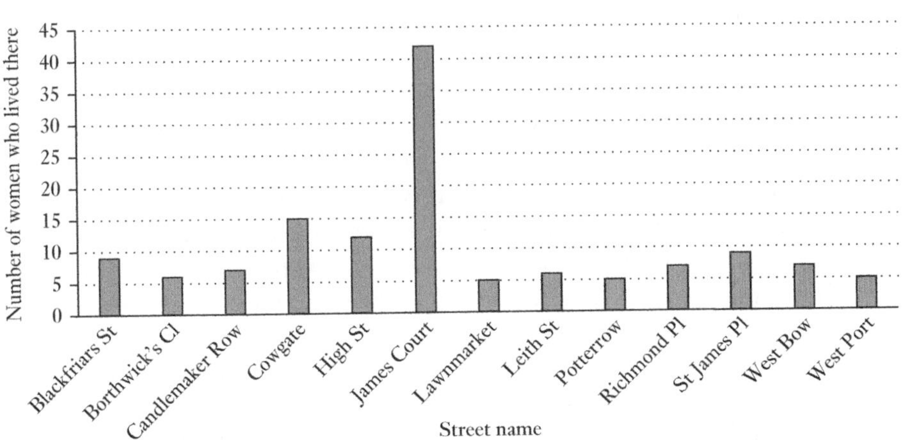

Figure 5.11 Home Addresses of Women Convicted for Importuning, Edinburgh, 1903–31.
Source: Edinburgh Burgh Court Records, 1903–31.

women's prostitution, or simply chose to turn a 'blind eye', remains uncertain. Nevertheless, whatever the individual situation in each lodging house, it is clear that lodging houses also played a role in facilitating prostitution in Edinburgh.

Whilst 'madams' were often associated with brothels, in a majority of the police reports, especially those relating to smaller flats, this 'madam'-type character did not exist. The small flats were often the women's own homes, and this can be seen by the number of witness statements which described the defendant as both a prostitute and a brothel-keeper. For example, Margaret Coutts was described by the police as 'a convicted prostitute and brothel-keeper.'[107] Whereas McArthur was labelled as the 'victim' during the immoral traffic trial, as a brothel-keeper she was seen as the one profiting from the exploitation of other women. McArthur's identity as both prostitute and brothel-keeper disrupted the assumed dichotomy between the two, highlighting the inadequacy of using the labels of 'victim' or 'villain' to describe individuals involved in prostitution and demonstrating how it was not always possible to draw a neat dividing line. The relationships which developed between women in these situations may have been ones of friendship and mutual support or, alternatively, more exploitative and business-oriented but, either way, the situation was clearly more complicated than a madam and prostitute dichotomy. In the larger brothels there was likely to be more scope for exploitation and a power dynamic more associated with the stereotypical 'madam/pimp-prostitute' relationship. However, several witness testimonies show that even in these situations the power relationship was not straightforward. For example, the larger brothel at 47 St. Stephen Street (mentioned above) was run by the seventy-five-year-old mother of one of the women who was working there as a prostitute.[108]

It was most frequently women who ran the brothels, but there were a few that were run by men or, more commonly, by a man and woman working together (often as husband and wife). There were even some court cases which described whole families living together in brothels, including grandparents and children.[109] For example, in November 1919 Patrick Stanley and Mary Stanley were accused of conducting their house at 30a Greenside Row in Edinburgh as a brothel and convicted of harbouring the prostitute Lily Barr. The police described how their house consisted of:

> Three apartments: one room, kitchen and bed closet off same, and with a bed in each apartment, during the said period the said Patrick Stanley and Mary Buckley or Stanley resided there with their children, Patrick Stanley aged 13, Thomas Stanley aged 10 and William Stanley aged 8 years.[110]

Rather than 'malicious madams', who, according to anti-white traffic propaganda, seduced women to work in their brothels and then forced them to stay against their will, the 'brothel-keepers' themselves could sometimes be the ones in difficult circumstances. For some women who were labelled as 'brothel-keepers', renting rooms to prostitutes may have been a necessary strategy to support their young families. For example, on 15 May 1925, Jane Meikle was charged with conducting her house at 40 Jamaica Street in Edinburgh as a brothel and harbouring a 'known prostitute' named Helen Thomson.[111] There are few details of the exact circumstances within the 'brothel' but it appears that there was only one woman working there, and it is likely that Jane Meikle was simply letting a room to this woman in order to help pay the rent since her husband had been killed during the First World War. However, the 1880 Industrial Schools Amendment Act and the 1908 Children Act meant that women in these situations were often harshly punished if the authorities discovered that they were allowing prostitutes to frequent their premises. Under the 1908 Act, children who were found to be residing in a 'brothel' or in 'immoral surroundings' could be forcibly removed and sent to an industrial school.[112] Consequently, George Shirran, the Chief Inspector of the Scottish Society for the Prevention of Cruelty to Children, petitioned the court to have the children removed from the home because he thought that Jane's brothel-keeping conviction meant that the children were 'living in circumstances calculated to cause, encourage or favour the seduction or prostitution of the said children.'[113] The petition was successful and Jane's two children, eight-year-old Elizabeth and seven-year-old Jeannie, were forcibly removed from her care and placed under the custody of the Minister of Pensions until the age of sixteen.

A similar case occurred in November 1919 when Mary and Stanley Buckley were charged with harbouring Lily Barr for the purposes of prostitution at their three-room residence at 30a Greenside Road in Edinburgh. Stanley was fined £10 with the alternative of 30 days imprisonment and Mary was fined £5 or 10 days. However, they were unable to pay their fines within the required seven-day period and were therefore both sent to gaol on 27 November 1919. It was decided that their children, Patrick, aged thirteen, Thomas, aged ten, and William, aged eight, should be removed from their care because they were 'living in circumstances calculated to cause, encourage, or favour their seduction or prostitution'. Subsequently, thirteen-year-old Patrick, who was described as having a 'bad character', was sent to the Mars Ship certified industrial school at Dundee and ten-year-old Thomas was sent to St. Joseph's certified industrial school in Haddingtonshire. There is nothing written about the fate of the youngest son, eight-year-old William.[114] Another similar case occurred in September 1915 when the three children of Margaret Fiddes were sent to an industrial school after she was imprisoned for sixty days for using her flat at 3 Northcote Street in Edinburgh for the purposes of prostitution.[115] In these and several other cases, there was little evidence to suggest that the potential danger posed to the children required the complete break-up of the family. Whilst the children may not have been living in ideal home environments, there may have been other, less detrimental ways to improve these families' living arrangements.

Rather than dangerous madams, the 'brothel-keepers' in these situations could be viewed as the victims of overzealous reformers who punished women whom they considered 'immoral mothers' and separated families unnecessarily. However, there were some cases in which the children's welfare was more obviously at risk and the removal of the children seemed more justifiable. For example, during 1916 and 1917 the probation report for Alexandria Stewart described how she solicited on the street with her eleven-year-old son and left the rest of her four children at home, 'with no one to look after them'.[116] The report also stated that Alexandria was frequently drunk, and on inspection of her home, the probation officer found it to be 'dirty', her 'children poorly clad and dirty', left alone in the house with only 'a small piece of bread' to eat.[117] Alexandria evidently had an alcohol addiction problem and was finding it difficult to care adequately for her four children by herself. In this instance, it seems that there was more evidence to support an intervention for the sake of the children's welfare.

Overall, the court records show that many brothels were little more than rooms to which women took the men they had solicited and they were frequently run by other poor working-class women and their families. Although many brothel-keepers certainly did exploit women, the majority of 'brothel-keepers' in these situations did not force the women to sell sex or treat them harshly, but rather took advantage of the higher rents that they could charge women who earned more money than the majority of other working-class tenants and who otherwise had difficulty finding accommodation. Arguably, this was not altogether that much different from other forms of rent exploitation that commonly occurred during the period.[118]

Community Attitudes towards Prostitution

The witness testimony given during the trial against John Kelly for living off the immoral earnings made by his wife is useful for illustrating how members of the local community could be sympathetic and understanding towards the plight of women involved in prostitution. In the case of Mary Kelly, her neighbour Jane Millar offered support and advice and was also willing to stand as a witness in court against Kelly's husband.[119] Similarly, the letter written by a concerned local resident, informing the police about the abusive behaviour of a local 'pimp', demonstrated the general hostility felt towards 'bullies' and the sympathy felt towards the 'victims' of these men.[120] In both situations, the neighbours were willing to defend the women involved in prostitution and recognised that these women needed help rather than condemnation.

However, these cases draw on the traditional notion of women as victims of 'evil bullies', and there is little evidence to indicate whether these neighbours would have been as sympathetic towards women who did not fit the victim stereotype. There is certainly evidence to suggest that not all neighbourhood relationships were friendly, especially if the women were causing a public nuisance and breaking gendered norms of respectable neighbourly behaviour. For example, in June 1917 Mrs Lithgow gave the following evidence against her neighbour, Jane Allan who was accused of keeping a brothel at 100 Marshall Street, Edinburgh, and harbouring Flora Wallis:

> About 2 months ago the woman Flora Wallis came to reside with accused, and shortly thereafter I became annoyed by men, mostly soldiers, who were brought to the house by the woman Wallis. I spoke to Mrs McPherson regarding the manner in which she was conducting her house, but she paid no attention. During the past month the conduct in the house became worse and I complained to the police as I was quite satisfied that accused was conducting her house as a brothel. I have a family of two young girls and a boy and in order to safeguard them and have a stop put to this immoral conduct, I am quite willing to appear at the police court as a witness.[121]

There was clearly no neighbourly solidarity in this situation; rather, Mrs Lithgow saw both Jane Allan and Flora Wallis as annoying pests who were a danger to her respectable young family.

In a few rare cases the Burgh Court records provide information about the family of a woman involved in prostitution and an insight into how they responded to the knowledge that their daughter was working in this fashion. Although surviving correspondence between parents, probation officers and magistrates is rare, the few documents that have survived show that the families often felt ashamed of their daughters. In 1920 John Livingston, the father of Elizabeth Livingstone or Emerson, wrote to the police to inform them that he could not take his daughter home, as requested.[122] He explained how the family had taken Elizabeth back 'a lot of times already and she made us sorry for it every time. There are four sisters here, all decent and hardworking lasses and it is more than likely they would leave the house if she came back. . . It might sound hard, but it is the only way.'[123] He also explained that his daughter had been married to a 'good husband' in New Zealand but had left him. John was evidently disappointed in his daughter's behaviour, and although the family was at first willing to forgive her if she changed her ways, her refusal to do so prevented him from allowing her to come home in case she disrupted the rest of his 'decent and hardworking' family. He appears to have seen prostitution as an indecent and lazy occupation, something to which a woman who had 'a good husband' did not need to resort.

Similarly, the parents of Margaret Ross described how 'they had given their daughter every chance and that unless she promised to mend her ways they will have no more to do with her'.[124] The Burgh Court Records described her parents as 'very respectable people' from Dundee, and it is clear that they could not reconcile their respectability with their daughter's behaviour. In these two cases, the parents refused to forgive their daughters unless they reformed. In the case of nineteen-year-old Elizabeth Moffat, her mother and sister both actively sought for 'Lizzie to go in a home' in the hope that it might spur her reformation.[125] In June 1916 Elizabeth's sister, Mrs Shepard, wrote to the probation officer to inform her that:

> Lizzie is misbehaving herself in a fearful way and making awful language to me and people of the street and I can't keep her in and I am not able to care for her . . . I told her dear Miss Hill that I would let you know about this carry on. She told me straight that she did not care neither [sic] for me, nor you, nor her mother . . . she will get me into trouble if she stays any longer here, a home is the place for her where there is [sic] no men.[126]

The letter suggests that Elizabeth resisted the reforming influence of her family and probation officer by continuing to see men and behaving in a 'fearful' and 'awful' manner. However, the family could not accept this type of disruptive behaviour and, like the Livingston family, were concerned about her corrupting influence. In both families, therefore, prostitution was seen as a potentially dangerous pollutant that threatened the reputation of their otherwise respectable families. Clearly, prostitution was not seen as an acceptable occupation by respectable working-class families. Nonetheless, in each case the families had tried on many occasions to give their daughters a second chance. It was their daughters' refusal to renounce their involvement in prostitution and to abide by their families' codes of respectability that caused the parents to forsake their daughters. However, the fact that they were repeatedly willing to offer second chances shows that prostitution was not necessarily seen as an unforgivable sin that resulted in irreversible exclusion from the family, and if their daughters had repented, they could have been welcomed back into the family.

Conclusion

By using case studies and extracts from a wide range of sources, it has been possible to piece together some of the reasons why women became involved in prostitution and what role it played in the course of their lives. Although each woman's story was unique, by exploring some of their collective and individual experiences, this chapter has highlighted several important themes. The women were mainly from working-class backgrounds and many experienced considerable hardship throughout their lives. In particular, ill-health, poverty, exploitation and abuse were experiences shared by many of the women involved in prostitution. Whilst rising wages, increasing female employment opportunities and the establishment of basic welfare benefits certainly helped some women during the early twentieth century, many did not benefit from these developments. Therefore, as in the nineteenth century, poverty, low wages, inequality and a lack of educational and economic opportunities remained a crucial underlying reason as to why women became, and remained, involved in prostitution.

Another significant theme is the importance that various institutions played in the lives of women engaged in prostitution, as the women frequently moved between reform homes, poorhouses, prisons and hospitals. The Criminal Conviction Registers show that many of the women became involved in a wide range of crimes and were often sent to gaol, a factor that made it hard to find other forms of 'respectable' work. In the latter half of the period studied here, women were increasingly placed on probation and sent to reformatories rather than to gaol but these institutions often failed to reform women in the intended way. Many women still had to resort to the poorhouse, and the records of these institutions show that the women often suffered ill-health and were unable to settle in one place for long. However, the chapter has also shown that women's involvement in prostitution was often only temporary and that their earnings from selling sex were frequently used to supplement their earnings from other occupations when employment was scarce. Consequently, some women only engaged in prostitution for relatively short periods during their lives and stopped once they married or found alternative steady employment. Moreover, the women's descriptions of themselves as cleaners, domestic servants or laundresses support the notion that the women involved in prostitution could identify with other working-class women and were not necessarily isolated from the rest of the working-class community. This flexibility and fluidity suggests that the women were not necessarily burdened with the stigma of having been involved in prostitution once they were no longer selling sex. The willingness of neighbours to sympathise with the plight of women involved in prostitution also suggests that the women were not necessarily outcasts from society. Although 'respectable' working-class families may have been ashamed of their daughters' involvement in prostitution, they were liable to forgive them if they reformed their behaviour.

Finally, the chapter has offered a rare glimpse into the experiences of the people involved in prostitution and questioned our understanding of relationships between 'bullies', 'brothel-keepers' and 'prostitutes'. The case studies have demonstrated the ways in which some 'bullies' violently abused, manipulated and exploited the women under their control. However, they have also shown that in some instances women managed to resist their control and used the law to help defend themselves. The relationships between 'bullies' and 'prostitutes' were often complicated and could involve situations in which power and control were not always in the hands of the men. Similarly, the relationships between 'brothel-keepers' and 'prostitutes' could be just as complex, and the women labelled as 'brothel-keepers' one day, could be labelled as 'prostitutes' another day. Although there were certainly elements of exploitation, the power balance between 'prostitutes' and 'brothel-keepers' was far from straightforward. The final chapter will explore these relationships further. The nature of the available sources has meant that this chapter has primarily focused on the experiences of women who were arrested and/or spent time in reformatories and poorhouses. However, the final chapter will examine the experiences of women who were less likely to come into contact with the authorities because they worked in more lucrative and clandestine locations, such as the Kosmo dance club.

Notes

1. Edinburgh City Archives (hereafter ECA), Edinburgh Burgh Court Records (EBCR), Case of James Clinton, 16 May 1919.
2. See the introduction for a detailed discussion and overview of feminist debates concerning prostitution.
3. Linda Mahood, *The Magdalenes: Prostitution in the Nineteenth Century* (London: Routledge, 1990); Judith Walkowitz, *Prostitution and Victorian Society: Women, Class, and the State* (Cambridge: Cambridge University Press, 1980); Victoria Harris, *Selling Sex in the Reich* (Oxford: Oxford University Press, 2010).
4. Glasgow City Archives (hereafter GCA), D-Hew 17/56 Glasgow Poor Law Records (hereafter GPLR), case of Mary Muirhead, p. 78,723.

5. Ibid.
6. GCA, D-Hew 16/12/12, GPLR, case of Mary Muirhead, p. 3,327.
7. Ibid.
8. National Records of Scotland (hereafter NRS), HH21/32 Duke Street Prison Register, 1907 and 1911.
9. GCA, D-Hew 16/12/12, GPLR, case of Mary Muirhead, p. 3,327.
10. ECA, EBCR, 2 February 1917.
11. GCA, Glasgow Magdalene Institute Annual Reports (hereafter GMIAR) for the years 1906, 1907, 1909, 1910.
12. Ibid.
13. ECA, EBCR, case of Margaret Ross, 8 March 1920; ECA, EBCR, case of Peggy Drummond, 12 December 1936.
14. For more on women's economic situation during this period see, for example, E. Breitenbach and E. Gordon (eds), *The World is Ill divided: Women's Work in Scotland in the Nineteenth and Early Twentieth Centuries* (Edinburgh: Edinburgh University Press, 1990).
15. GCA, GMIAR, 1906, 1907, 1909, 1910, 1915.
16. EBC, EBCR, case of Isabella Shepard, 27 October 1916, letter written by the probation officer, Reverend R. B. Mackinnon on 12 January 1917.
17. Ibid.
18. Ibid.
19. GCA, D-Hew 15/5/11–3167, GPLR case of Margaret Douglas.
20. GCA, D-Hew 17/424–25115, Glasgow Poor Law Records (hereafter GPLR), case of Agnes Fraser.
21. Ibid.
22. GCA, D-Hew 17/367–392, GPLR, case of Bridget Tolland.
23. ECA, EBCR, 15 October 1919, case of Elizabeth Prestell.
24. See, for example, Breitenbach and Gordon, *The World is Ill Divided.*
25. Ibid.
26. GCA, D-Hew 15/5/11–3167, GPLR, case of Margaret Mackie; GCA, D-Hew 17/424–25115, GPLR, case of Agnes Fraser.
27. ECA, EBCR, case of Margaret Robertson, 30 December 1914; ECA, EBCR, case of Margaret Campbell, 19 March 1920; ECA, EBCR, case of Jane Swanson, 1 December 1919.
28. GCA, T. PAR 1.16, p. 279, *Memorandum on A Social Evil in Glasgow, and the State of the Law for Dealing with Certain forms of Immorality*, pp. 5–6.
29. Ibid.
30. ECA, EBCR, case of Jane Swanson, December 1919.
31. Tony Henderson, *Disorderly Women in Eighteenth-Century London:*

Prostitution and Control in the Metropolis, 1730–1830 (London: Longman, 1999), p. 16.

32. Walkowitz, *Prostitution and Victorian Society*, p. 213.
33. GCA, D-Hew 16/7/7–2005 GPLR, case of Elizabeth Miller.
34. GCA, D-Hew 16/14/370–59733, GPLR, case of Ruby O'Connor.
35. Graham Walker, *Intimate Strangers: Political and Cultural Interaction Between Scotland and Ulster in Modern Times* (Edinburgh: John Donald, 1995), p. 65.
36. See, for example, Tom Gallagher, *Glasgow and the Uneasy Peace, Religious Tensions in Modern Scotland, 1819–1914* (Manchester: Manchester University Press, 1987); P. Panayi, *Immigration, Ethnicity and Racism in Britain, 1815–1845* (Manchester: Manchester University Press, 1994).
37. Walker, *Intimate Strangers*, p. 65.
38. NRS, Duke Street Prison Registers, 1903.
39. Ibid, 1911.
40. Ibid, 1921.
41. Ibid, 1931.
42. Walkowitz, *Prostitution and Victorian Society*, p. 196.
43. Ibid.
44. NRS, Duke Street Prison Registers, 1903.
45. Ibid, 1911.
46. Ibid, 1921.
47. Ibid, 1931.
48. GCA, D-Hew 16/13/358–53559, case of Elizabeth Erskine; GCA, D-Hew 16/6/3–733, case of Isabella Thompson; GCA, D-hew 16/6/3–720, case of Mary McAlister.
49. GCA, D-Hew 17/424–25115, case of Agnes Fraser; EBC, EBCR, case of Peggy Drummond, 12 December 1936.
50. Roger Davidson, *Dangerous Liaisons: a Social History of Venereal Disease in Twentieth-Century Scotland* (Amsterdam: Rodopi, 2000), p. 23.
51. Ibid, p. 18.
52. ECA, EBCR, case of Marion Ferguson, 28 June 1920; ECA, EBCR, case of Elizabeth Livingston, 22 March 1920.
53. Walkowitz, *Prostitution and Victorian Society*, p. 26.
54. See, for example, Neil McKeganey, 'Street Prostitution in Scotland: The Views of Working Women', *Drugs: Education, Prevention and Policy*, 13, 2 (2006) pp. 151–66; L. Holmes, 'A Tale of Three Cities: Regulating Street Prostitution in Scotland', *Scottish Affairs*, 52 (2005) pp. 71–88.
55. See, for example, T. C. Smout, *A Century of the Scottish People*

1830–1950 (London: Fontana, 1986); Brian Harrison, *Drink and the Victorians: The Temperance Question in England, 1815–1872* (London: Faber and Faber, 1971).

56. David Gutzke, '"The Cry of the Children": The Edwardian Medical Campaign against Maternal Drinking', *British Journal of Addiction* 79, 1 (1984) pp. 71–84.
57. David Gutzke, 'Gender, Class, and Public Drinking in Britain during the First World War', *Social History* 27, 54 (1994) pp. 367–91.
58. ECA, EBCR, case of Isabella McGregor, 25 August 1919.
59. ECA, EBCR, case of Isabella McGregor, letter written 17 December 1919.
60. ECA, EBCR, case of Mary McGravie, 13 July 1918.
61. GCA, D-Hew 16/6/6 p. 1565; D-Hew 15/5/11 p. 3,274; D-Hew 10/5/82 p. 144 GPLR case of Margaret Mackie.
62. See, for example, Norval Morris and David Rothman (eds), *The Oxford History of the Prison: The Practice of Punishment in Western Societies* (Oxford: Oxford University Press, 1995).
63. Bill Forsythe, 'Women Prisoners and Women Penal Officials 1840–1921', *British Journal of Criminology*, 33, 4 (1993) p. 532.
64. ECA, Edinburgh Police Criminal Conviction Registers (hereafter EPCCR) vol. 31, case of Madge Thompson.
65. ECA, EPCCR, vol. 31, case of Agnes Duff.
66. ECA, EPCCR, vol. 31, case of Janet Mannock; ECA, EPCCR, vol. 31, case of Janet Cranston.
67. NRS, HH21/32: Duke Street Prison Registers.
68. Walkowitz, *Prostitution and Victorian Society*, p. 212.
69. Frances Finnegan, *Poverty and Prostitution: A study of Victorian Prostitutes in York (Cambridge: Cambridge University Press, 1979)*, p. 109.
70. See, for example, Annmarie Hughes, 'Working Class Culture, Family and Domestic Violence on Clydeside, c. 1918–1939: A View from Below', *Scottish Tradition*, 27 (2002) pp. 60–90.
71. ECA, EPCCR, vol. 30, case of Mary Mullaney.
72. Ibid.
73. ECA, EPCCR, vol. 30, case of Jane Darroch.
74. Ibid.
75. ECA, EPCCR, vol. 29, case of Edith Boyd.
76. Edward Bristow, *Prostitution and Prejudice, the Jewish Fight against White Slavery, 1870–1939* (Oxford: Clarendon, 1982); Walkowitz, *Prostitution and Victorian Society*.
77. Bristow, *Prostitution and Prejudice*, p. 34.
78. ECA, EPCCR, vol. 30, case of Thomas Gallacher.

79. See for example, Bristow, *Prostitution and Prejudice*.
80. ECA, EPCCR, vol. 29, case of Henry Fair.
81. ECA, EPCCR, vol. 30, case of Robert Ross.
82. Harris, *Selling Sex in the Reich*, p. 78.
83. *The Scotsman*, 5 September 1902, p. 7.
84. Ibid, p. 7.
85. ECA, EPCCR, vol. 31, case of Ann Forbes.
86. Ibid. ['messages' is slang in Edinburgh and Glasgow for shopping].
87. NRS, JC31/1913/24, case of Otto Hall.
88. Ibid.
89. Ibid.
90. ECA. EBCR, case of James Clinton, 16 May 1919.
91. Ibid.
92. Ibid.
93. ECA, EBCR, case of John Kelly, 23 July 1919.
94. Ibid.
95. Ibid
96. Ibid.
97. ECA, EBCR, case of May McArthur, 29 November 1919.
98. William T. Stead, 'The Maiden Tribute of Modern Babylon', parts I-IV, *Pall Mall Gazette*, 6, 7, 8, 10 July 1885.
99. Evelyn Waugh's *Brideshead Revisited* (London: Chapman & Hall, 1945); Oscar Wilde, *The Picture of Dorian Gray* (London: Lippincott's, 1890).
100. Alain Corbin, *Women for Hire: Prostitution and Sexuality in France after 1850*, trans. Alan Sheridan (London: Harvard University Press, 1990); Harris, *Selling Sex in the Reich*.
101. *Singleton V Ellison* (1895) 59 JP 119, cited in Julia Laite, 'Prostitution in London, 1885–1930', PhD thesis (University of Cambridge, 2008), p. 69.
102. ECA, EBCR, case of Mary Watt, 8 March 1917.
103. ECA, EBCR, case of Jane Meikle, 22 May 1925.
104. ECA, EBCR, case of Margaret Foley, 1 December 1915.
105. ECA, EBCR, case of Margaret Robertson, 30 December 1914.
106. William Merrilees, *The Short Arm of the Law: The Memoirs of William Merrilees* (London: Long, 1966).
107. ECA, EBCR, case of Margaret Coutts and Margaret Jackson, 10 July 1919.
108. ECA, EBCR, case of Margaret Robertson, 30 December 1914.
109. ECA, EBCR, case of Patrick Stanley and Mary Stanley, 17 November 1919.
110. Ibid.

111. ECA, EBCR, case of Jane Meikle, 27 May 1925.
112. Linda Mahood, *Policing Gender, Class and Family: Britain, 1850–1940* (London: UCL Press, 1995).
113. Ibid.
114. ECA, EBCR, case of Mary and Stanley Buckly, 19 November 1919.
115. ECA, EBCR, case of Margaret Fiddes, 30 September 1915.
116. ECA, EBCR, case of Alexandria Stewart, 5 January 1918.
117. Ibid.
118. See, for example, J. Melling, *Rent Strikes: People's Struggle for Housing in West Scotland, 1890–1916* (Edinburgh: Polygon, 1983).
119. ECA, EBCR, case of John Kelly, 23 July 1919.
120. ECA, EBCR, case of James Clinton, 16 May 1919.
121. ECA, EBCR, case of Flora Wallis, 19 June 1917.
122. ECA, EBCR, case of Elizabeth Livingstone or Emerson, 13 March 1920.
123. Ibid.
124. ECA, EBCR, case of Elizabeth Livingstone or Emerson; ECA, EBCR, case of Margaret Ross, 8 March 1920.
125. ECA, EBCR, case of Elizabeth Moffat, 12 June 1916.
126. Ibid.

CHAPTER 6

Dance Clubs and Ice-cream Tubs: Clandestine Prostitution and the Kosmo Club[1]

The previous chapters have shown how wider socio-economic changes, especially developments in technology, commerce and entertainment, were as important as policing policies in shaping the ways in which prostitution was organised, controlled and experienced in Scotland during the early part of the twentieth century. A crucial element in all of this was the opening up of new opportunities for clandestine prostitution. By examining a particularly detailed court case relating to the Kosmo dance club in Edinburgh, this chapter will explore the role that dance clubs played in the development of new sites for clandestine prostitution and examine what influence this environment had on the experiences of the women who worked there. As we have seen, the experiences of women who sold sex are difficult to access and this is particularly true for those who worked clandestinely. The Kosmo trial, however, provides a rare glimpse of the ways in which these women negotiated the considerable dangers posed by this new environment and tells us more about the lives of women who were less likely to come to the attention of the police. The first half of the chapter will explore how various clandestine forms of indoor prostitution were organised and how these networks facilitated new methods for selling sex. The second section will focus on the experiences of women who worked at the Kosmo dance club and examine their relationships with the men who managed and frequented the club.

Clandestine Prostitution in Edinburgh and Glasgow

Whilst the previous chapters have primarily focused on prostitution that occurred on the street or in brothels, these were not the only locations in which prostitution took place. By the 1920s and 1930s new forms of indoor clandestine prostitution were occurring in ice-cream parlours, fish-and-chip shops, coffee shops and dance clubs. It was believed that the rooms above or behind these shops were used for prostitution and that these venues particularly attracted young women who were vulnerable to the advances of the 'immoral types' who owned and frequented these places. It was assumed that, once seduced by these men, the women would then engage in prostitution there. The venues that were most commonly singled out for suspicion were shops run predominantly by minority groups, especially the Italians who owned ice-cream parlours and fish-and-chip shops. It was these 'foreigners' who were described as 'immoral types', and the xenophobic nature of the criticism of these venues was never far from the surface.[2] Perhaps the best example of the fears associated with seemingly innocent venues such as ice-cream parlours was the 'Memorandum on a Social Evil in Glasgow, and the State of the Law for Dealing with Certain Forms of Immorality', published in 1911 by Glasgow Parish Council. The report described how it was 'well known that temperance and ice-cream shops [were] being used as brothels', and that 'most of the offenders against the Immoral Traffic Act [were] foreigners and Jews.'[3] The 'evidence' for this statement was provided by several descriptions of particular cases where women had been seduced in these types of premises. For example, the report detailed how one girl had been:

> leading an immoral life for about 6 months. She 'got into a bad company of girls' and was advised by a friend to 'go with Brazilian sailors for immoral purposes.' She was first taken advantage of in an ice-cream shop. She at first declined (but persuaded by her friend) . . . she gave way and allowed the Italian to have sexual intercourse with her in the back shop . . . she was also 'in the habit in the evenings of frequenting certain offices in the centre of the city and having immoral intercourse with the occupiers'.[4]

In the report, ice-cream parlours were seen as a location for immorality and, alongside the 'bad company of girls', the foreign men were ultimately held responsible. This emphasis on 'foreigners' resonated with the fears associated with the 'white slave trade' and with the belief that 'foreigners' were a major cause of sexual immorality.[5]

The report also highlighted the uncertainty surrounding what actually occurred at these venues, thus providing a good example of how the distinction between prostitution and promiscuity was often blurred. For example, the author of the report explained how 'ice-cream shops have a very black record because of the temptation offered to young girls . . . [F]rom the ice-cream shop it is but a step to the "farmed-out" house and the brothel, thence to the lock hospital or the poorhouse'.[6] It appears that the ice-cream parlours were seen as a 'first step' on the way to prostitution, as opposed to an actual site of prostitution. Rather than money, the report described how the Brazilians 'supplied [the girls] with chocolate, trumpery scarves, [and] cheap jewellery'.[7] Nevertheless, even if the boundaries between promiscuity and prostitution were blurred in the minds of those who feared that sexual immorality was rising, these types of venues were (rightly or wrongly) increasingly associated with prostitution.

Dance Clubs and Prostitution

A 'dance revolution' at the beginning of the twentieth century meant that social dancing became an important part of nightlife entertainment and the phenomenon of the dance club became particularly popular during the interwar period.[8] The arrival of American troops in Britain during the First World War introduced jazz and ragtime music to the British public, which was accompanied by new dances, such as the Charleston, the tango and the shimmy.[9] To facilitate this growing enthusiasm for dancing, new venues were created where, after the payment of a small entrance fee, men and women could go and dance to the music of a live band. This 'membership fee' meant that customers were officially classed as 'private members' and therefore alcohol could be served in compliance with licensing laws.[10] These venues were not designed for prostitution and most were never used for that purpose. However, as the dance clubs proliferated, so too did opportunities to use these new spaces for more illicit activities.

Although prostitution did not actually take place inside these clubs, within certain 'less respectable' venues a system of 'booking-out' was introduced. This system involved the payment of a set fee to hire a female 'dance partner' or 'dance instructress' for the evening. What took place during the evening, whether it was dancing, dinner, a car ride, or 'immoral relations', was allegedly a private matter. One of the most well-known of these 'less respectable' dance clubs where booking-out occurred was the Kosmo Club in Edinburgh, owned by Asher Barnard and managed by Edwin Jones, with the help of the floor manager James Black. It first opened in 1923 at number 20 Swinton Row in the East End of Edinburgh and was originally known as the Bohemian Dance Club until the name was changed to The Kosmo in 1928. At the Kosmo Club, a fee of thirty shillings was charged for the 'booking-out' service because it was supposedly equivalent to the sum of money that the woman could have earned had she been dancing with men individually (each dance cost six pennies, and the managers estimated that a woman could have taken part in 60 dances during one evening). From these thirty shillings the women kept one third whilst the Kosmo Club owner, Barnard, took two thirds.

Whilst the club was known as a popular destination for late night dancing and drinking, it had long been suspected that it also functioned as a place where men could buy sex. These suspicions did not go unnoticed by the police and the sergeant in charge of licensing in Edinburgh, William Merrilees, took it upon himself to investigate the goings-on at the club. After several nights' observation Merrilees was granted a warrant to search the club and believed he had found enough evidence to prove that the owners and managers were using this venue to profit from the prostitution of their employees. The Procurator Fiscal agreed and on 27 November 1933 the trial of Asher Barnard, Edwin Jones and James Black began in Edinburgh's Sheriff Court.

The charge against the three men was that they had 'conspired together with a view to gain from prostitution of employees engaged in the said club as dance partners, and that while acting in concert they did knowingly live wholly or in part off the earnings of prostitution.'[11] The papers from the Kosmo trial show that the police had indeed gathered considerable evidence to support the allegations that the accused were 'aiding and abetting prostitution'.[12] Business cards from suspected 'immoral boarding houses' were found in the club, and it was alleged that Barnard, Jones and Black had conspired with the owners of these 'immoral houses' to send women there for the purpose of prostitution.[13] Dance cards, which were used to calculate how many dances and 'bookings-out' each woman had undertaken, were provided as evidence to show that women were being 'booked-out' several times at once and on many different occasions during the same evening.[14] Taxi drivers also testified to the fact that the dance instructresses had often left 'twice in one night with different men'.[15] This contradicted the claim that the patron was paying to have the woman's company for the whole evening, clearly suggesting that these men were expecting more than just to dance in the short time for which they had paid. Other evidence included a box of pornography, condoms and evidence that the minutes and 'signing in' books, which were needed to prove that the Kosmo was a legitimate members' club, were in fact forged.[16] However, by far the most substantial evidence came from the witnesses. These included the police officers who had watched the club, men who had frequented the club, waiters, taxi drivers and, perhaps most importantly, the women who had worked as dance partners in the Kosmo club.[17]

Clandestine Networks

The witness statements provided considerable evidence to suggest not only that the Kosmo Club was being used for the purposes of prostitution but that it was part of a larger network that incorporated taxis, lodging houses, hotels, cafes, brothels, private flats and other dance clubs. The Kosmo Club's role was to function as an easily accessible central location where men could go to meet women without needing to solicit them publicly on the street. The men and women would then use a car to transport them to another venue, such as a lodging house, hotel or private flat, where the sexual transaction would take place. In a few instances, the men had their own cars, however, in the majority of cases they used taxis. The witness testimonies from the taxi drivers provide many references to the use of taxis as a means of transporting men and women from the club to various venues around the city. In some cases, the taxi itself was used as the location for sex, with several dance partners admitting that there had been 'immoral relations in the taxi'.[18] The compliance and discretion of these taxi drivers was vital, as they could potentially inform the police of any suspicious behaviour.

Clearly, the invention of – and widening access to – the motor car was an essential part of the organisation of this new type of clandestine prostitution. During the interwar period, the number of privately owned cars in the United Kingdom rose from nearly 110,000 in 1919 to 1,056,214 in 1930, before doubling again over the next eight years.[19] Although car ownership was primarily confined to the middle and upper classes, a growing second-hand-car market was beginning to allow some of the more affluent working-class wage earners to possess a car.[20] Additionally, the increasing use and availability of motorised taxis during the interwar period allowed those on a more modest income to hire personal transport for a short period.[21] The use of cars meant that men and women could be quickly and discreetly taken to venues away from the Kosmo Club for the actual sex act. Consequently, these dance clubs avoided contravening brothel legislation because no sex occurred on the premises.

After leaving the club, the women were driven to various addresses that were known by the police to function as brothels, such as 13 Hart Street, a suspected brothel run by Miss Thompson, and 14 Frederick Street, an 'immoral boarding house' run by forty-five-year-old Mrs Euphemia Sutherland. When Mrs Sutherland's 'immoral boarding house' was full, it was alleged that customers were instead sent to another suspected brothel on Leith Street run by Mrs Kemp.[22] Other brothels that were used by the dance partners included 6 East Claremont Street, run by forty-seven-year-old Marie Stewart, and 7 Hillside Crescent. In some instances the owner of the 'immoral boarding house' simply 'turned a blind eye' to the suspicious circumstances surrounding a man and a woman who came late at night claiming to be husband and wife. However, in other cases the owners actively encouraged men and women to go to their premises for prostitution by leaving their advertisement cards at the Kosmo Club and allowing couples to pay '10 shillings to occupy the room for 30 minutes'.[23] The women also mentioned visiting several hotels, such as the Hotel Royal and the Chimes Hotel.[24]

Another influential technology that was part of this clandestine network was the telephone. According to several witnesses, 'a system of phone booking' was in operation at the Kosmo Club.[25] For example, Robert Swan described how he 'got in touch with the instructresses by telephone'[26] after being told by his friend, Paul Slater, that 'if he telephoned for a girl that would be alright'.[27] He did not speak to the dance instructresses directly, but instead 'left a message for them to meet [him]. I had a car nearby, and they met me there.'[28] Agnes Dawson also explained how she was 'booked by telephone to go to an office in Leith',[29] and Florence Hunter confirmed that she 'had the experience of telephone booking twice'.[30] Although the more clandestine nature of the Kosmo Club meant that entering the club was less conspicuous than entering a brothel, the Kosmo Club's reputation was not sufficiently respectable for some men to risk discovery in such an establishment. The use of the telephone therefore allowed men almost complete secrecy.

The Kosmo Club's owner, Barnard, made sure that the dance partners did not have direct access to the telephone. When Florence Hunter was asked how often she used the telephone to arrange meetings with men, she replied that the women at the club were 'forbidden from using the telephone' and that arrangements were instead made by one of the managers.[31] Telephone use was becoming increasingly common by the 1930s, but it was unlikely that the women would have had access to a home telephone. For example, from data compiled using UK Post Office statistics, in 1930 the number of telephones per 100 people was as low as 4.1, and in 1935 the corresponding figure was still only 5.1.[32] The dance partners were therefore dependent on the Kosmo Club as a place where they could receive calls. Barnard's concern about the women having access to the telephone shows that he already realised the potential threat to his business if the 'middle man' could be cut out. As the century progressed and access to telephones became more widespread, this 'fear' would start to become realised.[33] This early use of the telephone therefore gives us a tantalising glimpse of how the 'call girl' industry began. Nevertheless, during the interwar period the location of a venue in the centre of the city remained an essential part of this clandestine network.

The Kosmo Club was not the only venue that used this booking-out system. As described in an article in *The Scotsman*, 'booking-out [was] not a system unique to the Kosmo Club and it was open to wide abuse.'[34] Whilst there has yet to be any substantial research into the system of 'booking-out' across British cities, Julia Laite has shown that a similar system functioned in London.[35] Within Edinburgh, booking-out was certainly occurring in various establishments across the city. For example, The Savoy on Cockburn Street also employed dance instructresses who could be 'booked-out' and The Havana Dance Club, located at 120 Princes Street and owned by Thomas Delworth, was the only other dance club with a 'booking-out' system that, like the Kosmo Club, stayed open until 4am. There appears to have been rivalry between these different clubs and Barnard feared that his dance partners and customers might leave his club in favour of one of his competitors. Several other dance clubs and halls also employed dance instructresses, such as The Palais, The Plaza, Dunedin and Maximes, although, according to the witness testimony of Helen Campbell who used to work as a dance instructress, only the latter two had a system of 'booking-out' similar to the Kosmo Club and the Havana. Whilst it is not clear whether all 'booking-out systems' were used as a form of clandestine prostitution, there appears to have been a distinction between those dance halls or clubs that were seen as 'respectable' and those which were suspected of being 'immoral'. The Kosmo and the Havana, with opening hours much later than those of the other venues, were apparently viewed as 'less respectable', and it is likely that it was only in these types of venues that 'booking-out' was synonymous with prostitution.

Life at the Kosmo Club

It has been widely acknowledged that the voices of the women involved in prostitution are difficult to recover because they were unlikely to have had access to a means of recording and preserving their experiences in a way that is accessible to historians. Although it is possible to learn more about the women's lives through the organisations and institutions which attempted to police, reform and care for them, these records are heavily mediated by the authorities and reformers who wrote them. This is also true of the witness testimonies given by the Kosmo dance partners, and it must be remembered that court testimony is a 'staged performance' and therefore not without its own methodological problems, stemming from the witness's need to vindicate herself in front of the bench and her peers in the public space of the courtroom.[36] Nonetheless, as long as we keep these limitations in mind, these sources can enable us to gain new insights into the lives of these women and offer a fuller, more personal picture of the realities of 'booking-out'.

One of the most detailed witness statements was given by twenty-four-year-old Elsie Bibby. Bibby originally came from Manchester and was described as 'a good looking blonde, of more than average height and of smart appearance'.[37] In her witness statement she explained how she was 'flabbergasted' when she realised that the club was nothing more than a 'sink', but she could not leave because she 'had not enough money'.[38] *The Scotsman* reported that 'her mother was not a widow. . . [but] her father did not live with them'.[39] It was also reported that she used to work as a chorus girl and a cafe supervisor.[40] This gives us some important information about her personal life, suggesting that she was from a single-parent working-class background and that a mixture of a sudden change in environment and the economic uncertainty that this had caused were the primary reasons why she chose to continue working at the Kosmo Club. Bibby's testimony also provides us with examples of her experience of being 'booked-out'. Bibby described how, on her first night, Black told her 'I will give you an address to go to', and when she asked what he meant by this, he told her to 'stay the night'.[41] She then explained how one customer 'took me towards Leith and started to pull me about. The car door was locked and I was yelling.'[42] On another occasion she described how a patron 'pushed me into the bedroom. He got rough. Said he wanted satisfaction'.[43] Bibby was adamant that the managers 'put their heads together and got the idea to book a girl for 30/- to get a clean woman from the club and not the street', and she re-emphasised this by adding that she had 'come to a nasty place. My virtue was for sale at any moment'.[44] The language used in this account may have been selected for its emotive currency with the jury. However, the traumatic events described in this testimony suggest that violence and intimidation were a regular part of life as a dance partner.

Another dance partner, Margaret Armour (known as Pearl), aged twenty-three, also experienced violence working at the Kosmo Club. She described an incident when an 'Egyptian used bad language, thrashed me about', and when she told Barnard that 'he had been nasty', he simply told her to 'go back to the box again' to wait for another man to 'book' her.[45] Florence Hunter (known as Flo), also aged twenty-three and described as being 'married, with a husband and two children', admitted that 'on some occasions the purpose of booking-out was immoral. But her husband '[didn't] know'.[46] In her testimony she recalled an occasion when, out in the countryside, two male patrons tried to force her out of the taxi and into the rain, which made the other dance partner so angry that she struck the patron, and the two women then ran away.[47] On another occasion, she recalled how she refused to be 'booked-out' by a man who wanted 'something of a very indecent nature, apart from ordinary fornication.'[48] These examples give an insight into some of the dangers dance partners faced but also highlight the strength and courage these women needed in order to survive in that environment. Although the women were faced with dangerous situations, they were able to defend themselves and refused to engage in activities which they rejected.

While three of the fourteen dance partners who were called as witnesses admitted that prostitution took place when they were 'booked-out', the other eleven witnesses recorded in the Sheriff's notes denied any immorality. For example, Marie McDonald, aged twenty-three, Eva Duckenfield, aged eighteen, Margaret Purdie, aged twenty, and Catherine D'Agostino, aged twenty-seven, all denied that 'booking-out' was for immoral purposes. Similarly, Helen Campbell, a thirty-two-year-old widow with two children, aged four and seven, insisted that she 'never had immoral relations with anyone'[49], and Agnes Dawson, aged twenty-nine, also denied immoral relations, even though the police had found her nude in bed with a patron of the Kosmo Club at 13 Hart Street (a known brothel).[50] Nancy Cuminisky explained that 'she could make enough money from dancing without needing to be "booked-out"', but she still maintained that the thirty shillings 'booking-out' fee was paid for the woman's company and not immorality.[51] If this was the truth, it seems strange that Nancy turned down thirty shillings for providing such (apparently) innocent company.

Nonetheless, it does appear that some women chose not to 'book-out'. Margaret Armour reported that not all of the instructresses 'booked-out' very often and that 'probably some of them preferred it that way.'[52] These women managed to defy the pressure placed on them to be 'booked-out' and instead chose not to engage in prostitution. Rather than selling sex, these women used the appearance of availability to attract men, encouraging them to buy drinks and pay for dances. This type of 'parasexuality' had long been used within the entertainment and hostelry business to encourage custom and, according to Lady Ada Cecil Chesterton, 'promiscuous' young women often made a habit of 'teasing' men in this way to get 'treats'.[53] The fact that the majority of the women that the club hired were in their teenage years or early-to-mid-twenties and described as 'good looking' supports the likelihood that the club used 'parasexuality' to promote business.[54]

However, in the case of some women, such as Nancy Cuminisky, who had been found naked in a brothel but denied that 'booking-out' led to prostitution, it is reasonable to assume that they may have been lying about the nature of their involvement in 'booking-out'.[55] There are several reasons why it may have been advantageous or necessary for these women to lie about their involvement in prostitution at the Kosmo Club. Firstly, it is likely that they did not want to be labelled as 'prostitutes' for various reasons. Not only would it have made them liable to future arrest; it is likely that they wanted to keep their involvement in prostitution a secret to avoid the stigma associated with commercial sex. Secondly, they may have been fearful of the consequences of incriminating Barnard. Not only would testifying against their boss lead to potential unemployment; it also appears that Barnard attempted to intimidate the women in other ways. For example, twenty-four-year-old Catherine Wallace and twenty-three-year-old Frances Robertson were labelled as 'hostile witnesses' because they were suspected of being influenced by

Barnard, who had been seen talking to them on George IV Bridge the evening before their court appearance.[56]

Bernard's ability to solicit such authority throws into question whether the women were really free to choose if, and when, they engaged in prostitution whilst working at the Kosmo Club. Moreover, Pearl Armour explained that whilst there was 'no compulsion to be booked out . . . she depended on booking-out principally for her income. Women who depended entirely on what they made from dances might not make 10d a night. They got 2d for each dance'.[57] By examining the dance cards which documented each woman's weekly earnings, the lawyers showed that without the extra money they earned from being 'booked-out', the women's wages were considerably lower. For example, Nancy Cuminisky only earned £1 10s 3d and Georgina McArthney only 16s 8d without 'booking-out', whereas Elsie Bibby earned £3 4s 1d a week because of the 'booking-out' fees she received.[58] The increased wages received though 'booking-out' provided these women with a much higher level of economic comfort than was possible for women working in traditional working-class occupations.[59] Considering that in 1935 the average weekly earnings of a male manual worker was estimated at £3 4s 6d, and that women on average earned far less than men, the fee of thirty shillings per booking was a large amount of money, even after deductions were made by Bernard.[60]

On the one hand, the evidence suggests that 'booking-out' was not a system of forced prostitution. On the other hand, it highlights how problematic the notion of 'choice' was in view of the women's poor economic conditions and the economic advantage that 'booking-out' offered. Considering that these women had to provide for themselves, and in some situations for their entire families (as in the case of Helen Campbell, a widow with two young children), choosing not to earn these higher wages may not have been a viable option. The reasons why these women chose to engage in prostitution were, therefore, undoubtedly rooted in wider socio-economic factors, such as poverty, inequality, low wages and limited opportunities for social advancement. Nonetheless, whether women sold sex, parasexuality, or a mixture of the two ultimately depended on their individual decisions, and this lack of clarity or control over women's sexual and commercial activities did not sit easily on the minds of middle-class observers.

Negotiating Power and Resistance

William Merrilees, the police sergeant in charge of the Edinburgh licensing department and of the investigation of the Kosmo Club, made several accusations about the 'viciousness' of Barnard and his control over the women.[61] However, police memoirs as a source must be used cautiously. Whilst the authors of memoirs typically profess to tell the truth, 'there are problems in judging where fact and fiction collide in these works'.[62] In his memoir, Merrilees attempted to depict a heroic image of himself as a man who significantly reduced vice in Edinburgh, and his depiction of Barnard as a dangerous bully may have been exaggerated in an effort to sensationalise the importance and success of his mission to rid the city of vice. Moreover, Merrilees appears to have had a personal vendetta against Barnard and the Kosmo Club. Merrilees' description of arresting Barnard demonstrates just how much contempt he felt for the man and the satisfaction he gained from securing his arrest. For example, Merrilees described how, when he read the warrant for his arrest, Bernard at first possessed:

> contempt, confidence, and a sort of boys-will-be-boys attitude . . . [H]e was so sure of himself . . . but as I continued to read, a change came over the man. The import of it all and the terms of the charge began to sink in, and like a pricked balloon Asher Barnard collapsed. Quite suddenly this big-shot, this racketeer, for so long invulnerable, who claimed as friends, inmates and supporters some of the most influential names in Scotland, broke down like a snivelling child. Indeed, he actually fouled his clothing in abject fear.[63]

Police memoirs are therefore clearly not without personal bias and should not be taken at face value. However, in addition to Merrilees' statements, the powerful influence that Barnard and the other managers wielded over the women who worked at the Kosmo Club is also demonstrated throughout the witness testimonies.

These testimonies describe a variety of methods that were used to control the women's activities, including a list of rules which forbade them to use the telephone, to visit the rival Havana Club or to loiter around the coffee stalls on the Mound (an area where 'street walkers' solicited men).[64] Many of the statements explain how the dance partners were not allowed to live in their own flats and were instead forced to reside in lodgings chosen by Barnard.[65] In his defence, Barnard insisted that this measure was intended to protect the women and to ensure that they lived in respectable accommodation.[66] However, as pointed out during the trial, it would also have served to restrict their privacy and to monitor their activities outside the club, effectively meaning that they could not work without Barnard making a profit. However, the witness testimony also suggests that the women often ignored these rules. For example, Armour explained that the dance partners (including herself) knew the rules but 'they were not carried out'.[67] Another witness admitted that:

> these rules were not always obeyed. She knew of three girls who had been threatened with dismissal unless they left a flat they were staying in, and they had preferred to leave the club . . . there was quite a lot done underhand by the girls.[68]

Armour also explained that she 'wasn't employed for compulsory service. I led my own life'[69], and Flo Hunter described how she told Barnard: 'I was not going to take anybody anywhere'.[70] Similarly, twenty-three-year-old Frances Robertson described how she 'broke the rules by taking drink';[71] twenty-four-year-old Marie McDonald was temporarily dismissed for attending the Havana Club and living in her own lodgings;[72] and seventeen-year-old Elizabeth Harcus refused to be 'booked-out' by men who asked her to do something she did not like.[73] The extent to which women broke the rules depended on their individual circumstances. Nevertheless, this evidence indicates that women were capable of determining at least some aspects of their situation, demonstrating a level of agency which can be overlooked if the label of 'silent victim' is too quickly applied to all those who engaged in prostitution.

The trial concluded with the conviction of the defendants, with Bernard receiving an eighteen-month prison sentence and Black and Jones receiving a three-month sentence each. The witness statements given by the dance partners played an important part in securing the convictions, and the fact that several of the dance partners were willing and able to testify against Barnard in the court room demonstrates their ability to resist his influence. Although Barnard succeeded in intimidating some women so that they would not testify against him, he could not bully all of them. Similarly, the testimony of the dance partners also suggests that they were capable of challenging not only the power and authority of Barnard but also that of the police, the Procurator Fiscal and other lawyers. For example, during her cross-examination by the Procurator Fiscal, Agnes Dawson repeatedly criticised the police, complaining that she 'didn't have a chance to say anything' when questioned by the officers because 'if you didn't say yes, your statement was thrown in front of you and you were called a liar.'[74] Her willingness to accuse the police of misconduct and to argue with the Procurator Fiscal in court demonstrated a considerable amount of self-assurance. John Carter Wood has described how increased reporting of abuses of police powers during the 1920s, in cases such as the excessive interrogation and sexual harassment of Irene Savidge by police in 1928, meant that public awareness of such abuses had increased – potentially leading to more complaints, both founded and unfounded.[75] It is possible, therefore, that Agnes Dawson was drawing on these references to help her to voice her experience of police misconduct to help her defence. If her claims were true, then it also shows how vulnerable these women were, not only in relation to dance club managers, but also to pressure from the police. Nonetheless, although she was vulnerable in relation to these competing powers, her ability to strongly defend herself in court shows that she was far from a silent victim.

Julia Laite has shown that in Metropolitan London the increased criminalisation of prostitution during the early twentieth century forced women off the streets and into more clandestine environments, which consequently resulted in the break-up of women's support and friendship networks.[76] However, the previous chapters have shown that prostitution in Edinburgh and Glasgow was not increasing criminalisation and that wider socio-economic and technological development was more influential in shaping the new forms of clandestine prostitution that emerged. Moreover, the potential for isolation and abuse was more dependent on whether women were working alone under the control of an abusive 'pimp', rather than on whether they were working clandestinely. Chapter five has shown that for those women who did work alone under the control of a 'pimp', this type of arrangement was most likely to result in the women being isolated and vulnerable to abuse.[77] However, the women working in the Kosmo Club were not isolated from each other and had many opportunities to work and live together, especially in light of Bernard's rules which required that many of the women lived together in the same flat. For example, at least three of the dance partners lived at 13 Hermitage Place in Leith and another two lived together in Hart Street.[78] It is difficult to confirm, but if the women lived and worked together, it is possible to speculate that friendships might have developed between some of them. The witness testimony shows that the women were often 'booked-out' in pairs or in small groups, and for most women it is fair to assume that this kind of group work would have been safer than working alone and, therefore, preferable.[79] However, a statement made by Pearl Armour, which described how she was 'not on talking terms with the other girls at all, I had no time for them and they had no time for me', suggests that not all of their working relationships were friendly. Nevertheless, her use of the words 'they' and 'them' suggests that at least some of the dance instructresses did form a collective unit, albeit one from which she was seemingly excluded.[80]

It appears, therefore, that both the environments of the street and of the dance club allowed women to form support networks, and whether or not women preferred to work alone or to form friendships depended on the individuals involved rather than on the inherent qualities of these different types of spaces. In both locations the women were vulnerable to abuse from customers, however, there was some limited protection at the Kosmo Club. Furthermore, the more comfortable environment of the Kosmo Club was likely to be preferable to working on the street, especially as the amount women could earn at the club was often substantially higher. However, the women forfeited a substantial amount of their earnings to Bernard and were subjected to rules which limited their personal freedoms. Moreover, not all women who wanted to work at the Kosmo club would have been able to, as only young and attractive women with dance hostess skills were seen as suitable employees.

Perceptions of Prostitution

The Kosmo trial is also useful for gauging public attitudes towards prostitution. The trial attracted considerable attention; large crowds gathered outside the court each day, and detailed reports of the trial appeared in several newspapers, such as *The Times* and the *Manchester Guardian*.[81] Moreover, the wide range of newspapers from across Scotland that covered the trial, such as the *Dundee Courier, The Daily Express (Scotland)* and *The Glasgow Herald*, shows that it was of considerable interest throughout Scotland. Merrilees even suggested that newspapers in New York and Australia covered the case.[82] The trial occupied considerably more column space than was usually given to criminal trials, suggesting that, unsurprisingly, the public were particularly interested in prostitution and immorality in the city.

The articles focused primarily on reporting the details of the trial, especially the witness testimonies. The reports were mainly sympathetic towards the women, with little critical or degrading language used to describe the dance partners. Instead, the reports focused on the women's experiences of exploitation and abuse at the hands of the Kosmo managers. In contrast, the male managers, and in particular Barnard, were demonised as 'white slavers'. The accounts followed a particular press narrative that had developed around the rhetoric of 'white slavery', a narrative which had become prominent after the highly publicised crusade against white slavery that was instigated by W. T. Stead's 1885 article, 'The Maiden Tribute of Modern Babylon'.[83] Adrian Bingham has shown how the use of recurring narratives allowed the reader to 'consolidate stereotypes of "deviants"' – and Barnard, a wealthy Jewish man who had moved to Scotland from England, certainly appeared to fit the character of the 'evil outsider' who sold innocent young women into sexual slavery.[84] Bingham explains how the press – although particularly interested in 'criminal and morally transgressive activities' – had to use 'a euphemistic style that drew a veil around the most explicit details' and show support for 'the law, the police, and conventional morality'.[85] Similarly, this white slavery narrative which focused on the immorality of Barnard allowed for the discussion of an illicit subject matter, whilst 'stirring up hostility to individuals seen to be breaking moral codes of behaviour'.[86]

The Kosmo trial is a particularly valuable source for analysing the different ways in which people, especially the women themselves, articulated their understanding of prostitution during this period. For example, the following court dialogue between the Procurator Fiscal and Pearl Armour demonstrates how differently the two understood prostitution:

Procurator Fiscal (P. F.): The crown says that you are a prostitute. Have you anything to say about that?
Pearl Armour (P. A.): I would not like to say.
(P. F.): Are you seeking to go back on the answer you gave me?
(P. A.): I am going back on nothing. I understand that a prostitute is a street woman who takes any man who comes along.
(P. F.): Let me put it more clearly. Any woman who hires out her body for gain is a prostitute?
(P. A.): As you put it, the only answer is yes.
(P. F.): Then you now stand confessed as a woman without virtue?
(P. A.): You are putting it that way.[87]

Whilst Armour made a clear distinction between what she did, as opposed to what a prostitute did (something she considered to be defined by indiscriminate street solicitation), the Procurator Fiscal argued that any woman who hired out her body was a prostitute and therefore necessarily without virtue. Armour, however, refused to be labelled as such.

Another extract from the cross-examination demonstrates this ambiguity further. Armour was asked whether she had 'ever solicited with any man for the hire of her body for payment of money?' Armour insisted that she had not solicited with *any* man and, when questioned about whether she had ever importuned or been convicted for prostitution, she replied 'never; I never had to yet', thus suggesting that she saw importuning as something separate from what she did, an undesirable activity in which she did not need to engage.[88] It appears, therefore, that Pearl and the Procurator Fiscal shared some similar notions about the role that importuning and being convicted of prostitution played in defining what constituted being a prostitute. However, it is equally clear that the Procurator Fiscal had little understanding or appreciation of the complex distinctions the women used to define prostitution, respectability and status.

Similarly, another comment from the Procurator Fiscal demonstrates the variety of connotations associated with the label 'prostitute'. In the following address to the jury, the women were no longer portrayed as immoral liars, but as the poor victims of 'white slavers':

> men are sitting back and watching the degradation of women and taking the spoils of that degradation – a case of white slavers taking young women into their employment without considering their moral upbringing – a case of placing them in the line of temptation in the hope they would succumb without consideration as to whether they were willing or not.[89]

In this account, men became the true villains and it was acknowledged that many of the women were involved in prostitution for reasons beyond their control. This clearly demonstrates how the meaning behind the phrase 'white slavery' had evolved from the nineteenth-century literal meaning (referring to a woman who had been physically forced or trapped into prostitution abroad) to a more symbolic interpretation and usage.[90] Nevertheless, this use of white slavery terminology shows that it was still necessary to label women as victims in order to voice empathy towards them. Another address given to the jury (this time by Barnard's lawyer, Mr D. P. Blades) again shows just how variable the connotations of 'prostitute' could be, even within one court case:

> One of the cruellest things done in this case was the indiscriminate branding of these Kosmo dance partners as prostitutes. These women might be of lowly origin, but they are not entitled to be stigmatized and branded as the lowest of womankind without positive proof.[91]

The question of whether these women were 'prostitutes' was obviously an important element in determining whether the defendants were guilty of aiding prostitution. However, the question of whether it was fair to label 'prostitutes' as the 'lowest of womankind' remained unasked. There was evidently a fine, but very symbolic, line between being a dance partner and a 'prostitute'. The status of those who crossed that line and engaged in prostitution was perceived as lower than that of dance partners and, unless they were victims of white slavery (literally or symbolically), there was little sympathy for those who could unmistakably be labelled as 'prostitutes'. However, the witness testimony shows that this sentiment was not shared by all and, for the women involved in commercial sex, this 'fine line' could be, and was, drawn at different boundaries.

As we have seen in the previous chapters, one of the most important of these boundaries was that between indoor and outdoor prostitution. The witness testimony given by Elsie Bibby provides some insight into the importance of these distinctions. During the trial, Bibby described how men came to the Kosmo club because they could 'get a clean woman from the club not the street', implying that street prostitution was more commonly associated with venereal disease.[92] If the dance instructresses were to become associated with 'street prostitutes', this would ruin the impression that they only worked in the club and were therefore 'clean' (something worth a higher price). This method of labelling and categorising clearly demonstrates that a hierarchy did exist among the different methods of prostitution. However, this apparent separation between indoor and outdoor prostitution was not always adhered to, especially if independent soliciting could be more economically advantageous. For example, Barnard explained that he was concerned about the reputation of his dance instructors being damaged if they were seen loitering near the coffee stalls, implying that some women from the Kosmo Club also solicited on the street.[93] With Barnard taking two thirds of their earnings in the club, it may have been more profitable for the women to work independently on the street. This suggests that there was some flexibility, but also that distinctions were complex.

These deliberations about what constituted prostitution highlight the anxiety about female sexuality during this period, most noticeably articulated through terms such as 'flappers', 'the modern girl' and 'amateur prostitutes'.[94] Concerns about women's sexuality and behaviour in the public sphere were not new to the twentieth century but, during the Victorian period, moralists had found it easier to label women as either 'innocent' or 'fallen', depending on their virginal status before marriage. However, as the number of women engaging in pre-marital sex appeared to increase during the twentieth century, this muddied the previously black and white distinction.[95] G. M. Hall's 1933 study of prostitution highlighted contemporaries' concerns about changing sexual behaviour and voiced a commonly held fear that young women were increasingly engaging in pre-marital sex as part of courtship.[96] The growing uncertainty was heightened by the fact that an increasing number of 'respectable' women were enjoying new forms of night-time entertainment, meaning that women who had no intention of engaging in promiscuous sex, paid or otherwise, were also attending clubs like the Kosmo. For example, Edinburgh City Councillor John McDiarmid Airlie was reported to have visited the club with his wife.[97]

The trial, therefore, raises several questions about identity, especially regarding the labelling of women as 'prostitutes'. The lawyers' testimony demonstrates how difficult this process was and suggests that contemporaries were well aware that not all women involved in prostitution fitted the stereotypical characteristics of the 'common prostitute' or 'fallen woman'.

Barnard's defence lawyer, Mr Blades, was keen to point out that 'one act of illicit intercourse does not make a woman a prostitute, otherwise everyone in this country who has been divorced on the grounds of adultery is a prostitute.'[98] However, the Procurator Fiscal, James Adair, was a little more certain about how to identify 'prostitutes', claiming that often 'you can tell at a glance' who is a prostitute because 'the Babylonian stamp is on them, and nothing will efface it.'[99] However, he was prepared to admit that some women (in this case, Pearl Armour) did not 'look like a member of the profession'.[100] Visual representation was evidently important, and when these visual signifiers were no longer obvious, it was only because a particular woman, such as Pearl Armour, 'quite brazenly gloried in the fact' that her involvement in prostitution was 'her own business', that it was possible to identify her as a prostitute.[101] The Procurator Fiscal's open disgust towards this situation revealed his anxiety about losing control over how these women were to be identified and about the power that Armour had to choose, change or hide her identity.[102] Clearly, the increasing number of young, unchaperoned women, out after dark, all wearing similar clothes and dancing in the same clubs, was making it more difficult to distinguish between 'respectable' and 'unrespectable' women, a factor which aided the establishment of 'booking-out' as a system of clandestine prostitution.

The Role of Men as Managers and Clients

The owner of the Kosmo Club, Asher Barnard, was born in Canterbury on 1 January 1884 to a Jewish family. In 1885 the family moved to Portsmouth, where he was educated and worked alongside his father, who was employed as a shop assistant and tailor's cutter. He moved to Edinburgh in 1905. In 1916 he was called up for army service, but declared unfit, so he instead taught soldiers how to drive.[103] During this period he married and had two children and set up a number of small businesses. In May 1923 he opened the dance club which would later become known as the Kosmo Club.

The manager, Edwin Jones, was described in the newspapers as a fifty-two-year-old married man with two children. Jones was reported to have been mainly employed in 'odd-jobs', such as 'cleaning, lights and fires', and his wife had worked as a cook at the club.[104] He resided at St. James Place, close to the Kosmo Club, and his rent was paid by Barnard. Before working at the Kosmo Club, he had worked as a stableman in Manchester and also as an 'outsider' for the Prince of Wales in Marlborough House, London.[105] The floor manager, twenty-seven-year-old James Black, was reported to have come from Inverness and was married with a two-year-old child.[106] Before his employment at the Kosmo Club, he had been a gardener and a Royal

Scots Trooper. He had served as a Lance Corporal with the Scots Guards in Scotland and India for several years and claimed that he would have been promoted had he not been transferred to the Army Reserves due to the army's funding cut in 1926.[107] He described his duties at the Kosmo Club as 'keep[ing] records of dances, good order and discipline', but insisted that he knew nothing of what the girls did when 'booked-out'.[108]

Before the jury's announcement of the verdict, there was considerable debate over whether or not they could find Barnard guilty but not Black and Jones (because the jurors were aware that Barnard could not have conspired to profit from prostitution without co-conspirators). The jury did eventually find Black and Jones guilty as well, sentencing them to three months in prison each, whereas Barnard received an eighteen-month prison sentence. However, after the trial a petition was sent by the members of the jury to explain that they had not understood that they could convict the men separately. An appeal launched by Jones and Black then found that these two men were not guilty and their sentences were dropped.[109]

This series of events raises questions concerning why the jury felt that Black and Jones were less responsible than Barnard. The most obvious reason was that Barnard was the owner, whereas Black and Jones were only employees. However, these factors seem to have already been brought into consideration in the original trial and were the reason behind Black and Jones receiving a three-month sentence each, as opposed to the eighteen-month sentence given to Barnard. Moreover, there was considerable evidence to suggest that Black was more instrumental in the day-to-day management of the club than Barnard. For example, on several occasions Black was described as the person who arranged to which brothels the patrons and instructresses would go, and to whom the money was paid.[110] The lack of public hostility felt towards these two men is therefore intriguing, considering that they were also involved in the exploitation of women; yet Barnard was the only one to be heavily demonised. In comparison to Edwin Jones and James Black, who were Scottish 'family men' and one of whom had been in the Scots Guards, Barnard was English, Jewish, an outsider, and therefore possessed some of the typical characteristics of the traditionally demonised white slaver.[111] Arguably, this case could exemplify the role that xenophobia and anti-Semitism played in creating villains within Scottish society in the interwar period.[112]

Although less prominent, issues concerning the relationship between race and sexuality was also prevalent in the trial testimony. Returning again to the notion of white slavery, Barnard's lawyer Mr Blades defended Barnard from accusations that he was a white slaver by arguing that the fact that Barnard 'protected Pearl from the last final calamity that can befall her, sexual intercourse with a man of colour', meant he could not be a white slaver.[113] This demonstrates Blades' open prejudice towards 'men of colour' and his apparent belief that the sexual exploitation of white women by 'coloured' men was an inherent characteristic of white slavery. The importance of race was not only stressed by Mr Blades; Pearl herself was also reported to have stated that 'she declined to have anything to do with a coloured man. She had not got so low as that yet.'[114] Prejudice towards different ethnic minorities was clearly an important issue when negotiating what she understood to be acceptable sexual activity.

Men who Bought Sex

Information about the men who bought sex is often difficult to obtain, as the men did not commit any legal offence and were of little interest to voluntary organisations who were more concerned about reforming the women who sold sex, rather than the men who bought it. There is, therefore, little evidence available to provide a detailed profile of the men who visited 'prostitutes' or any documentation of their experiences. However, the testimony from the Kosmo trial does provide some information about the male patrons of the Kosmo Club. Considering that the thirty shillings' fee that was charged to 'book-out' Kosmo dancers amounted to roughly half the weekly wage of a manual labourer during this period, the majority of working-class men could not afford to 'book-out' Kosmo dancers. The Kosmo clients who were able to afford this fee therefore represented only a small minority of the men who bought sex. Nevertheless, their witness testimony does reveal some interesting insights into their attitudes towards prostitution and 'booking-out'.

Robert Swan, a twenty-four-year-old bookmaker, appeared not to see 'booking-out' as prostitution:

> **Procurator Fiscal (P. F.)**: What was your purpose?
> **Robert Swan (R. S.)**: to have a night out.
> **(P. F.)**: Explain the purpose for which you booked out the girl?
> **(R. S.)**: Well, of course, that all depended on myself. It is a matter of what I wanted, not really what the girl wanted. I am not saying anything against the girls in the matter. I wanted immorality, but I am not saying that I always got it. I was responsible for that.
> **(P. F.)**: What was the purpose for that?
> **(R. S.)**: What I wanted was immorality. I don't say I necessarily got it, but that is what I wanted.
> **(P. F.)**: And that was the purpose you had in view when you booked them out?
> **(R. S.)**: Certainly.

(P. F.): Was it one girl in particular that you wanted to see?
(R. S.): Always.
(P. F.): And the arrangement you had was a private and personal one between yourselves?
(R. S.): Certainly . . . Of course, if I ever thought of taking her out through the day, it doesn't necessarily follow it would be for immoral purposes. She is a very nice little girl, and all that sort of thing.
(P. F.): Although ultimately on occasions you did have immoral relation with the girl, that was not the sole purpose of your companionship with her?
(R. S.): Oh no, I wouldn't say that against the girl, oh no.[115]

Swan displayed a certain degree of respect for the 'girl' and appeared not to have labelled her as a prostitute. Although his attempts to redirect blame away from the dance partner suggest that he wanted to protect her reputation, his description of how 'it is a matter of what I wanted, not really what the girl wanted' and how she was a 'little girl' suggests that he assumed control in the relationship. However, his comment that, although he wanted immorality, he did not necessarily get it, implies that he was aware of the dance hostesses' power to deny him sex. Moreover, his emphasis on their 'private and personal relationship', which only sometimes led to sex, rather than describing it as the straightforward purchase of sex, suggests that Swan wanted to believe that he was involved in a scenario similar to a normal courtship rather than prostitution. Perhaps he felt guilty or uneasy about the realities of prostitution or, alternatively, the insinuation that he had to pay for sex may have been socially embarrassing. Either way, his involvement in 'bookmaking', which itself was a slightly dubious occupation that was often on the wrong side of the law, perhaps made him more comfortable with less clear-cut notions of morality.

However, not all of the men were ready to admit that they 'booked-out' women. For example, Robert Murray, a thirty-eight-year-old bookmaker, denied knowing Flo Hunter or going with her to the Stewart Boarding House for immoral relations, adding that he was 'a married man' who 'didn't go with another woman'.[116] Alternatively, men such as twenty-one-year-old Robert Glenny admitted that he had 'booked-out' women for 'immoral purposes', but denied his moral responsibility by stating that he 'hardly insisted'.[117] This suggests these men felt guilty or embarrassed about their behaviour once it was exposed to public scrutiny and therefore lied about their behaviour or blamed the dance partners.

One particularly interesting patron was Councillor John McDiarmid Airlie. As the councillor for the central St. Giles ward in Edinburgh and a member of the city's committee for streets and buildings, Airlie was in a position that would have given him considerable power regarding the licensing of clubs such as the Kosmo. Airlie was reported to have been to the Kosmo Club on many occasions and had apparently known Barnard well enough to ask him for a loan of £200.[118] Airlie insisted that he only ever went to the Kosmo Club with his wife and that he never 'booked-out' women.[119] However, the friendship between Barnard and Airlie understandably raised suspicions of corruption, albeit suspicions that ultimately could not be proved.[120] Although Merrilees made claims that Barnard was protected by people in authority, no efforts were made to implicate the councillor in the trial.

As described earlier, male customers could be abusive towards the dance hostesses. However, there were also several instances in which the men appear to have treated the women well. For example, George Ferguson, a twenty-seven-year-old clerk, described how he had asked for his thirty shillings back from Flo Hunter because she told him she could not find them a hotel. However, when Flo told him that she would 'get the sack' if she went back without any money, he agreed that she could keep the money and that nothing would happen that night.[121] The relative safety of the club would have reduced the amount of violence the women were likely to encounter but this protection did not necessarily extend to areas outside the club. It is likely that many instances of violence and abuse went unreported, which means that it is difficult to know more about the hidden abuse that these women may have suffered, or to make any broad claims about the behaviour and attitudes of male clients. Nonetheless, these examples demonstrate the complexity of the different power relationships between the dance partners and the patrons.

Conclusion

The Kosmo trial provides us with a valuable case study for examining indoor, more clandestine kinds of prostitution – something which by its very nature is often more difficult for historians to access. As new technologies, such as the telephone and the motor car, became more widely available, those involved in the sex industry took advantage of these technologies to develop new methods of clandestine prostitution. The Kosmo Club trial therefore highlights an important turning point in the organisation of prostitution, a period characterised by the development of networks between the dance clubs, boarding houses, hotels and taxis drivers and a process that laid the foundation for how prostitution would develop during the second half of the twentieth century. Moreover, clubs such as the Kosmo took advantage of the fact that distinctions between parasexuality, promiscuity and prostitution had become more blurred during the interwar period, as an increasing number of unchaperoned young women ventured into the city to enjoy night-time entertainment. On the one hand, the increased anxiety and confusion surrounding female sexuality and the presence of the 'flapper' helped the development of 'booking-out' as a new form of clandestine prostitution. On the other hand, clubs such as the Kosmo were instrumental in providing a location in which these boundaries between 'respectability' and 'deviance' could be broken down.

The Kosmo trial also reveals more about the role that men played in prostitution, as both business managers and clients. Whilst Barnard was demonised as a 'white slaver', Black and Jones were attributed with less blame. The fact that Barnard was an outsider, due to his English and Jewish origins, may have made him a more convenient and reassuring culprit than Scottish men. Unlike the 'pimps' who often physically abused the women, rather than using violence, the Kosmo managers relied on their ability to take advantage of women in poor economic circumstances who needed the higher wages that 'booking-out' provided. Although less is known about the male clients, the chapter has shown how their attitudes towards, and relationships with, dance partners were often complex. Whilst some clients were abusive or indifferent towards the dance partners, others appear to have treated them more respectfully.

Whilst it has been argued that in London the increased criminalisation of prostitution led to the development of more dangerous types of clandestine prostitution, the Kosmo trial has shown that this was not necessarily the case in Edinburgh. In venues such as dance clubs the women could work together in more comfortable surroundings, often with little interference from the police. Although Barnard certainly exploited the dance partners economically and the women were vulnerable to abuse from customers, working at his club was safer than working alone under the control of a pimp and was not necessarily more dangerous than other kinds of street or brothel prostitution. What is more, the dance partners' witness statements highlight the many ways in which they managed to negotiate these dangers and were able to defend themselves, both in the courtroom and in their everyday lives.

Through the use of the dance partners' witness statements, this chapter has offered a rare insight into the lives of women who engaged in prostitution via 'booking-out'. One of the most difficult aspects of researching the history of prostitution is the lack of opportunities to understand the realities of the women's lives. However, the Kosmo case allows us to capture fragments of the women's experiences and to explore some of the ways in which they resisted attempts made by the police, magistrates and club owners to label and to control them. Whilst both the prosecution and the newspapers used the 'white slavery' narrative to describe the case, the notion that these women were all victims of evil 'white slavers' who forced them into prostitution is misleading. To focus on these women solely as victims detracts from the complexity of their experiences and the multifaceted reasons behind their involvement in commercial sex.

Notes

1. This chapter was developed from an original article published in *Twentieth Century British History*, see Louise Settle, 'The Kosmo Case: Clandestine Prostitution in Britain during the Interwar Period', *Twentieth Century British History*, 25, 4 (2014), pp. 562–84.
2. See, for example, Panikos Panayi, *Immigration, Ethnicity and Racism in Britain, 1815–1845* (Manchester: Manchester University Press, 1994).
3. Glasgow City Archives (hereafter GCA), T. PAR 1.16, p. 279; *Memorandum on the Social Evil in Glasgow*, 1911, p. 10.
4. Ibid.
5. Edward Bristow, *Prostitution and Prejudice, the Jewish Fight against White Slavery, 1870–1939* (Oxford: Clarendon, 1982).
6. GCA, T. PAR 1.16, *Memorandum on the Social Evil in Glasgow*, p. 4.
7. Ibid, p. 10.
8. See, for example, Judith Walkowitz, *Nights Out: Life in Cosmopolitan London* (London: Yale University Press, 2012).
9. Martin Pugh, *We Danced All Night: A Social History of Britain Between the Wars* (London: Bodley Head, 2008), p. 219.
10. 1921 Licensing (Scotland) Act.
11. National Records of Scotland (hereafter NRS) HH16/1 'Criminal case file: Asher Barnard, Edwin Jones, James Black, Indictment, 1933–1934'.
12. NRS, JC34/1/155, Trial Transcript, taken for the Sheriff Court at the trial of Asher Barnard, James Black and Edwin Jones, 27 November 1933 (hereafter, Trial Transcript).
13. NRS, JC34/1/155, List of Productions in the Sheriff and Jury DIET.
14. NRS, JC34/1/155, Trial Transcript, witness testimony of Jean Fairbairn or Smith, p. 49.
15. NRS, JC34/1/155, Trial Transcript, witness testimony of Godfred Peterseen, p. 38.
16. Ibid.
17. NRS, JC34/1/155, List of Witnesses in the Court DIET, p. 6.
18. Edinburgh City Archives (hereafter ECA) ACC827, Trial Transcript taken by Edinburgh Police at the request of William Merrilees, 27 November 1933 (hereafter Trial Transcript), p. 123.
19. W. Knox, 'Transport and Scottish Society 1840–1940', in *A History of the Scottish People*, National Museum of Scotland Multimedia Team

(eds) (Edinburgh Scottish Cultural Resources Access Network) www.scran.ac.uk.

20. Ibid.
21. James Cooper, Ray Mundy and John Nelson, *Taxi! Urban Economies and the Social and Transport Impacts of the Taxicab* (Farnham: Ashgate, 2001).
22. ECA, ACC827, Trial Transcript, p. 112.
23. ECA, ACC827, Trial Transcript, pp. 351 and 329; ECA, ACC827, Trial Transcript, p. 112.
24. ECA, ACC827, Trial Transcript, p. 138.
25. *Daily Express*, 2 December 1933, p. 8.
26. ECA, ACC827, Trial Transcript, witness testimony of Robert Swan, p. 221.
27. *Daily Express* 2 December 1933, p. 8.
28. ECA, ACC827, Trial Transcript, witness testimony of Robert Swan, p. 221.
29. ECA, ACC827, Trial Transcript, witness testimony of Agnes Dawson, p. 70.
30. ECA, ACC827, Trial Transcript, witness testimony of Florence Hunter, p. 122.
31. Ibid.
32. S. N. Broadberry, *Market Services and the Productivity Race, 1850–2000: British Performance in International Context* (Cambridge: Cambridge University Press, 2006), p. 112. Data table compiled from the UK Post Office statistics.
33. Ibid.
34. *The Scotsman*, 8 December 1933, p. 8.
35. Julia Laite, *Common Prostitutes and Ordinary Citizens: Commercial Sex in London, 1885–1960* (Basingstoke: Palgrave Macmillan, 2012, pp. 139–40.
36. Shani D'Cruze, *Crimes of Outrage: Sex Violence and Victorian Women* (London: UCL Press, 1998).
37. *The Scotsman*, 30 November 1933, p. 8.
38. NRS, JC34/1/155, witness testimony of Elsie Bibby, pp. 22–24.
39. Ibid, p. 27.
40. *The Scotsman*, 1 December 1933, p. 13.
41. NRS, JC34/1/155, witness testimony of Elsie Bibby, p. 22.
42. Ibid, p. 23.
43. Ibid, p. 26.
44. Ibid, pp. 23 and 26.
45. NRS, JC34/1/155, witness testimony of Margaret Armour, p. 5.
46. NRS, JC34/1/155, witness testimony of Florence Hunter, p. 19.

47. ECA, ACC827, Trial Transcript, p. 211.
48. ECA, ACC827, Trial Transcript, witness testimony of Florence Hunter, p. 212.
49. ECA, ACC827, Trial Transcript, witness testimony of Helen Campbell, p. 81.
50. NRS, JC34/1/155, witness testimony of Agnes Dawson, p. 10.
51. NRS, JC34/1/155, witness testimony of Nancy Cuminisky, p. 9.
52. ECA, ACC827, Trial Transcript, witness testimony of Margaret Byres Armour, p. 40.
53. Peter Bailey, 'The Victorian Barmaid as Cultural Prototype', *Gender & History*, 2 (1990), pp. 148–72; Ada Cecil Chesterton, *Women of the Underworld* (1928), p. 158.
54. *The Scotsman*, 30 November 1933, p. 8.
55. NRS, JC34/1/155, witness testimony of Agnes Dawson, p. 10.
56. ECA, ACC827, Trial Transcript, p. 196.
57. NRS, HH16/1 Press Reports, *Glasgow Herald*, 28 November 1933.
58. ECA, ACC827, Trial Transcript, witness testimony of Nancy Cuminisky, 62; Georgina McArthney, 102; Elsie Bibby, p. 166.
59. Esther Breitenbach and Eleanor Gordon (eds), *The World is Ill divided: Women's Work in Scotland in the Nineteenth and Early Twentieth Centuries* (Edinburgh: Edinburgh University Press, 1990).
60. David Metcalf, Stephen J. Nickell and Nicos Floros, 'Still Searching for an Explanation of Unemployment in Interwar Britain', *Journal of Political Economy*, 90, 2 (1982), pp. 386–99.
61. Ibid.
62. Paul Lawrence, '"Scoundrels and Scallywags, and Some Honest Men . . .": Memoirs and the Self-Image of French and English Policemen, c. 1870–1939', in Barry S. Godfrey, Clive Emsley and Graeme Dunstall (eds), *Comparative Histories of Crime* (Cullompton: Willan 2003), p. 126.
63. Merrilees, W., *The Short Arm of the Law, the Memoirs of William Merrilees* (London: Long, 1966), p. 94.
64. ECA, ACC827, Trial Transcript, witness testimony of Asher Barnard, pp. 410–11.
65. NRS, HH16/1 Kosmo Club Trial Press Reports of Trial (hereafter Press Reports), *Dundee Courier and Advertiser*, 7 December 1933.
66. NRS, JC34/1/155, witness testimony of Barnard, p. 57.
67. ECA, ACC827, Trial Transcript, witness testimony of Margaret Armour, p. 31.
68. Ibid.
69. Ibid, p. 29.

70. ECA, ACC827, Trial Transcript, witness testimony of Florence Hunter, p. 124.
71. ECA, ACC827, Trial Transcript, witness testimony of Frances Robertson, p. 30.
72. ECA, ACC827, Trial Transcript, witness testimony of Marie McDonald, p. 109.
73. ECA, ACC827, Trial Transcript, witness testimony of Elizabeth Harcus, p. 32.
74. ECA, ACC827, Trial Transcript, witness testimony of Agnes Dawson, p. 67.
75. John Carter Wood, 'The Third Degree: Press Reporting, Crime Fiction and Police Powers in 1920s Britain', *Twentieth Century British History*, 21, 4 (2010), pp. 464–85.
76. Laite, *Common Prostitutes and Ordinary Citizens.*
77. For further discussion and examples of women's relationships with 'pimps' see, Louise Settle, 'Policing the "Social Evil": Prostitution in Edinburgh and Glasgow, 1892–1939', PhD Thesis (University of Edinburgh, 2013), pp. 175–188.
78. NRS, JC34/1/155, schedule from the court DIET, p. 2.
79. See, for example, ECA, ACC827, Trial Transcript, witness testimony of Georgina McArthney, p. 93.
80. ECA, ACC827, Trial Transcript, witness testimony of Pearl Armour, p. 45.
81. *The Scotsman*, 8 December 1933, p. 9. *The Times*, 8 December 1933, p. 11; *The Times*, 25 January 1934, p. 4. NRS, HH16/1 Press Reports, *Manchester Guardian*, 30 November 1933; 7 December 1933.
82. Merrilees, *The Short Arm of the Law*, p. 104.
83. William T. Stead, 'The Maiden Tribute of Modern Babylon', parts I–IV, *Pall Mall Gazette*, 6, 7, 8, 10 July 1885.
84. Adrian Bingham, *Family Newspapers? Sex, Private Life and the British Popular Press, 1918–1978* (Oxford: Oxford University Press, 1995, 2009), p. 159.
85. Ibid, pp. 125 and 132.
86. Ibid, p. 160.
87. NRS, HH16/1 Press Reports, *Daily Express (Scotland)* 1 December 1933.
88. ECA, ACC827, Trial Transcript, witness testimony of Pearl Armour, p. 34.
89. NRS, HH16/1 Press Reports, *Dundee Courier and Advertiser*, 7 December 1933.
90. See, for example, Edward Bristow, *Prostitution and Prejudice*;

Katarina Leppänen, 'Movement of Women: Trafficking in the Interwar Era', *Women's Studies International Forum*, 30 6 (2007), pp. 523–33.

91. NRS, HH16/1 Press Reports, *Daily Express (Scotland,)* 8 December 1933.
92. NRS, JC34/1/155, witness testimony of Elsie Bibby, p. 23. For further literature on the connections between prostitution and venereal disease see, for example, Richard Davenport-Hines, *Sex, Death and Punishment: Attitudes to Sex and Sexuality in Britain since the Renaissance* (London: Collins, 1990); Adrian Bingham, 'The British Popular Press and Venereal Disease During the Second World War', *The Historical Journal*, 48 4 (2005), pp. 1,055–1,076; Mary Spongberg, *Feminizing Venereal Disease: The Body of the Prostitute in Nineteenth-Century Medical Discourse* (London: Macmillan, 1997).
93. NRS, JC34/1/155: witness testimony of Asher Barnard, p. 57.
94. Samantha Caslin, 'Flappers, Amateurs and Professionals: The Spectrum of Promiscuity in 1920s Britain', in Kate Hardy, Sarah Kingston, Teela Sanders (eds), *New Sociologies of Sex Work* (Ashgate, 2010).
95. Carol Dyhouse, *Girl Trouble: Panic and Progress in the History of Young Women* (London: Zed Books, 2014), p. 70.
96. G. M. Hall, *Prostitution: A Survey and a Challenge* (London: Williams & Norgate, 1933), Dyhouse, *Girl Trouble*, pp. 106–107.
97. ECA, ACC827, trial transcript, witness testimony of John McDiarmid Airlie, p. 212.
98. ECA, ACC827, Trial Transcript, Mr Blades, p. 466.
99. ECA, ACC827, Trial Transcript, Procurator Fiscal, p. 462; James Adair would later become a prominent member of the Wolfenden Committee, which in its 1957 report commended the increased penalisation of solicitation offences. See R. Davidson and G. Davis, *The Sexual State: Sexuality and Scottish Governance, 1950–1980* (Edinburgh: Edinburgh University Press, 2012).
100. Ibid.
101. Ibid.
102. See, for example, Julia Laite, 'Taking Nellie Johnson's Fingerprints: Prostitutes and Legal Identity in Early Twentieth-Century London', *History Workshop Journal*, 65 (2008), pp. 96–116.
103. *The Scotsman*, 6 December 1933, p. 8.
104. NRS, HH16/1 Press Reports, *Dundee Courier and Advertiser*, 6 December 1933.
105. Ibid.
106. Ibid.

107. ECA, ACC827, trial transcript, witness testimony of James Black, p. 349.
108. NRS, JC34/1/155 Appeal by Edwin Jones and James Black against conviction for the crime of aiding and abetting prostitution, p. 231.
109. Ibid.
110. NRS, HH16/1 Press Reports, *Glasgow Herald*, 29 November 1933; NRS JC34/1/155, witness testimony of Barnard, p. 11.
111. NRS, HH16/1 Press Reports, *Dundee Courier and Advertiser*, 6 December 1933.
112. For more on anti-Semitism in Scotland and its links with increased immigration see, for example, Ben Barber, 'The Trial of Oscar Slater (1909) and Anti-Jewish Prejudices in Edwardian Glasgow', *History: Journal of the Historical Association*, 88 (2003), pp. 262–879.
113. ECA, ACC827, trial transcript, witness testimony of Mr Blades, p. 463.
114. ECA, ACC827, trial transcript, witness testimony of Jean Fairbairn, p. 463.
115. ECA, ACC827, trial transcript, witness testimony of Robert Swan, p. 226.
116. ECA, ACC827, trial transcript, witness testimony of Robert Murray, p. 148.
117. NRS, JC34/1/155, witness testimony of Robert Glenny, p. 35.
118. NRS, HH16/1 Press Reports, *Daily Express*, 1 December 1934.
119. ECA, ACC827, trial transcript, witness testimony of John McDiarmid Airlie, p. 212.
120. NRS, JC34/1/155, witness testimony of Barnard, p. 59.
121. ECA, ACC827, trial transcript, witness testimony of George Ferguson, pp. 145–7.

CHAPTER 7

Conclusion

The turbulent socio-economic environment in Edinburgh and Glasgow during the early twentieth century, especially the renegotiation of women's role in the public sphere and changes in technology and entertainment, greatly influenced the organisation of prostitution and the experiences of those involved. The policing of prostitution was also influenced by these wider social changes, but the introduction of probation also meant that many aspects of the nineteenth-century 'Glasgow System' that had relied on the informal cooperation between the law and voluntary organisations became integrated into official policy. Whilst the treatment of women under this twentieth-century penal-welfare system was arguably less repressive than under the nineteenth-century system, the focus on reforming women according to middle-class standards of respectable femininity remained constant. By exploring the experiences of the women who sold sex, this book has found that whilst abuse, exploitation and poverty affected many of the women involved in prostitution, they also found numerous ways to negotiate the challenges posed by the individuals and institutions that attempted to control or exploit them. The conclusions that can be drawn from this research about the effectiveness of various policies and the influence they had on the lives of women is particularly relevant to current debates concerning the merits and drawbacks of the decriminalisation and legalisation of prostitution. This final chapter will bring these various themes together and explore how this historical research can help inform current debates about prostitution.

Rather than prostitution becoming increasingly criminalised during the early twentieth century, as was the case in London, this research has shown that there was no strong demand or support for a sustained 'crackdown' on prostitution in Edinburgh and Glasgow prior to the Second World War. On the contrary, the police's response was often apathetic, seeing prostitution as a moral issue for the concern of the Kirk and conscience, rather than a matter for the police. Women apprehended for soliciting were often allowed to leave with only a caution, or they were given fines and short prison sentences. Enthusiasm for increased criminalisation was shown only during short-lived moments of enhanced public concern, and often only in relation to 'brothel-keepers' and 'pimps'. These characters were viewed with particular disgust because of their perceived exploitation and abuse of vulnerable women. Nonetheless, although there may have been more enthusiasm to catch 'bullies' and brothel-keepers, especially during periods of moral panic concerning 'white slavery', this was often a difficult and lengthy process, as reflected in the low conviction rates throughout the period.

The persistent presence of prostitution in central business and commercial areas in Edinburgh and Glasgow shows that the police were unable forcibly to determine the location of prostitution. Whilst the higher number of arrests in central areas may partly have reflected the police's policy to target women working in the most visible areas, the amount of solicitation in these areas remained relatively high, despite efforts to deter it. The concentrated number of men passing through the city centre, thanks to the location of transport hubs and commercial entertainment venues in this area, gave women a better chance of successfully soliciting customers. Considering that many women only received a caution or a fine when caught in these central areas, it is fair to assume that it may have been a risk worth taking in light of the considerable financial benefits. Whilst the women involved in prostitution were subject to arrest by the police and were therefore not completely free to move as they pleased, the threat of such action was not sufficient to deter them from working in the most profitable areas of the city centre. Although 'respectable' members of society may have wanted prostitution hidden from sight or restricted to the outskirts of the city, in reality the police were unable to achieve this.

As the twentieth century went on, the increasing number of unchaperoned young single women going out after nightfall to the cinema, ice-cream parlour or dance hall made it easier for women who were soliciting to blend in. These larger social changes also made it easier for women to sell sex clandestinely, especially when the use of the car or the telephone could further hide any public transactions, and new venues, such as the Kosmo Dance Club, opened up across Scottish cities to take advantage of these new opportunities. Overall, therefore, the larger socio-economic factors, such as the location of entertainment venues and the increasing availability of cars and telephones, were in many ways just as important in determining the organisation of prostitution as were policing policies – something that should be kept in mind when considering the merits of criminalisation and the police's realistic ability to abolish prostitution.

The police and magistrates in Edinburgh and Glasgow often worked together with voluntary organisations and the probation service to implement a more penal-welfare-oriented approach towards prostitution. Senior police officers in both Glasgow and Edinburgh were particularly keen on using probation sentences to send women to reform homes rather than to gaol. By giving probation sentences to the women convicted of prostitution offences, the magistrates ensured that these women would be placed under the supervision of a probation officer in their own home or in a reform home. The close connection that existed between the newly emerging probation service and the religious voluntary organisations that had previously been involved in 'rescuing the fallen' meant that this system resulted in the formal adoption of an informal system that had been in operation in Edinburgh and Glasgow since the early nineteenth century. Although the 1907 Probation of Offenders Act had introduced new powers and procedures to the probation service, the individuals and organisations involved in probation remained virtually the same, and the 'probationers' were often sent to the same voluntary reform homes that had been used during the nineteenth century.

Whilst there had been considerable improvements in the living conditions of these reform institutions since the nineteenth century, the 'inmates' were still subjected to hard work for little or no pay, and the basic principle of reforming women in accordance with middle-class standards of respectable femininity remained the same. In institutions such as the Edinburgh and Glasgow Magdalene Asylums, the women were trained only in basic literacy, Bible studies and domestic skills and, once they left, they received help in finding work as servants or laundresses, or returned to their families. Even those 'inmates' who were given help to emigrate abroad were still expected to remain within a domestic setting, regardless of the increasing opportunities available for women in new 'white collar' occupations. Some of the organisations involved in probation, such as the National Vigilance Association of Scotland (Eastern Division) were critical of institutionalisation and instead embraced more scientific methods, such as the individual casework approach that characterised the new professional outlook towards social work. However, even when women were placed under the supervision of these more progressive organisations and were allowed to remain in their own homes, the basic principle of removing them from the precarious position they had occupied in the public sphere and restoring them to their 'rightful' place within the domestic sphere remained central.

Whether probation was a more desirable option than prison for those women who were convicted of prostitution offences largely depended on the women's individual circumstances. On the one hand, a probation sentence could result in the loss of freedom for periods much longer than the maximum prison sentence for solicitation offences, and the probationers were subjected to a long list of rules which restricted where they could live or with whom they could socialise. If probation officers felt that any of the rules had been broken, they could report this to the magistrates and the woman could be sent to prison in accordance with their original sentence. Arguably, this penal-welfare approach extended the authorities' basis for disciplinary intervention by acquiring detailed knowledge, not only of the offenders, but also of their families, therefore encouraging the increased surveillance and control of women.[1] The fact that many women chose to break the probation bonds and risk imprisonment shows that, for some women at least, this type of invasive control of their personal lives was intolerable.

On the other hand, some women used probation as an opportunity to avoid prison and to gain the skills and references that would help them find employment outside prostitution. Although the employment opportunities they were subsequently qualified for restricted them to the field of domestic labour, this focus on preparing women to fulfil roles in the domestic sphere was by no means exceptional to reform homes during this period. Outside the few environments in which this domestic sphere ideology was being challenged, such as during the unique situation created by the need for female labour during the First World War or within the small field of well-educated middle-class women who were entering professional life, most working-class women had few opportunities beyond the home or strictly defined 'women's' occupations. Therefore, the chance that these women had to gain training and employment offered them a realistic alternative to sex work that did not involve resorting to the poor law. Moreover, it meant that the women avoided spending time in prison. Although the reform homes may have left much to be desired, in the period examined here the living standards were much higher than they had been during the nineteenth century and were certainly a lot better than in gaol. As the lengthy conviction histories of women who were repeatedly sent to gaol demonstrate, a short prison sentence did little to help women exit prostitution, and in many cases it hindered them in obtaining and retaining stable employment.

Nevertheless, regardless of the potential benefits that the probation system offered some women, the ways in which these women were judged and treated according to whether they met a particular standard of respectable femininity was (and remains) highly problematic. Whilst some officials showed sympathy towards the young 'newly fallen' women who were seen as 'victims' and therefore given cautions or probation sentences, those labelled as 'common prostitutes' were more likely to be subjected to frequent arrests.

This gendered assessment of a woman's supposed 'character' therefore became part of the official legal system which labelled and treated women differently according to whether they were considered 'common prostitutes' or 'amateurs' – a distinction which had long-lasting implications for the treatment of 'sexually deviant' women by the state. By focusing on women's 'character', the authorities and the rest of society were able to emphasise the 'flaws' of the individual woman rather than the wider socio-economic inequalities that led her to become (and remain) involved in prostitution – an issue that is still a problem today.

This book has explored some of the wider socio-economic reasons why women became, and remained, involved in prostitution and examined how this involvement influenced their lives. The heavily mediated nature of the available sources, such as police, court and reform organisations' records, means that it is only possible to gain small glimpses into the women's life-stories from the moments when they interacted with particular organisations and authorities. However, rather than seeing this methodological difficulty as an impenetrable barrier, a position which has often resulted in researchers ignoring the experiences of the women who are central to the history of prostitution, this research has used a collective biography approach to learn more about women's experiences. Whilst the lives of women such as Mary Muirhead, Mabel Jamieson and Elsie Bibby were unique and complex, some common themes can be drawn from looking at these women as a group. By examining the records of over eight hundred women involved in prostitution, it has been possible to learn more about their backgrounds and the course of their lives. The majority of the women were from working-class homes and had experienced poverty or an unstable upbringing, with many of them having lost one or both parents. The death or desertion of a spouse was another common factor that led women to enter prostitution, especially if they had young children. The majority of the women came from Scotland but there was some movement from throughout Britain, and women with an Irish heritage were noticeably over-represented, suggesting that the difficulties and prejudices associated with immigration may have played a role here. Many of the women spent time in various institutions, including poor houses, gaol and reform institutions, and by the latter part of the period younger women were especially likely to have been placed on probation or to have spent time in reform homes. The criminal records show that many of the women were also involved in other types of petty crime, especially crimes relating to theft or alcohol. However, the extent to which these women engaged in petty crime or were drinking alcohol to any greater extent than other working-class women during this period remains uncertain.

The social profile and experiences of the women often depended on the type of prostitution in which they engaged. Those employed in more clandestine types of prostitution, in venues such as dance clubs, were often younger and less impoverished than those who worked on the streets. For example, women who worked at the Kosmo Club in Edinburgh earned at least ten shillings per 'booking' and could make several pounds a week, whereas women working on the streets made much less, often earning only a few shillings per transaction. These women's experiences, therefore, were quite different and the women themselves made distinctions between different 'classes of prostitutes'. Whereas Mary Muirhead experienced extreme poverty and entered prostitution to provide for herself and her children after being abandoned by her husband, other women such as Elsie Bibby earned high enough wages to avoid the poorhouse – although neither was able to avoid exploitation altogether, and the distinctions between indoor and outdoor prostitution could be somewhat fluid.

Despite the potential dangers that all the women encountered, most were not forced to the outskirts of society, either physically or socially. The women worked on some of the most prominent streets in the city centre and the police were unable to deter them from working in these prosperous areas. Although the middle classes and aspirational working classes may have tried to keep their distance from 'immorality', the women involved in prostitution in Edinburgh and Glasgow were not necessarily isolated from working-class life; instead, they lived in working-class areas and engaged in a wide range of activities alongside other working-class men and women. Moreover, the prison, police and poor law records show that women frequently moved in and out of prostitution and other working-class occupations according to their economic circumstances at a particular time, meaning that Tony Henderson's notion of the 'makeshift economy' was as relevant to women working in prostitution during the early twentieth century as it had been during the eighteenth.[2] Whilst the long criminal histories of women such as Jane Darroch, Mary Mullaney and Edith Boyd show that a considerable minority of these women relied on petty crime, casual labour and prostitution to survive, the relatively short records of other women, such as Mary Clark, demonstrate that it was also possible for women to enter prostitution whilst young and with few prospects, but to leave as soon as they married or found better employment. Unfortunately the nature of the available records makes it difficult to learn much about these women's lives outside of their involvement in prostitution. Although the authorities may have increasingly tried to label women as 'common prostitutes', the testimony of women such as Pearl Armour demonstrates that the women themselves did not necessarily view the selling of sex as their main source of employment or identity.

In London, the increased criminalisation of prostitution during the early-twentieth century forced women into more clandestine forms of prostitution, which consequently made them more isolated and vulnerable to abuse.[3] Whilst this was certainly true for the women in Edinburgh and Glasgow who were forced into working alone with pimps, this was not always the case for the women who chose to work in other clandestine environments, such as the Kosmo Club. Although the 'dance partners' lost some of their freedom and a percentage of their wages to the owners of these establishments, they did not appear to be any more isolated from other women than those who worked on the street. Moreover, although in all settings there were men who violently abused women, as well as others who treated them respectfully, venues such as the Kosmo Club offered some limited protection. However, the fact that much of the abuse women faced was not reported to the police, coupled with the authorities' general lack of interest in the activities of the male customers, means that there are few sources available to make solid conclusions about the behaviour of men and the level of danger women faced in particular settings. More research is therefore needed on the history of the men who bought sex, although, given the severe shortage of available source material, this will be difficult for anyone researching the period before living memory.

By far the most dangerous environment for women was to work and live alone with a pimp. The case studies of men such as Thomas Gallacher and Henry Fair have demonstrated the appalling ways in which these men used violence and emotional manipulation to force women to engage in prostitution. However, the relationships between 'pimps' and 'prostitutes' could sometimes be more complicated than traditionally understood. In some situations women were involved in romantic attachments with the men who acted as their 'pimps' and also benefited from the protection they provided. In other situations, it was not always clear if the man was actually a 'pimp', or merely the partner of a woman who engaged in prostitution. Nonetheless, despite the increased concerns about the dangers of pimps and their involvement in 'white slavery', there is little evidence to suggest that the involvement of 'bullies' in prostitution increased significantly during this period. This ambiguity regarding the nature of relationships between 'prostitutes' and others involved in commercial sex also applied to 'brothel-keepers'. Whilst some brothel-keepers certainly did exploit and manipulate women, in many situations the brothels were run by other women selling sex, or by poor individuals and families who needed extra money from renting rooms. In these circumstances it was not always clear who held the power and the arrangement could be more about convenience and mutual benefit rather than there being a clear-cut distinction between the exploiter and the exploited.

Examining the complexity of these relationships has highlighted the many ways in which women engaged in various forms of resistance. Several previous studies of prostitution have emphasised the ways in which the women involved in prostitution were victims of both class and gender discrimination due to their poor socio-economic circumstances and their inequality within a patriarchal society.[4] However, although these factors are important, to focus only on these issues risks denying these women's historical agency. Whilst this book has shown that these socio-economic factors continued to play a large role in the experiences of women during the twentieth century, that was not the whole story. Many of the women resisted the attempts of the police, voluntary organisations and probation workers to control and shape their behaviour and they were not 'silent victims'. Similarly, many women found the courage to testify in court against their abusive 'bullies' or to break the rules of brothel and dance club managers. Other women decided to endure the arduous regimes of the reform homes in order to take advantage of the training and employment opportunities that would result from playing by the rules. Whether through the use of violence, evasion of arrest, testifying in court, absconding from reform homes or from probation, refusing to abide by the rules laid down for them, or tactically embracing them to receive employment opportunities, these women were fully capable of asserting their agency. In many cases this resistance was fleeting, with the contravention of probation rules resulting in a prison sentence, or an escape from an abusive bully causing harsh reprimands. Nonetheless, these examples show how the women involved in prostitution used the resources available to them to determine the course of their own lives, even if these resources were minimal and their options limited.

In terms of a comparison between Edinburgh and Glasgow, the different nature of the surviving sources in each city makes a like-with-like comparison difficult. Nevertheless, this book has demonstrated many similarities in the organisation of prostitution and comparability in the methods of formal and informal policing of it that occurred in each city. Whilst the lives of the women in either city were shaped by their unique urban environments, similar wider socio-economic factors continued to affect their lives, regardless of each city's particularities. Recent research on prostitution in the late twentieth century has shown how Edinburgh and Glasgow adopted very different strategies towards policing prostitution.[5] Whereas Glasgow developed a zero-tolerance policy, partly because of the strong influence of anti-prostitution feminists within the city council, Edinburgh adopted a more pragmatic approach, first creating an informal tolerance zone in Leith, and then encouraging prostitution to move indoors by relaxing the enforcement of licensing laws in the 'saunas' and 'massage parlours' that were used for clandestine prostitution. Clearly there are some links here between the various types of informal toleration that occurred in Edinburgh during the first and second halves of the twentieth century, whereas there was a more drastic shift in approach in Glasgow during the latter half of the twentieth century. However, the details of these processes remain unclear, and more research is needed to establish the underlying reasons behind these post-World-War-Two changes.

The book has shown that, in some respects, the policing, organisation and experiences of women involved in prostitution in Scotland were similar to those in England. However, the fact that this book focuses on Edinburgh and Glasgow and the research on prostitution in England during the twentieth century concentrates primarily on London, makes it difficult to compare the whole of Scotland and England. Further research is therefore needed to make such comparisons more substantial, especially relating to non-urban prostitution. Nevertheless, the book has highlighted some important differences between the two countries. In Scotland, it was the Procurator Fiscal who decided which cases would be brought to court, rather than the police, as was the case in England. Additionally, no proof of annoyance was required in solicitation cases and Scots law required two witnesses to give evidence before a conviction could be made, rather than one, as in England. These differences made it less likely that the Scottish police could be accused of malpractice or corruption. However, the most important difference was the formal use of the cautioning system in Scotland. This system allowed women several chances before they were arrested and possibly sent to prison. In conjunction with increased cooperation among the police, magistrates, the probation service and voluntary workers, this cautioning system gave women more opportunities to avoid arrest and imprisonment. There has been no comparable research on the role of probation and voluntary services in the regulation of prostitution in England, which makes it difficult to compare the two countries. Nonetheless, it appears that the long tradition of religious and voluntary organisations within Scottish society has helped to shape the distinctly 'penal-welfare' nature of prostitution policing polices in Scotland.

The Kosmo Club case study has demonstrated not only how new forms of clandestine prostitution developed alongside changes in entertainment and technology, but also how the narrative of 'white slavery' that originated in the nineteenth century continued to play an important role in Scottish prostitution discourses during the early twentieth century. Even today, issues surrounding forced prostitution and human trafficking often feature prominently within discourses on prostitution. Whilst trafficking is a serious issue and deserves full public attention, it should not be at the expense of helping other women involved in prostitution.[6] Firstly, this focus on trafficking does not represent the experiences of women who have chosen to work in the sex industry and who call for more workers' rights and the decriminalisation of prostitution. Secondly, focusing on trafficking directs attention away from the more deep-rooted socio-economic factors, such as gender inequality, racism, low wages and diminishing opportunities for social mobility which commonly contribute to women becoming involved in prostitution and limit the number of alternative choices available to them. Thirdly, focusing upon the 'character' and culpability of individual women, or of the men who exploit them, further detracts attention from the large underlying socio-economic causes behind women's reliance on this type of income. This is especially true for economic migrants that are doubly penalised, not only by economic inequality, but also by racism and xenophobia.

Neil McKeganey's research on prostitution in twenty-first-century Scotland found that the majority of women entered prostitution out of 'dire need'.[7] The reasons behind this 'dire need' included poverty, the necessity of providing for dependants, domestic and sexual abuse, lack of alternative options and drug addiction. These factors seem remarkably similar to those described in this book. Despite the improvements in the general standard of living over the past seventy-five years and the introduction of the welfare state, poverty, inequality and the various associated problems, such as drug addiction, homelessness, social exclusion, family dysfunction, lack of education and employment opportunities, still play a crucial role in determining why many women unwillingly enter prostitution and have difficulty leaving it.[8] The central aspect of any policy about prostitution must not shy away from addressing these wider socio-economic issues, especially in relation to the problem of low wages and the need for increasing access to affordable childcare, training and further education.

In the meantime, whilst it may take a long time for new policies to be put in place that would enable the creation of a more equal society, (and current governmental policies in Britain seem to be moving in the opposite direction,) some more immediate and practical steps could be taken to improve the lives of the women currently involved in sex work. This research and various other studies have shown that blanket criminalisation policies do little to decrease the demand for prostitution or to protect women.[9] On the contrary, several studies have demonstrated that the criminalisation of prostitution makes sex work more dangerous. If women have to hide from the police, they are less likely to seek medical help or protection when they are in danger from clients or other third parties. Moreover, criminalisation can force women to work with pimps and it means that women soliciting on the street have less time to judge which customers may be dangerous. The illegality of prostitution also encourages criminal gangs to become involved, subjecting women to the more dangerous environment of organised crime. Even when the laws in place are intended to criminalise the male customers rather than the women sex workers (as in the case of the Swedish model, where buying, but not selling sex, is illegal), many of the same problems still occur. Moreover, this book has shown that wider socio-economic changes, especially in entertainment and technology, were often more important in shaping the organisation of prostitution than the judicial system, which was typically ineffective at controlling prostitution. Those involved in prostitution were quick to take advantage of new spaces and technologies that would allow them to avoid detection and to maximise profits, meaning the police were left trying to keep up with these changes. This still remains a serious issue today, and although the policy of 'zero-tolerance' may seem to offer a good solution in theory, in reality the law's ability to control prostitution will always be limited.

However, this is not to say that the law cannot play a role. When used in a more targeted way, the law can be effective in ensuring that women are not being trafficked into prostitution or working underage, and it can be used to ensure that women are working in safe environments and are not exploited by 'pimps'. Other laws could also be used to regulate the ways in which the sale of sex is advertised and represented in the public sphere and unionisation could help enforce fairer wages and working conditions, helping to avoid the type of 'mega-brothels' that have developed in countries such as Germany. As well as the law, education would also need to play an important role in changing attitudes towards prostitution and the women involved. A focus on the men who buy sex, and the reasons why they buy sex, may be an especially helpful approach here. However, a crucial aspect of this whole approach would be to provide specialised services to those women who are unsure if they should begin this type of work or decide they want to leave prostitution. Here we could learn something from the approach used in Edinburgh and Glasgow during the early twentieth century. Although there were many negative aspects to the penal-welfare approach, there were also some positive sides. The ways in which voluntary organisations gave women food and shelter, offered them advice and counselling, trained them in new skills and found them employment did help some women to leave prostitution. This approach was certainly more helpful than giving women fines and short prison sentences. If this model could be updated and adapted so that the obligatory and punitive aspects were removed, extra services such as counselling and drug rehabilitation programmes were provided, and the emphasis on education and training were modified to fit with contemporary needs and expectations, rather than focusing on preparing women to enter domestic labour, it could be a much more realistic way of protecting women from working in prostitution against their will or because of 'dire need'. Voluntary organisations could still play an important role, but rather than relying only on charitable donations, these services could also be funded by the taxes raised through legalised prostitution and by the savings made from not sending women through the criminal justice system. This approach would also mean that those women who choose to work in the sex industry could do so more safely and would not be penalised and stigmatised by the criminalisation of prostitution. If suitably updated, aspects of the approach practised in Scotland during the early twentieth century could have contemporary relevance in the early twenty-first century as well.

Notes

1. David Garland, *Punishment and Welfare: a History of Penal Strategies* (Aldershot: Gower, 1985).
2. Tony Henderson, *Disorderly Women in Eighteenth-Century London: Prostitution and Control in the Metropolis, 1730–1830* (London: Longman, 1999).
3. Julia Laite, *Common Prostitutes and Ordinary Citizens: Commercial Sex in London, 1885–1960* (Basingstoke: Palgrave Macmillan, 2012).
4. See, for example, Frances Finnegan, *Poverty and Prostitution: A study of Victorian Prostitutes in York* (Cambridge: Cambridge University Press, 1979).
5. Lucy Holmes, 'A Tale of Three Cities: Regulating Street Prostitution in Scotland', *Scottish Affairs*, 52 (2005) pp. 71–88.
6. See Jo Doezema, 'Loose Women or Lost Women? The Re-Emergence of the Myth of 'White Slavery' in Contemporary Discourses of 'Trafficking in Women', *Gender Issues*, 18, 1 (2000) pp. 23–50.
7. Neil McKeganey, 'Street Prostitution in Scotland: The Views of Working Women', *Drugs: Education, Prevention and Policy*, 13, 2 (2006) pp. 151–66.
8. See, for example, J. Davis, *Off the Streets: Tackling Homelessness among Female Street-based Sex Workers* (London: Shelter, 2004).
9. Jane Scoular and Teela Sanders (eds), Regulating Sex/Work: From Crime Control to Neo-Liberalism? *Journal of Law and Society Special Issues* (2010); M. Goodyear and L. Cusick, 'Protection of sex workers', *British Medical Journal* (2007) pp. 334, 52–3; Laite, *Common Prostitutes and Ordinary Citizens*.

Bibliography

Archive Sources

Edinburgh City Archive

Edinburgh Burgh Court Records, 1900–1939 (not catalogued).
Edinburgh Magdalene Asylum Ladies' Committee Minutes: SL237/2/3.
Edinburgh Magistrates Minutes: SL/12/3.
Edinburgh Police Criminal Conviction Registers (not catalogued).
Edinburgh Police General Order books: ED006/2.
Edinburgh Police Return of Crimes: ED006/1.
Kosmo Trial Transcript: ACC827.
Minutes of the Edinburgh Town Council, SL/1.

Glasgow City Archive

Glasgow Magdalene Institute Annual Reports: T-PAR.
Glasgow Magdalene Institute Home Committee Minutes: TD1776/1.
Glasgow Police Annual Reports: DTC 7/19/1.
Glasgow Police City and Burgh Specimen Charge Book: SR22/63/40.
Glasgow Police General Order Books: NMSR22/43.
Glasgow Police Instruction Books: SR22/60/13.
Glasgow Poor Law Records: D-Hew.
Memorandum on the Social Evil in Glasgow, 1911: T. PAR 1.16, p. 279.
The Origins and Development of the Glasgow Magdalene Institute, Glasgow, 1905: PA11/2/8.

National Records of Scotland

Appeal by Edwin Jones and James Black against conviction for the crime of aiding and abetting prostitution: JC34/1/155.
Bill of suspension and liberation by Alfred Joseph Vaughn, Ivy Summerhayes or Vaughn: JC31/1919/7.

Bill of Suspension and Liberation by Otto Hall: JC31/1913/24.
Criminal Case file: Asher Barnard, Edwin Jones, James Black: HH16/1.
Duke Street Prison Registers: HH21/32, 1903–1931.
Judiciary appeal by John James McIntyre, P. F. Glasgow V William Thomson: JC31/1912/10.
Press Report Cuttings from the Kosmo Trial: HH16/1.
Street Offences Committee File: HH60/263.
Transcript of Verdict and Ensuing Discussion in the Kosmo Club Trial: HH16/1 C/112/1.
Trial transcript taken for the Sheriff Court at the trial of Asher Barnard, James Black and Edwin Jones: JC34/1/155.

National Library of Scotland

Family Care Papers, Newspaper Cuttings: Acc.11191 1928.
Minutes of the Ladies' Committee National Vigilance Association of Scotland (Eastern division) 1913–1926: Acc.11191/2.
Women Patrols Papers: HH31/16/1–13.

Imperial War Museum

Women's Work Collection, The Annual Report of the Women Patrols For Scotland 1914–1920: EMP 42/3.

Women's Library

The Association for Moral and Social Hygiene (AMSH): Papers on Solicitation Laws in Scotland 1892–1955 3: AMS/b/04/02.

Newspapers

Daily Express
Dundee Courier and Advertiser
Evening Standard
Glasgow Herald
Manchester Guardian
The Pall Mall Gazette
The Scotsman
The Times

Acts

Burgh Police (Scotland) Act 1892 (55&56 Vict. c. 55).
Criminal Justice Administration Act 1914 (4 & 5 Geo.5, c. 58).
Criminal Law Amendment Act 1885 (48&4 Vict. c. 69).
Criminal Law Amendment Act 1912 (3&4 Geo 5, c. 38).
Defence of the Realm Act 1914 (4&5 Geo. 5, c. 29).
Edinburgh Burgh Police (Scotland) Act 1898 (58&59 Vict. c. 152).
Edinburgh Municipal and Police Act 1879 (42&43 Vict. c. cxxxii).
Glasgow Police (Further Powers) Act 1892 (55&56 Vict. c. 165).
Immoral Traffic (Scotland) Act 1902 (1&2 Geo 5, c. 20).
Licensing (Scotland) Act 1903 (3 Edw 7, c. 25).
Probation of Offenders Act 1907 (3 Edw. 7, c. 25).
Licensing (Scotland) Act 1921.
Probation of Offenders (Scotland) Act (21 & 22 Geo. 5, c. 30).

Published Books (Primary)

Acton, W., *Prostitution Considered in its Moral, Social, and Sanitary Aspects* (2nd edn, reprint, London: Routledge, 1972).
Chesterton, A. C., *Women of the Underworld* (London: Stanley Paul & Co., 1928).
Cockerill, A. W., *The Memoirs of Percy Sillitoe* (London: W. H. Allen, 1975).
Colquhoun, R., *Life Begins at Midnight* (London: Long, 1962).
Hall, G. M., *Prostitution: A Survey and a Challenge* (London: Williams & Norgate, 1933).
Logan, W., *The Great Social Evil and its Causes, Extent, Results and Remedies* (London: Hodder & Stoughton, 1871).
McNee, D., *McNee's Law* (London: Collins, 1983).
Merrilees, W., *The Short Arm of the Law, the Memoirs of William Merrilees, O.B.E., Chief Constable, the Lothians and Peebles Constabulary* (London: Long, 1966).
Muir, E., *Scottish Journey* (London: Heinemann/Gollancz, 1935).
Rolph, C. H. (ed.), *Women of the Streets, A Sociological Study of the Common Prostitute* (London: Secker & Warburg, 1955).
Tait, W., *Magdalenism: An Inquiry into the Extent, Causes and Consequences of Prostitution in Edinburgh* (Edinburgh: P. Rickard, 1840).
Waugh, E., *Brideshead Revisited* (London: Chapman & Hall, 1945).
Wilde, O., *The Picture of Dorian Gray* (London: Lippincott's, 1890).

Published Books (Secondary)

Anderson, A., *Tainted Souls and Painted Faces: The Rhetoric of Fallenness in Victorian Culture* (London: Cornell University Press, 1993).

Arnot, M., E. Bartels, V. Beechey, L. Birke, S. Himmelweit, E. Hitelegg, D. Leonard, S. Ruehl and A. Speakman (eds), *The Changing Experience of Women* (Oxford: Robertson, 1982).

Bailey, P., *Leisure and Class in Victorian England: Rational Recreation and the Contest for Control, 1830–1885* (London: Routledge, 1978).

Banerjee, S., *Under the Raj: Prostitution in Colonial Bengal* (New York: Monthly Review Press, 1998).

Barrie, D., *Police in the Age of Improvement: Police Development and the Civic Tradition in Scotland, 1775–1865* (Cullompton: Willan, 2008).

Barry, K., *The Prostitution of Sexuality* (New York: New York University Press, 1995).

Bartley, P., *Prostitution, Prevention and Reform in England, 1860–1914* (London: Routledge, 2000).

Bell, D., and G. Valentine (eds), *Mapping Desire* (London: Routledge, 1995).

Bernstein, L., *Sonia's Daughters: Prostitutes and Their Regulation in Imperial Russia* (Berkeley: University of California Press, 1995).

Bingham, A., *Family Newspapers? Sex, Private Life and the British Popular Press, 1918–1978* (Oxford: Oxford University Press, 2009).

Bland, L., *Banishing the Beast* (London: Penguin Books, 1995).

Bourke, J., *Working-Class Cultures in Britain 1890–1960: Gender, Class and Ethnicity* (London: Routledge, 1994).

Braybon, G., *Out of the Cage: Women's Experiences in Two World Wars* (London: Pandora Press, 1987).

Braybon, G., (ed.), *Evidence, History and the Great War: Historians and the Impact of 1914–18* (Oxford: Berghahn Books, 2003).

Breitenbach, E. and E. Gordon (eds), *The World is Ill divided: Women's Work in Scotland in the Nineteenth and Early Twentieth Centuries* (Edinburgh: Edinburgh University Press, 1990).

Bridge, G. and S. Watson (eds), *A Companion to the City* (Oxford: Blackwell Publishers, 2000).

Bristow, E., *Prostitution and Prejudice, the Jewish Fight against White Slavery, 1870–1939* (Oxford: Clarendon, 1982).

Bristow, E., *Vice and Vigilance: Purity Movements in Britain Since 1700* (Basingstoke: Palgrave Macmillan, 1977).

Broadberry, S. N., *Market Service and the Productivity Race, 1850–2000: British Performance in International Context* (Cambridge: Cambridge University Press, 2006).

Brophy, J. and C. Smart (eds), *Women-in-Law: Explorations in Law, Family and Sexuality* (London: Routledge & Kegan Paul, 1985).
Brogden, M., *On the Mersey Beat* (Oxford: Oxford University Press, 1991).
Butler, A., *Daughters of Joy, Sisters of Misery: Prostitutes in the American West, 1865–1890* (Urbana: University of Illinois Press, 1985).
Cameron, E., *Impaled Upon A Thistle: Scotland Since 1889* (Edinburgh: Edinburgh University Press, 2012).
Certeau, M., *The Practice of Everyday Life* (London: California University Press, 1984).
Clark, E. P., *The Cambridge Urban History of Britain* (Cambridge: Cambridge University Press, 2000).
Clark, H. and E. Carnegie, *She was aye Workin': Memories of Tenement Women in Edinburgh and Glasgow* (Oxford: White Cockade in association with the People's Story, City of Edinburgh Council, and the People's Palace, Glasgow City Council, 2003).
Cohen, S., *Folk Devils and Moral Panics: The Creation of the Mods and Rockers* (Oxford: Basil Blackwell, 1987).
Collins, M., *Modern Love: An Intimate History of Men and Women in Twentieth-Century Britain* (London: Atlantic, 2003).
Connelly, M., *The Response to Prostitution in the Progressive Era* (Chapel Hill: University of North Carolina Press, 1980).
Cook, H., *The Long Sexual Revolution* (Oxford: Oxford University Press, 2004).
Cooper, J., R. Mundy and J. Nelson, *Taxi! Urban Economies and the Social and Transport Impacts of the Taxicab* (Farnham: Ashgate, 2001).
Cooter, R., M. Harrison and S. Sturdy (eds), *Medicine and Modern Warfare* (Amsterdam: Atlanta, 1999).
Corbin, A., *Women for Hire: Prostitution and Sexuality in France after 1850*, trans. Alan Sheridan (London: Harvard University Press, 1990).
Cowley, R., *A History of the British Police: From its Earliest Beginnings to the Present Day* (Stroud: History Press, 2011).
Cox, P., *Gender, Justice and Welfare: Bad Girls in Britain, 1900–1950* (Basingstoke: Palgrave Macmillan, 2003).
Cree, V. E., *From Public Streets to Private Lives: The Changing Task of Social Work* (Aldershot: Avebury, 1995).
Criticher, C., *Moral Panics and the Media* (Milton Keynes: Open University Press, 2003).
Cross, G., *A Social History of Leisure since 1600* (State College, PA: Venture, 1990).
Culleton, C., *Working-Class Culture, Women, and Britain, 1914–1921* (Basingstoke: Macmillan, 1999).

D'Cruze, S., *Crimes of Outrage: Sex Violence and Victorian Women* (London: UCL Press, 1998).

Daniels, K., *So Much Hard Work: Women and Prostitution in Australian History* (Sydney: Fontana, 1984).

Davenport-Hines, R., *Sex, Death and Punishment: Attitudes to Sex and Sexuality in Britain since the Renaissance* (London: Collins, 1990).

Davidoff, L. and C. Hall, *Family Fortunes: Men and Women of the English Middle Class, 1780–1850* (London: Hutchinson, 1987).

Davidson, R., *Dangerous Liaisons: a Social History of Venereal Disease in Twentieth-Century Scotland* (Amsterdam: Rodopi, 2000).

Davidson, R. and G. Davis, *The Sexual State: Sexuality and Scottish Governance, 1950–1980* (Edinburgh: Edinburgh University Press, 2012).

Davidson, R. and L. Hall (eds), *Sex Sin and Suffering: Venereal Disease and European Society since 1870* (London: Routledge, 2001).

Davies, A., *City of Gangs: Glasgow and the Rise of the British Gangster* (London: Hodder & Stoughton, 2013).

Davies, A., *Leisure, Gender and Poverty* (Milton Keynes: Open University Press, 1992).

Davies, A., *The Gangs of Manchester: the Story of the Scuttlers, Britain's First Youth Cult* (Preston: Milo Books, 2008).

Davis, J., *Off the Streets: Tackling Homelessness among Female Street-based Sex Workers* (London: Shelter, 2004).

Delap, L., *Knowing Their Place: Domestic Service in Twentieth Century Britain* (Oxford: Oxford University Press, 2011).

Donnelly, D. and K. Scott (eds), *Policing Scotland* (Cullompton: Willan, 2005).

Donzelot, J., *The Policing of Families* (Baltimore: Johns Hopkins University Press, 1997).

Dyhouse, C., *Girl Trouble: Panic and Progress in the History of Young Women* (London: Zed Books, 2014), p. 70.

Faley, J., *Up oor Close: Memories of Domestic Life in Glasgow Tenements, 1910–1945* (Wendlebury: White Cockade, 1994).

Farmer, L., *Criminal Law, Tradition and Legal Order: Crime and the Genius of Scots Law 1747 to the Present* (Cambridge: Cambridge University Press, 1997).

Finnegan, F., *Poverty and Prostitution: A study of Victorian Prostitutes in York* (Cambridge: Cambridge University Press, 1979).

Finnegan, F., *Do Penance or Perish: Magdelene Asylums in Ireland* (Oxford: Oxford University Press, 2001).

Foucault, M., *Discipline and Punish: The Birth of the Prison* (London: Penguin, 1979).

Foucault, M., *Madness and Civilization: A History of Insanity in the Age of Reason* (London: Tavistock, 1967).

Foucault, M., *The History of Sexuality* (Harmondsworth: Penguin, 1981).
Francis, D., *Red Light Neon: a History of Vancouver's Sex Trade* (Vancouver: Subway, 2006).
Gallagher, T., *Glasgow and the Uneasy Peace, Religious Tensions in Modern Scotland*, 1819–1914 (Manchester: Manchester University Press, 1987).
Garland, D., *Punishment and Welfare: A History of Penal Strategies* (Aldershot: Gower, 1885).
Gibson, M., *Prostitution and the State in Italy, 1860–1915* (Athens, OH: Ohio State University Press, 1986).
Giddens, A., D. Held, D. Hubert, D. Seymour and J. Thompson (eds), *The Polity Reader in Social Theory* (Cambridge: Polity Press, 1995).
Gilfoyle, T., *City of Eros: New York City, Prostitution, and the Commercialization of Sex, 1790–1920* (London: W. W. Norton, 1992).
Grant, D., *The Thin Blue Line: The Story of the City of Glasgow Police* (London: Long, 1973).
Grant, M., *Playing the Whore: The Work of Sex Work* (London: Verso, 2014).
Grayzel, R. S., *Women and the First World War* (Harlow: Longman, 2002).
Guy, D. J., *Sex & Danger in Buenos Aires: Prostitution, Family, and Nation in Argentina* (Lincoln: University of Nebraska Press, 1991).
Hall, L., *Sex, Gender and Social Change in Britain since 1880* (Basingstoke: Palgrave Macmillan, 2000).
Hamilton, D., *The Healers: A History of Medicine in Scotland* (Edinburgh: Mercat, 1981).
Harris, V., *Selling Sex in the Reich: Prostitution in German Society, 1914–1945* (Oxford: Oxford University Press, 2010).
Harrison, B., *Drink and the Victorians: The Temperance Question in England, 1815–1872* (London: Faber &Faber, 1971).
Henderson, T., *Disorderly Women in Eighteenth-Century London: Prostitution and Control in the Metropolis, 1730–1830* (London: Longman, 1999).
Henriot, C., *Prostitution and Sexuality in Shanghai: A Social History, 1849–1949* (Cambridge: Cambridge University Press, 2001).
Hershatter, G., *Dangerous Pleasures: Prostitution and Modernity in Twentieth Century Shanghai* (Berkeley: University of California Press, 1997).
Howell, P., *Geographies of Regulation: Policing Prostitution in Nineteenth Century Britain and the Empire* (Cambridge: Cambridge University Press, 2009).
Hughes, A., *Gender and Political Identities in Scotland, 1919–1939* (Edinburgh: Edinburgh University Press, 2009).
Humphries, S., *A Secret World of Sex: Forbidden Fruit: The British Experience 1900–1950* (London: Sidgwick & Jackson, 1988).
Hunt, A., *Governing Morals: A Social History of Moral Regulation* (Cambridge: Cambridge University Press, 1999).

Hutter, B. W. and Williams, G. (eds), *Controlling Women: The Normal and the Deviant* (London: Croom Helm, 1981).

Jackson, L., *Child Sexual Abuse in Victorian England* (London: Routledge, 2000).

Jackson, L., *Women Police: Gender, Welfare and Surveillance in the Twentieth Century* (Manchester: Manchester University Press, 2006).

Jackson, L., (with Bartie, A.), *Policing Youth: Britain 1945–70* (Manchester: Manchester University Press, 2014).

Jeffreys, S., *The Idea of Prostitution* (Melbourne: Spinifex Press, 1997).

Jeffreys, S., *The Industrial Vagina: The Political Economy of the Global Sex Trade* (Oxford: Routledge, 2009).

Jeffreys, S., *The Spinster and her Enemies, Feminism and Sexuality, 1880–1930* (London: Pandora, 1985).

Jordan, J. and I. Sharp (eds), *Josephine Butler and the Prostitution Campaigns: Diseases of the Body Politic* (London: Routledge, 2003).

Klein, J., *Invisible Men, the Secret Lives of Police Constables in Liverpool, Manchester and Birmingham, 1900–1939* (Liverpool: Liverpool University Press, 2010).

Kohn, M., *Dope Girls: The Birth of British Drug Underground* (London: Granta, 1992).

Laite, J., *Common Prostitutes and Ordinary Citizens: Commercial Sex in London, 1885–1960* (Basingstoke: Palgrave Macmillan, 2012).

Lefebvre, H., *The Production of Space* (Oxford: Basil Blackwell, 1991).

Levine, P., *Prostitution, Race and Politics: Policing Venereal Disease in the British Empire* (London: Routledge, 2003).

Levine, P., *Victorian Feminism, 1850–1900* (London: Century Hutchinson, 1987).

Luddy, M., *Prostitution and Irish Society, 1800–1940* (Cambridge: Cambridge University Press, 2007).

Mahood, L., *Policing Gender, Class and Family: Britain, 1850–1940* (London: UCL Press, 1995).

Mahood, L., *The Magdalenes: Prostitution in the Nineteenth Century* (London: Routledge, 1990).

McHugh, P., *Prostitution and Victorian Social Reform* (London: Croom Helm, 1979).

McLaren, A., *The Trials of Manhood: Policing Sexual Boundaries, 1870–1930* (Chicago: University of Chicago Press, 1997).

McNay, L., *Foucault and Feminism: Power, Gender and the Self* (Cambridge: Polity Press, 1992).

Melman, B., *Flappers and Nymphs: Women and the Popular Imagination in the Twenties* (Basingstoke: Palgrave Macmillan, 1998).

Melling, J., *Rent Strikes: People's Struggle for Housing in West Scotland, 1890–1916* (Edinburgh: Polygon, 1983).
Morris, N. and D. Rothman (eds), *The Oxford History of the Prison: The Practice of Punishment in Western Societies* (Oxford: Oxford University Press, 1995).
Mort, F., *Dangerous Sexualities: Medico-Moral Politics in England since 1830* (London: Routledge, 1987).
Nagle, J., *Whores and Other Feminists* (London: Routledge, 1997).
Nead, L., *Myths of Sexuality: Representations of Women in Victorian Britain* (Oxford: Basil Blackwell, 1988).
Nolland, L., *A Victorian Feminist Christian: Josephine Butler, the Prostitutes and God* (Carlisle: Paternoster, 2004).
O'Connell, D., *Prostitution, Power and Freedom* (Cambridge: Polity, 1998).
Okin, S. M., *Justice, Gender and the Family* (New York: Basic Books, 1989).
Osler, A., *Introduction to the Probation Service* (Winchester: Waterside, 1995).
Pacione, M., *Glasgow: The Socio-Spatial Development of the City* (Chichester: John Wiley and Sons, 1995).
Panayi, P., *Immigration, Ethnicity and Racism in Britain, 1815–1845* (Manchester: Manchester University Press, 1994).
Pearson, M., *The Age of Consent: Victorian Prostitution and Its Enemies* (Newton Abbot: David & Charles, 1972).
Petrow, S., *Policing Morals: The Metropolitan Police and the Home Office, 1870–1914* (Oxford: Clarendon, 1994).
Philip, N., *Working Girls: An Illustrated History of the Oldest Profession* (London: Bloomsbury, 1991).
Porter, R. and L. Hall, *The Facts of Life: The Creation of Sexual Knowledge in Britain 1650–1950* (New Haven: Yale University Press, 1995).
Prochaska, F. K., *Women and Philanthropy in Nineteenth-Century England* (Oxford: Clarendon, 1980).
Pugh, M., *We Danced All Night: A Social History of Britain Between the Wars* (London: Bodley Head, 2008).
Ringdal, N., *Love for Sale: A World History of Prostitution* (New York: Grove Press, 2004).
Robb, G. and N. Erber (eds), *Disorder in the Courts: Trials and Sexual Conflict at the Turn of the Century* (Basingstoke: Macmillan, 1995).
Rosen, R., *The Lost Sisterhood: Prostitution in America, 1900–1919* (London: Johns Hopkins University Press, 1982).
Rossiaud, J., *Medieval Prostitution* (Oxford: Basil Blackwell, 1988).
Scott, J., *Gender and the Politics of History* (New York: Columbia University Press, 1988).

Self, H., *Prostitution, Women and Misuse of the Law: the Fallen Daughters of Eve* (London: Frank Cass, 2003).

Sheilds, R., *Places on the Margin: Alternative Geographies of Modernity* (London: Routledge, 1991).

Smout, T. C., *A Century of the Scottish People, 1830–1950* (London: Fontana, 1986).

Spongberg, M., *Feminizing Venereal Disease: The Body of the Prostitute in Nineteenth-Century Medical Discourse* (London: Macmillan, 1997).

Srebnik, A. G. and R. Levy (eds), *Crime and Culture: An Historical Perspective. Advances in Criminology* (Aldershot: Ashgate, 2005).

Strange, C., *Toronto's Girl Problem: The Perils and Pleasures of the City, 1880–1930* (Toronto: University of Toronto Press, 1995).

Symanski, R., *The Immoral Landscape* (Toronto: Butterworths, 1981).

Thane, P. (ed.), *The Origins of British Social Policy* (London: Croom Helm, 1978).

Thomas, B., *The Last Picture Shows, Edinburgh: Ninety Years of Cinema Entertainment in Scotland's Capital City* (Edinburgh: Moorfoot, 1994).

Trudgill, E., *Madonnas and Magdalens: The Origins and Developments of Victorian Sexual Attitudes* (London: Heinemann, 1976).

Valverde, M., *The Age of Light, Soap, and Water: Moral Reform in English Canada, 1885–1925* (Toronto: Toronto University Press, 2008).

Vanstone, M., *Supervising Offenders in the Community: A History of Probation Theory and Practice* (Aldershot: Ashgate, 2004).

Varga, S., *Edinburgh New Town* (Stroud: Tempus, 2007).

Vicinus, M. (ed.), *Suffer and be Still: Women in the Victorian age* (London: Methuen, 1972).

Walker, G., *Intimate Strangers: Political and Cultural Interaction Between Scotland and Ulster in Modern Times* (Edinburgh: John Donald, 1995).

Walkowitz, J. R., *City of Dreadful Delight: Narratives of Sexual Danger in Late-Victorian London* (London: Virago, 1992).

Walkowitz, J. R., *Prostitution and Victorian Society: Women, Class, and the State* (Cambridge: Cambridge University Press, 1980).

Walkowitz, J. R., *Nights Out: Life in Cosmopolitan London* (London: Yale University Press, 2012).

Weeks, J., *Sexuality* (London: Tavistock, 1986).

Wilson, A., (ed.), *Rethinking Social History: English Society, 1570–1920 and its Interpretation* (Manchester: Manchester University Press, 1993).

Wiener, M., *Reconstructing the Criminal: Culture, Law and Policy in England, 1830–1914* (Cambridge: Cambridge University Press, 1990).

Wood Hill, M., *Their Sisters' Keepers: Prostitution in New York City, 1830–1870* (London: University of California Press, 1993).

Zedner, L., *Women, Crime and Custody in Victorian England* (Oxford: Clarendon, 1991).

Zweiniger-Bargielowska, I., *Women in Twentieth-Century Britain* (Harlow: Longman, 2001).

Book Chapters

Bland, L., 'In the Name of Protection: The Policing of Women in the First World War', in J. Brophy and C. Smart (eds), *Women in Law: Explorations in Law, Family and Sexuality* (London: Routledge, 1985) pp. 23–49.

Bland, L., '"Cleansing the Portals of Life": The Venereal Disease Campaign in the Early Twentieth Century', in M. Langan and B. Schwarz (eds), *Crises in the British State, 1880–1930* (London: Hutchinson, 1985) pp. 196–7.

Caslin, S., 'Flappers, Amateurs and Professionals: The Spectrum of Promiscuity in 1920s Britain', in K. Hardy, S. Kingston and T. Sanders (eds), *New Sociologies of Sex Work* (Aldershot: Ashgate, 2010).

Emsley, C., 'Sergeant Goddard: The Story of the Rotten Apple, or a Diseased Orchard?' in A. Srebnick, and R. Levy (eds), *Crime and Culture: A Historical Perspective* (Aldershot: Ashgate, 2005) pp. 85–104.

Farmer, L., '"The genius of our law": Criminal Law and the Scottish Legal Tradition', in D. Sugarman (ed.), *Law in History: Histories of Law and Society* Vol. II (Aldershot: Ashgate, 1996) pp. 97–115.

Hart, A., 'Constructing a Spanish Red-Light District: Prostitution, Space and Power', in D. Bell and G. Valentine (eds), *Mapping Desire* (London: Routledge, 1995) pp. 195–207.

Lawrence, P., '"Scoundrels and Scallywags, and Some Honest Men . . .": Memoirs and the Self-Image of French and English Policemen, c. 1870–1939', in B. S. Godfrey, C. Emsley and G. Dunstall (eds), *Comparative Histories of Crime* (Cullompton: Willan, 2003) pp. 125–44.

Smart, C., 'Law and the Control of Women's Sexuality: The case of the 1950s', in P. Hutter and G. Williams (eds), *Controlling Women: The Normal and the Deviant* (London: Croom Helm, 1981) pp. 40–60.

Thoms, D., 'Motor Car Ownership in Twentieth Century Britain: A Matter of Convenience or a Marque of Status?', in D. Thoms, L. Holden and T. Claydon (eds), *The Motor Car and Popular Culture in the Twentieth Century* (Aldershot: Ashgate, 1998) pp. 42–9.

Articles

Adler, M. W., 'The Terrible Peril: A Historical Perspective on the Venereal Diseases', *British Medical Journal*, 281 (1980) pp. 206–11.

Ashworth, G. J, White, P.E and Winchester, H.P.M., 'The Red-Light District in the West European City: A Neglected Aspect of the Urban Landscape', *Geoforum*, 19 (1988) pp. 201–12.

Bailey, B., 'The Victorian Barmaid as Cultural Prototype', *Gender* & *History*, 2 (1990) pp. 148–72.

Barber, B., 'The Trial of Oscar Slater (1909) and Anti-Jewish Prejudices in Edwardian Glasgow', *History: Journal of the Historical Association*, 88 (2003) pp. 262–79.

Bartley, P., 'Preventing Prostitution: The Ladies' Association for the Care and Protection of Young Girls in Birmingham, 1887–1914', *Women's History Review*, 7, 1 (1998) pp. 37–60.

Beardsley, E. H., 'Allied Against Sin: American and British Responses to Venereal Disease in World War One', *Medical History*, 20 (1976) pp. 189–202.

Beran, K., 'Revisiting the Prostitution Debate: Uniting Liberal and Radical Feminism in Pursuit of Policy Reform', *Law and Inequality: A Journal of Theory and Practice*, 19 (2012) pp. 19–56.

Bingham, A., 'The British Popular Press and Venereal Disease during the Second World War', *The Historical Journal*, 48, 4 (2005) pp. 1055–76.

Bowler, A. E., Leon, C. S., Lilley, T. G., '"What Shall We Do with the Young Prostitute? Reform Her or Neglect Her?" Domestication as Reform at the New York State Reformatory for Women at Bedford, 1901–1913', *Journal of Social History*, 47, 2 (2013) pp. 458–81.

Brooks-Gordon, B., 'Bellwether Citizens: The Regulation of Male Clients of Sex Workers', *Journal of Law and Society* 37, no. 1 (2010) pp. 145–70.

Cox, P., 'Compulsion, Voluntarism, and Venereal Disease: Governing Sexual Health in England after the Contagious Diseases Acts', *Journal of British Studies*, 46, 1 (2007) pp. 91–115.

Davidoff, L., 'Mastered for Life: Servant and Wife in Victorian and Edwardian England', *Journal of Social History*, 7, 4 (1974) pp. 406–28.

Davidson, R. and G. Davis, '"A Festering Sore on the Body of Society": The Wolfenden Committee and Female Prostitution in Mid-Twentieth-Century Scotland', *Journal of Scottish Historical Studies*, 24 (2005) pp. 80–98.

Davidson, R., '"The Sexual State": Sexuality and Scottish Governance, 1950–1980', *Journal of the History of Sexuality*, 13, 4 (2004) pp. 500–21.

Davies, A., 'The Scottish Chicago? From "Hooligans" to "Gangsters" in Inter-War Glasgow', *Cultural and Social History*, 4 (2007) pp. 511–27.

Davies, A., 'Street Gangs, Crime and Policing in Glasgow in the 1930s: The Case of the Beehive Boys', *Social History*, 23, 3 (1998) pp. 251–68.

Davies, A., 'Glasgow's "Reign of Terror": Street Gangs, Racketeering and Intimidation in the 1920s and 1930s', *Contemporary British History*, 21, 4 (2007) pp. 405–27.

Davis, J., 'A Poor Man's System of Justice: The London Police Courts in the Second Half of the Nineteenth Century', *The Historical Journal*, 27 (1984) pp. 309–35.

Doezema, J., 'Loose Women or Lost Women? The Re-Emergence of the Myth of "White Slavery" in Contemporary Discourses of "Trafficking in Women"', *Gender Issues*, 18, 1 (2000) pp. 23–50.

Farley, M., '"Bad for the body, bad for the heart": Prostitution Harms Women Even if Legalized or Decriminalized', *Violence Against Women*, 10 (2004) pp. 1087–125.

Forsythe, W., 'Women Prisoners and Women Penal Officials 1840–1921', *British Journal of Criminology*, 33, 4 (1993) p. 532.

Gilfoyle, T., 'The Urban Geography of Commercial Sex: Prostitution in New York City, 1790–1860', *Journal of Urban History* 13, 4 (1987) pp. 371–93.

Goodyear, M. and Cusick, L., 'Protection of sex workers', *British Medical Journal* (2007) pp. 334, 52–53.

Gronewold, S., 'Beautiful Merchandise: Prostitution in China, 1860–1936', *Women and History*, 1 (1982), 1–114.

Gutzke, D., '"The Cry of the Children": The Edwardian Medical Campaign Against Maternal Drinking', *British Journal of Addiction* 79, no. 1 (1984) pp. 71–84.

Gutzke, D., 'Gender, Class, and Public Drinking in Britain during the First World War', *Social History* 27, 54 (1994) pp. 367–91.

Heilmann, A., 'Gender and Essentialism: Feminist Debates in the Twenty-First Century' *Critical Quarterly*, 53, 4 (2011) pp. 78–89.

Holmes, L., 'A Tale of Three Cities: Regulating Street Prostitution in Scotland', *Scottish Affairs*, 52 (2005) pp. 71–88.

Howell, P., 'A Private Contagious Diseases Act: Prostitution and Public Space in Victorian Cambridge', *Journal of Historical Geography*, 263 (2000) pp. 376–402.

Hubbard, P. and T. Sanders, 'Making Space for Sex Work: Female Street Prostitution and the Production of Urban Space', *International Journal of Urban and Regional Research*, 27, 1 (2003) pp. 75–89.

Hubbard, P. and M. Whowell, 'Revisiting the Red Light District: Still Neglected, Immoral and Marginal?' *Geoforum*, 39 (2008) pp. 1743–55.

Hughes, A., 'Working Class Culture, Family and Domestic Violence on Clydeside, c. 1918–1939: A View from Below', *Scottish Tradition*, 27 (2002) pp. 60–90.

Innes, S., 'Constructing Women's Citizenship in the Interwar Period: the Edinburgh Women Citizens' Association', *Women's History Review*, 13, 4 (2004) pp. 621–47.

James, J., 'Mobility as an Adaptive Strategy', *Urban Anthropology*, 4 (1975) pp. 349–64.

Laite, J., 'Taking Nellie Johnson's Fingerprints: Prostitutes and Legal Identity in Early Twentieth-Century London', *History Workshop Journal*, 65 (2008) pp. 96–116.

Laite, J., 'The Association for Moral and Social Hygiene: Abolitionism, and Prostitution Law in Britain, 1915–1959', *Women's History Review*, 17, 2 (2008) pp. 207–23.

Larence, P., 'Images of Poverty and Crime: Police Memoirs in England and France at the end of the Nineteenth Century', *Crime, History and Societies*, 4 (2000) pp. 63–82.

Leith Walk Research Group, 'Leith Walk and Greenside, A Social History', University of Edinburgh, 1978–1979.

Leppänen, K., 'Movement of Women: Trafficking in the Interwar Era', *Women's Studies International Forum*, 30, 6 (2007) pp. 523–33.

Levine, P., 'Walking the Streets in a Way no Decent Woman Should', *Journal of Modern History*, 66, 1 (1994) pp. 34–78.

Logan, D., 'An "Outstretched Hand to the Fallen": The Magdalen's Friend and the Victorian Reclamation Movement: Part I. "Much More Sinned against than Sinning"', *Victorian Periodicals Review*, 30, 4 (1997) pp. 368–87.

Mahood, L. and B. Littlewood, '"The Vicious Girl" and the "Street-Corner Boy": Sexuality and Gendered Delinquent in the Scottish Child-Saving Movement 1850–1940', *Journal of History of Sexuality*, 4, 4 (1994) pp. 549–78.

Mahood, L. and B. Littlewood, 'Prostitutes, Magdalenes and Wayward Girls: Dangerous Sexualities of Working Class Women in Victorian Scotland', *Gender and History*, 3, 2 (1991) pp. 160–75.

McKeganey, N., 'Street Prostitution in Scotland: The Views of Working Women', *Drugs: Education, Prevention and Policy*, 13, 2 (2006) pp. 151–66.

McKewon, E., 'The Historical Geography of Prostitution in Perth, Western Australia', *Australian Geographer*, 34, 3 (2003) pp. 297–310.

McLaughlin, L., 'Discourses of Prostitution/Discourses of Sexuality', *Critical Studies in Mass Communication*, 8, 3 (1991) pp. 249–72.

McNeill, F., 'Remembering Probation in Scotland', *Probation Journal*, 52, 1 (2005) pp. 23–38.

Metcalf, D., Nickell, S. J. and Floros, N. 'Still Searching for an Explanation of Unemployment in Interwar Britain', *Journal of Political Economy*, 90, 2 (1982) pp. 386–99.

Mort, F., 'Cityscapes: Consumption, Masculinities, and the Mapping of London', *Urban Studies*, 35 (1998) pp. 889–907.

Mort, F., 'Mapping Sexual London: The Wolfenden Committee on Homosexual Offences and Prostitution 1954–57', *New Formations*, 37 (1999) pp. 92–113.

Mumm, S., '"Not worse than other girls": The Convent-based Rehabilitation of Fallen Women in Victorian Britain', *Journal of Social History*, 29, 3 (1996) pp. 527–47.

Overall, C., 'What's Wrong with Prostitution? Evaluating Sex Work', *Signs*, 17, 4 (1992) pp. 705–24.

Robertson, S., 'What's Law got to do with it? Legal Records and Sexual Histories', *Journal of the History of Sexuality*, 14, 1/2 (2005) pp. 161–85.

Sanders, T., 'Blinded by Morality? Prostitution Policy in the UK', *Capital & Class* 29, 2 (2005) pp. 9–15.

Sangster, J., 'Incarcerating "Bad Girls": The Regulation of Sexuality Through the Female Refuges Act in Ontario, 1920–1945', *Journal of the History of Sexuality*, 7, 2 (1996) pp. 239–75.

Settle, L., 'The Social Geography of Prostitution in Edinburgh, 1900–1939', *Journal of Scottish Historical Studies*, 33, 2 (2013) pp. 234–59.

Settle, L., 'The Kosmo Case: Clandestine Prostitution in Britain during the Interwar Period', *Twentieth Century British History*, 25, 4 (2014) pp. 562–84.

Scoular, J., 'What's Law Got to do with it? How and Why Law Matters in the Regulation of Sex Work', *Journal of Law and Society*, 37, 1 (2010) pp. 12–39.

Scoular, J. and Sanders, T. (eds), Regulating Sex/Work: From Crime Control to Neo-Liberalism? *Journal of Law and Society Special Issues* (2010).

Shumsky, N. and L. Springer, 'San Francisco's Zone of Prostitution, 1880–1934', *Journal of Historical Geography*, 1 (1981) pp. 71–89.

Slater, S., 'Pimps, Police and Filles de Joie: Foreign Prostitution in Interwar London', *The London Journal*, 32, 1 (2007) pp. 53–74.

Slater, S., 'Containment: Managing Street Prostitution in London, 1918–1959', *Journal of British Studies*, 49, 2 (2010) pp. 323–57.

Taylor, H., 'Rationing Crime: The Political Economy of Criminal Statistics since the 1850s', *Economic History Review*, 3 (1998) pp. 569–90.

Towers, B. A., 'Health Education Policy 1916–1926: Venereal Disease and the Prophylaxis Dilemma', *Journal of Medical History*, 24, 1 (1980) pp. 70–87.

Valverde, M., 'The Love of Finery: Fashion and the Fallen Woman in Nineteenth-Century Social Discourse', *Victorian Studies*, 32, 2 (1989) pp. 169–88.

Vickery, A., 'Golden Age to Separate Spheres? A Review of the Categories and Chronology of English Women's History', *The Historical Journal*, 36, 2 (1993) pp. 383–414.

Walkowitz, J., 'Going Public: Shopping, Street Harassment, and Streetwalking in Late Victorian London', *Representation*, 62 (1998) pp. 1–30.

Walkowitz, J., 'Male Vice and Feminist Virtue: Feminism and the Politics of Prostitution in Nineteenth-Century Britain', *History Workshop Journal*, 13 (1982) pp. 79–93.

Woollacott, A., '"Khaki Fever" and its Control: Gender, Class, Age and Sexual Morality on the British Home Front in the First World War', *Journal of Contemporary History*, 29 (1994) pp. 325–47.

Wood, J. C., 'The third Degree: Press Reporting, Crime Fiction and Police Powers in 1920s Britain', *Twentieth Century British History*, 21 (2010) pp. 464–85.

Unpublished Theses

Laite, J., 'Prostitution in London, 1885–1930', PhD thesis (University of Cambridge, 2008).

Settle, L., 'Policing the "Social Evil": Prostitution in Edinburgh and Glasgow, 1892–1939', PhD thesis (University of Edinburgh, 2013).

Websites

Knox, W., 'Transport and Scottish Society 1840–1940', in *A History of the Scottish People*, National Museum of Scotland Multimedia Team (eds), (Edinburgh Scottish Cultural Resources Access Network) www.scran.ac.uk (last accessed 1 December 2012).

NLS geocoding site http://geo.nls.uk/urbhist/mapbuilder.html (last accessed May 2015).

Sarah Bromberg, *Feminist Issues in Prostitution* (1997) from feministissues.com (last accessed May 2015).

The International Prostitute's Collective, http://www.prostitutescollective.net/ (last accessed 1 May 2015).

The Oxford Dictionary of National Biography, http://www.oxforddnb.com/index.jsp (last accessed 30 May 2015).

http://www.nswp.org (last accessed 30 May 2015).

http://www.scot-pep.org.uk/ (last accessed 30 May 2015).

Index

Note: f indicates a figure; t indicates a table; page numbers in *italics* indicate illustrations

abolitionism, 1, 10, 187
adoption societies *see* National Vigilance Association
age of consent, 4, 100
Airlie, Councillor John McDiarmid, 172, 176–7
alcohol
  abuse, 126–7, 131, 132, 133, 146, 189
  dance clubs, 158, 167
  see also public houses
Allan, Jane, 147
Anderson, Mary, 101
anti-Semitism, 174
armed forces
  attitudes to prostitution, 2
  venereal diseases, 4, 21, 61, 105
  see also 'khaki fever'; sailors; soldiers
Armour, Isabella Shepard, 85, 116–17
Armour, Margaret (Pearl), 163, 164, 165, 166, 167, 168, 170, 173, 174, 175, 190
Armstrong Eliza, 141
Ashworth, G., 75, 76
assault, 131, 134, 135; *see also* violence
Association for Moral and Social Hygiene (AMSH), 10
asylums *see* Magdalene Asylums

Barnard, Asher, 11, 158, 159, 161, 162, 163, 164–5, 165–6, 167, 169, 172, 173, 174, 177, 178
Barr, Lily, 144, 145
Baxter, Mrs (probation officer), 87
Bibby, Elsie, 162–3, 165, 190
Bingham, Adrian, 169
Birmingham, 23, 28, 65
Black, James, 158, 159, 163, 167, 173–4, 178
Blades, D. P., 171, 173
Blair, Bethany, 101
Bland, Lucy, 105
boarding houses, 159, 160, 176, 177
Boyd, Edith, 131–3, 190
Boyle, Jemima, 87
Bradshaw, Mary, 65, 66
Brash, Ann, 136
Brash, Lewis, 136
breaches of the peace, 3, 21, 129, 130, 131, 132, 135
Brennet, Margaret, 71
Bristow, Edward, 134
Brogden, Mike, 32, 33
brothel-keepers, 39, 40, 42, 43, 46, 70, 114, 144–6, 150, 160, 186, 191
brothels, 4, 42, 46–7, 128, 141–6
  definition, 43, 142
  Edinburgh, 2, 33–4, 40, 41–2, 43–4, 62–3, 68–71, 72, 103, 160, 164
  families and, 144
  Glasgow, 44, 71, 72, 73, 74t
  locations, 71
  London, 43
  'mega-brothels' (Germany), 195
Brown, Mabel, 101–2
Brown, Rachel, 101
Buckley, Mary *see* Stanley, Mary
'bullies', 43, 45–6, 139–40, 141, 147, 150, 186, 191; *see also* pimps
Burgh Police (Scotland) Act (1892), 4–5, 17, 19f, 35, 36, 37, 40
Butcher, Mary, 87

'call girls', 161
Cambridge, 7
Campbell, Helen, 162, 164
cars, 69, 160, 186; *see also* taxis
Carson, Freda, 28
Cass, Elizabeth, 31
cautioning system, 30–1, 42, 65, 193
charities, 86–7
Chesterton, Lady Ada Cecil, 164
children
  in brothels, 144, 145–6
  Magdalene Asylums and, 94
  NVASED and, 101
  and probation service, 83
  as prostitutes, 141
  of prostitutes, 117
Children Act (1908), 145
Children Charter (1908), 94
cinemas, 62, 67
Clark, Mary Ann, 133, 190
Clinton, James, 113, 137–8, 140
coffee stalls/shops, 60, 157
Colquhoun, Robert, 26
condoms, 126
Contagious Diseases Acts, 4
convents, 102

courts
Burgh Courts, 6, 30, 35, 64, 66, 68, 69, 88, 116, 147, 148
Glasgow 71
Police Court, 35
see also magistrates
Coutts, Margaret, 144
Cox, Pamela, 105
Cranston, Janet, 129
Cree, Viviene, 8, 95
Criminal Amendment Act (1885), 4
Criminal Conviction Registers, 126, 129, 130, 133, 136, 149
Criminal Justice Administration Act (1914), 82, 83
criminal justice system, 8, 86–7
Criminal Law Amendment Act (1885), 100, 142
Criminal Law Amendment Act (1912), 5, 134
Cuminisky, Nancy, 164, 165

D'Agostino, Catherine, 164
dance clubs
Edinburgh *see* Edinburgh: Kosmo dance club
London, 161–2
dance halls, 62, 67, 76, 100
Darroch, Janet, 131–2, 133, 190
Davidson, Roger, 7–8, 67
Davis, Gayle, 8, 67
Dawson, Agnes, 161, 164, 167–8
de Certeau, Michel, 65
Defence of the Realm Act (DORA), 21, 105
Delaney, Catherine, 30
Dickson, Jemina, 96
Douglas, Margaret, 117
Drummond, Peggy, 116, 126
Duckenfield, Eva, 163–4
Duff, Agnes, 129

Edinburgh
brothels, 2, 33–4, 40, 41–2, 43–4, 62–3, 68–71, 72, 128, 142, 144, 145, 147, 160, 164
Burgh Court, 30–1
Criminal Conviction Registers, 11, 129, 130, 133–4, 136
East End, 62–5, 66
entertainment venues, 61–2, 75
Kosmo dance club, 11, 156, 158–79, 191, 193; booking-out system, 159, 160–2, 163–4, 167, 173, 175–6, 178, 190; clients, 175–7, 178; life at, 162–5; managers, 173–5, 178; negotiating power and resistance, 165–9; payment of women, 165, 190; and perceptions of prostitution, 169–73
lodging houses, 143–4
Magdalene Asylum, 84–5, 87, 89, 90, 91, 92, 94, 98, 99, 102–3, 128
Municipal and Police Act (1879), 17–18, 35, 142
National Vigilance Association of Scotland, Eastern Division (NVASED), 100–1
New Town, 53, 54, 55–9, 60–4, 65, 66
Old Town, 53–4, 59, 60, 64
police, 22–3, 26, 27–8, 33–4, 192–3
Police Criminal Conviction Registers, 129
poor law records, 11
probation service, 81, 83, 84
prosecutions, 19–20, 44–5, 46
railway station, 61
sentencing, 35–6
shebeens, 62
South Side, 54
Street Offences Committee, 22, 26, 31, 32
tenement flats, 62–3
women patrols, 104–5
Edinburgh Town Council Provost's Committee, 39
Edinburgh Women's Citizen Association, 39
Emerson, Elizabeth *see* Livingston, Elizabeth
Emsley, Clive, 34–5
England *see* Birmingham; Cambridge; Liverpool; London; Manchester; Oxford; York
entertainment
Magdalene Asylums, 98–9
venues, 2, 52, 61, 62, 67, 68, 73, 74, 75, 186, 195
see also dance clubs; dance halls; theatres
Erskine, Elizabeth, 125
Evening Dispatch, 101

Fair, Henry, 135, 191
families, 96, 101, 114, 115, 116–17, 118, 120–1, 131, 137, 140–1, 147–9; *see also* children; fathers; mothers
fathers
occupations, 96, 114, 115, 131, 137
see also families
femininity, 87, 90, 187
feminists, 2, 4, 9–10
Ferguson, George, 177
Ferguson, Marion, 126
Fiddes, Margaret, 145–6
Finnegan, Frances, 9, 130
First World War
asylums, 88
'khaki fever', 20, 104, 105
public houses, 127
sexual attitudes, 20–1, 61
fish-and-chip shops, 157
flappers, 172, 178
Fraser, Agnes, 117

Gallacher, Thomas, 134–5, 191
Gardiner, Helen, 88
Garland, David, 86, 97
Garvie, Helen, 27–8
gender
and behaviour, 97
boundaries of, 52, 65, 76
and conditioning, 87
equality of, 10
see also men; women
Germany
'mega-brothels', 195
'pimp–prostitute' relationships, 135

Gibbons, Mary, 61
Glasgow
  Broomielaw, 72, 73
  brothels, 40, 43, 71, 72, 73, 74t
  cautioning system, 31–2
  criminal statistics, 73
  Dalbeth Home, 128
  Duke Street Prison Registers, 71, 118–19, 121, 122f, 123, 124f, 129–30
  geography of prostitution, 71–5
  lock hospital, 126
  lodging houses, 143
  Magdalene Institute, 83, 89, 90, 91, 93, 94–5, 96, 98, 99
  Police Act (1866), 142
  police attitudes, 23–4, 26, 192, 193
  police districts map (1933), 75f
  Police (Further Powers) Act (1892), 5, 18
  police General Orders, 33
  Police Instruction Book, 31–2
  poor law records, 11
  probation service, 81, 83
  prosecutions, 19–20, 44, 45, 46
  Sauchiehall Street, 72, 73
Glasgow Parish Council
  'Memorandum on a Social Evil in Glasgow, and the State of the Law for Dealing with Certain Forms of Immorality', 44, 71, 157
'Glasgow system', 8, 185
Glenny, Robert, 176
Goddard, Sergeant George, 34–5

Hall, G. M., 172
Hall, Lesley, 105
Hall, Nellie, 136–7, 140
Hall, Otto, 136–7
Hamilton, Miss (Edinburgh Magdalene Asylum Ladies' Committee), 98, 103
Hannan, Robert, 42
Harcus, Elizabeth, 167
Harris, Victoria, 9, 10, 135
Henderson, Tony, 118, 190
Hope, Jessie, 30
hospitals *see* lock hospitals
hotels, 5, 160, 161, 177; *see also* boarding houses
housing, 71–2
Howell, Philip, 7, 67
Hubbard, Phil, 65
Hunter, Florence (Flo), 161, 163, 167, 176, 177

ice-cream parlours, 44, 62, 157–8
immigration, 121, 136, 189
Immoral Traffic (Scotland) Act (1902), 5, 6, 39–40, 44, 71, 113, 135, 136, 137, 140, 157
Immoral Traffic (Scotland) Amendment Bill (1910), 134
industrial schools, 95, 127
Industrial Schools Amendment Act (1880), 145
informants, 26
institutions, 127–9, 133, 149; *see also* industrial schools; lock hospitals; Magdalene Asylums; poorhouses; prisons; reform homes; rescue homes
Ireland, immigration from, 121, 189

Jamieson, Mabel, 115, 116, 120, 127
Jeffreys, Sheila: *The Spinster and her Enemies, 1880–1930*, 10
Jones, Edwin, 158, 159, 167, 173, 174, 178
Juvenile Delinquency Board, 83

Kelly, John, 138–9, 146
Kelly, Mary, 28, 138–9, 140, 146
'kerb crawling', 69
'khaki fever', 20, 104, 105
Klein, Joanne, 23, 28

Laite, Julia, 6, 9, 10, 21, 43, 168
law, 3–6, 17, 21, 22, 195; *see also* criminal justice system
Lee, Charlotte, 101
Lefebvre, Henri, 65
Leith, 67–8, 69, 168, 193
Leonard, Margaret, 85
Licensing (Scotland) Act (1903), 41
Lind, Hilda, 29
Lindsay, May, 88
List, Ida, 101
Littlewood, Barbara, 7
Liverpool, 7, 23, 28, 32, 33, 67
Livingston, Elizabeth, 126, 147–8
Livingston, John, 147–8
lock hospitals, 94, 126
lodging houses, 143–4
London
  brothels, 43
  clandestine venues, 22
  criminalisation of prostitution, 6, 76, 168, 190–1
  dance clubs, 161–2
  'economies of makeshift', 118, 119, 190
  police corruption, 34–5
  'red-light' zone, 71
  research, 193
  solicitation statistics, 21

McAllister, Mary, 125
McArthney, Georgina, 165
McArthur, May, 32, 113, 137–8, 140–1, 144
McCormack, Annie, 102
McDonald, Marie, 163–4, 167
McGravie, Mary, 128
McGregor, Isabella, 88, 127–8
McIntosh, Alexander, 72
McKeganey, Neil, 194
McKenzie, Agnes, 118, 126
McKenzie, Jane, 88
McKewon, Elaine, 61
Mckie, Margaret, 118, 128
Mckinnlay, Elizabeth, 89
McKinnon, Reverend, 84, 85
McLaughlin, Sarah, 96
McLeachy, Maggie, 101

Mclean, Catherine, 71
McNee, David, 26
Magdalene Asylums, 89–100, 128
  daily life, 98–100
  domestic training, 90–1, 187
  and NVASED, 100, 102
  and probation service, 83, 84–5
Magdalenes, 93–8
  behaviour, 97
  discipline, 98
  education, 90, 99, 187
  emigration, 92
  employment, 92, 96
  families, 96
  food, 99
  paternal occupations, 96
  pregnancy, 94
  recreational activities, 98–9
  surveillance, 105
  training, 90–1
magistrates, 35–6, 38, 81, 82, 84, 88, 187
Mahood, Linda, 7, 8, 9, 10, 19, 90, 95, 96, 98
'makeshift economy', 118, 119, 190
Manchester, police attitudes, 23, 28
Mannock, Janet, 129
marriage, 114, 117, 131, 136, 138, 139, 140
'massage parlours', 192
Maxwell, Katie, 100
medical profession, 2
Meikle, Jane, 145
men
  and brothels, 141
  and cars, 69
  earnings of, 165
  Kosmo Club management, 173–5
  payment for sex, 118, 175–7, 194–5
  as probation officers, 84
  prosecution of, 6, 39–40, 42
  see also 'bullies', fathers; pimps
Merrilees, William, sergeant, later Chief Constable, 28–9, 30, 33–4, 40, 41, 142–3, 159, 165–6, 177
migrants, 72, 194
Millar, Jane, 139
Miller, Elizabeth, 120
Milner, Marjory, 85
Mitchell, Helen, 89
Moffat, Elizabeth, 148
Monclif, Kitty, 92
Montgomery, Sarah, 65
Moor, Daisy, 66
Mort, Frank, 97
mothers: occupations, 131; *see also* families
Muir, Edwin, 52, 64
Muirhead, Mary, 114–15, 116, 117, 120, 125, 190
Mullaney, Mary, 131, 133, 190
Municipal and Police Act (1879), 4–5, 17–18
Murray, Robert, 176

National Union of Women Workers (NUWW), 100, 104
National Vigilance Association (NVA), 4, 100; *see also* Scottish National Vigilance Association
National Vigilance Association of Scotland, Eastern Division (NVASED), 8, 96, 97, 100–4, 105, 187; *see also* Scottish National Vigilance Association
New York, 71, 169
newspaper reports, 4, 11–12, 67, 72, 101, 105, 169, 178

O'Connor, Ruby, 120
orphans, 96, 116
Oxford, 67

Paisley, 83, 120f
Pall Mall Gazette, 141
parasexuality, 164, 165
parents, 114
  abuse by, 116–17
  contact with, 30, 85, 115, 116, 117, 118, 147–9
  loss of, 96, 116, 189
  see also families; fathers; mothers
parks, 5, 21, 66, 76, 104
Paterson, Ada, 101
Paterson, Miss (matron), 83
Paton, Ann, 30
philanthropy, 7, 86
pimps, 28, 40, 43, 45, 46, 113, 146–7, 168, 186, 191, 194
  case studies, 134–41
  see also 'bullies'
police
  attitudes, 1, 2, 7, 22–39, 46, 59–60, 65, 67, 73, 186–7, 192–3
  bribery, 143
  and brothels, 142–3
  Burgh Police (Scotland) Act (1892), 4–5, 17, 19f, 35, 36, 37, 40
  corruption, 28, 33–4, 193
  General Orders, 23, 33, 40–1
  Glasgow districts map (1933), 75f
  and Kosmo dance club, 159, 166, 167
  and the law, 5
  memoirs, 6–7
  Municipal and Police Act (1879), 4–5, 35
  and NVASED, 103
  as probation officers, 83
  Royal Commission into Police Powers and Procedures (1906), 35
Police Court Missionaries, 82
poor law records, 11, 114, 117, 128, 190
poorhouses, 93, 95, 114, 115, 126, 128, 149
poverty, 3, 9, 10, 24, 96, 115, 116, 124, 128, 133, 149, 165, 185, 189, 194
pregnancy, 94, 101
Pretsell, Elizabeth, 117
Priscilla (NVASED 'girl'), 101
prisons, 188
  Magdalenes, 95
  overcrowding, 86
  pimps, 136

registers, 71, 118–19, 121, 122f, 123f, 124f, 129–30
Probation of Offenders Act (1907), 82, 187
Probation of Offenders (Scotland) Act (1931), 83
probation service, 82–4, 188–9
and Christian charities, 86–7
development, 81
'Glasgow System', 8, 185
and Magdalene Asylums, 90, 92
penal-welfare-oriented approach to, 187
and prostitution, 84–9
selection criteria, 85
Procurator Fiscal, 5, 44, 193
Kosmo dance club trial, 159, 167, 170–1, 173, 175–6
promiscuity, 20, 157–8, 164
prostitutes
abuse, 28, 139, 177, 191
agency, 9, 192
ages, 123, 124f
alcohol abuse, 126–7, 131, 132, 133, 146, 189
arrests, 20, 21, 31–2, 67
assaults by, 131
birth places, 120f, 121
child, 141
convictions, 17, 18t, 19f, 21, 22, 31, 32, 39, 53f, 54, 55f, 56f, 57f, 58f, 59f, 65, 130, 131, 132
criminal records, 129–31, 133, 189
earnings, 118
experiences, 2, 9
fines, 4–5, 24, 35, 36, 37–8, 38
friendships, 168
health, 124–6
home addresses, 63f, 143f
identities, 173, 189, 190
imprisonment, 36, 37
institutionalisation, 133
labelling, 5, 26, 29, 144, 170, 171, 172, 188–9
movement, 65
nationalities, 122f, 123f
occupations, 119, 131, 149
relationship with pimps, 135–7
sentencing, 35–9, 86, 88, 128, 129, 186, 188
services for, 195–6
social class, 2, 4, 116, 119, 148, 190
suicide, 131, 133
symbolism, 1–2, 10, 171
venereal disease, 61, 105, 126, 172
victim stereotype of, 29
prostitution
attitudes to: community, 1–2, 33, 146–9, 150; police, 1, 2, 7, 22–39, 59–60, 65, 67, 73, 186–7, 192–3
clandestine, 6, 11–12, 22, 43, 47, 76, 119, 133, 159–62, 168, 186, 190, 191, 192
criminalisation, 6, 10, 17–19, 22, 65, 76, 168, 186, 190–1, 194
forced, 193
historiography, 2, 10
indoor, 22, 42–3, 46, 62, 69–70, 76, 142, 156–7, 171–2, 177, 192
and the law, 3–6, 9–10
locations, 2, 6, 7, 22, 41, 70, 76, 121, 157, 160–1, 186, 190
outdoor, 17–22, 46, 65–7, 69–70, 76, 171–2, 190
payment, 2, 190
penalties, 4–5, 18, 24
perceptions, 169–73
prosecutions, 18t, 21–2
reasons for, 2–3, 9, 10, 23–4, 28, 85, 96, 114–15, 116–19, 136, 149, 165, 189, 194
regulation, 81
'restriction', 76
safety issues, 10
social geography, 52–76
and time, 66–7
women's experiences of, 113–49
'zero-tolerance' policy to, 192, 195
public houses, 41, 62, 72, 73, 126, 127
Purdie, Margaret, 164

race, and sexuality, 174–5
racism, 194; *see also* anti-Semitism; xenophobia
railway stations, 61
Ramsay, Helen, 87
red light districts, 65, 69, 71, 75
reform homes, 24, 86, 87, 88, 102, 132, 187, 188, 192; *see also* Magdalene Asylums
reformers, 1, 2, 4, 29, 76, 103, 124, 127, 146, 162
rehabilitation programmes, 82, 84, 86, 102, 106, 195
religious organisations, 2, 7, 8, 81, 82, 83–4, 103, 187, 193
rescue homes, 83, 115
restaurants, 62
Riley, Annie, 101
Robb, PC Alexander, 27–8
Robertson, Frances, 164–5, 167
Robertson, Margaret, 42
'rookeries', 72
Ross, Margaret, 116, 148
Ross, Robert, 135
Ross, Roderick, Chief Constable, 22, 26, 27, 32–3

sailors, 23, 62, 66, 68
Salvation Army, 83, 84, 92, 96, 100
San Francisco, 67
Sanders, Teela, 65
'saunas', 192
Savidge, Irene, 31, 167
schools *see* industrial schools
The Scotsman, 72, 161, 162–3
Scottish Girls' Friendly Society, 100
Scottish National Vigilance Association (SNVA), 4, 8, 81, 89
Scottish Society for the Prevention of Cruelty to Children, 145
Scottish Union of Women Workers (SUWW), 104
servants, 91, 119f, 149, 187
sexuality
attitudes to, 20–1, 29
control of, 95
parasexuality, 164, 165

sexuality (*cont.*)
 and race, 174–5
 women, 20–1, 29, 95, 172
 see also femininity; promiscuity
shebeens, 62
Shirran, George, 145
Shumsky, Neil Larry, 67
Sillitoe, Percy, Chief Constable, 24, 26, *27*
Singleton v. *Ellison*, 142
Smith, Andrew Donnan, Chief Constable, 24, *25*, 42, 45–6
Smith, Nina, 101
social class
 boundaries of, 52, 53, 65, 67, 76
 and car ownership, 160
 and charity, 86–7
 and dance clubs, 163, 175
 and domestic ideology, 90, 92, 93
 and female behaviour, 82, 87–8, 97, 187
 and housing, 71
 of Magdalenes, 96
 NVASED and, 101
 and prisons, 129
 and prostitution, 2, 4, 116, 119, 148, 190
 and public houses, 127
 and women patrols, 105
'social purity movement', 4, 124, 126, 134
social work/workers, 60, 81, 86, 103, 187
soldiers, 20, 21, 60, 61, 62, 69, 70
Springer, Larry M., 67
Stag, Miss (probation officer), 84
Stanley, Mary, 144, 145
Stanley, Patrick, 144, 145
Stead, W. T.: 'The Maiden Tribute of Modern Babylon', 4, 141, 169
Stevenson, James Verdier, Chief Constable, 23–4, *25*, 34, 40, 45
Stewart, Alexandria, 146
Stewart, Peter, 72
Stewart, Robina, 83
Stirling, Helen, 69
support networks, 116, 120, 168
Swan, Robert, 161, 175–6
Swanson, Jane, 118

Tait, William, 2–3, 9, 53
taxis, 159, 160
technologies, 2, 52, 56, 168, 177, 185, 195; *see also* telephones
telephones, 161, 166, 177, 186
tenement flats, 62–3
theatres, 62
theft, 130, 132, 133
Thompson, Isabella, 84–5
Thompson, Ruby, 101, 103
Thompson, William, 42
Thomson, Helen, 145
Thomson, Isabella, 125
Thomson, Jane, 87
Thomson, Madge, 129
Thomson, Mary, 61
Thomson, William, 71
Tolland, Bridget, 117
trafficking, 5, 193–4; *see also* white slavery

unemployment, 116, 164
United States *see* New York; San Francisco

vagrancy laws, 3
Vanstone, Maurice, 86
Vaughn, Alfred Joseph, 71
venereal disease
 armed forces, 4, 21, 61, 105
 brothels, 141
 Magdalenes, 94
 prostitutes, 29, 105, 126, 172
 treatments, 126
violence
 dance clubs, 163, 177
 pimps, 134–5, 138, 139
 see also assault
voluntary organisations, 8, 82, 187, 193, 195; *see also* religious organisations

Walkowitz, Judith, 9, 123, 130, 134
Wallace, Catherine, 164–5
Wallace, Elizabeth, 87
Wallis, Flora, 147
Watt, Mary, 42
Waugh, Evelyn: *Brideshead Revisited*, 141
white slavery, 4, 36, 134, 141, 169–70, 171, 174–5, 178, 186, 193; *see also* trafficking
Wilde, Oscar: *The Picture of Dorian Gray*, 141
Wilson, Agnes, 102
Wilson, Margaret, 88, 128
Wilson, Molly, 85
Winter, Elizabeth, 66
witness statements, 5, 6, 11, 22–3, 26–7, 28, 41, 42, 62, 68, 69, 70, 71, 72–3, 126, 136, 137, 138, 142, 144, 146, 147, 159, 161, 162–3, 166–7, 169, 175–6
women
 as brothel-keepers, 144, 145
 and childcare, 117–18
 Edinburgh Women's Citizen Association, 39
 and employment, 20, 23, 103, 128, 188
 and femininity, 87
 as probation officers, 83, 84
 and public houses, 127
 and sexuality, 20–1, 29, 95, 172
 wages, 20, 23, 90, 117, 118, 140, 149, 165, 175, 178, 190, 191, 194, 195
 see also femininity; feminists; mothers
women patrols, 104–6
Wood, Cecelia, 66
Wood, John Carter, 167
Woollacott, Angela, 105

xenophobia, 157, 174, 178, 194; *see also* anti-Semitism; racism

York, 9, 130
Young, Elizabeth, 66